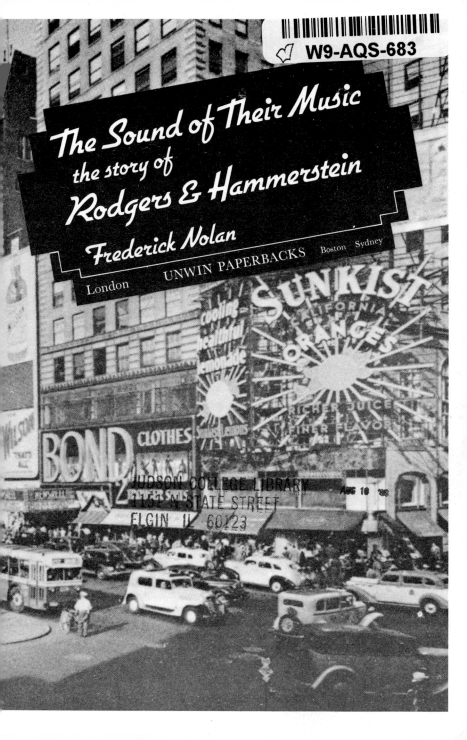

The Sound of Their Music
the story of
Rodgers & Hammerstein

Frederick Nolan

London   UNWIN PAPERBACKS   Boston   Sydney

First published in Great Britain by
J. M. Dent & Sons Ltd. 1978
First published in Unwin Paperbacks 1979

UNWIN® PAPERBACKS
40 Museum Street, London WC1A 1LU

British Library Cataloguing in Publication Data

Nolan, Frederick
   The sound of their music.
   1. Rodgers, Richard
   2. Hammerstein, Oscar, b. 1895
   3. Composers – United States – Biography
   I. Title
   782.8'1'0922   ML410.R6315   79-41077

   ISBN 0-04-782003-9

Acknowledgments
Special thanks to Alice Regensburg of the Lynn Farnol Group, Theodore C.
Fetter, Bill Richards and Esther Brumberg of the Museum of the City of
New York, Donna Bassi of The American Society of Composers, Authors
and Publishers, Roberts Jackson of Culver Pictures, Eddie Patman of 20th
Century Fox Films Ltd, Robert Dirskovski of W. H. Allen & Co. Ltd, the
staff of the British Film Institute, Seymour Britchky, Frank Jones and to
Heidi Nolan, who did the typing and the index.

Picture sources
AC   Author's collection
ASCAP   American Society of Composers, Authors and Publishers
CP   Culvers Pictures
LFG   Lynn Farnol Group
NFA   National Film Archive/Stills Library
TMC   Theatre and Music Collection, Museum of the City of
          New York

Times Square, 1938, is reproduced on the title page by permission of
Culver Pictures

Printed in Great Britain by
Hazell Watson & Viney Ltd, Aylesbury, Bucks

Preface

The man responsible for this book is Lorenz Hart, that brilliantly gifted lyricist who was Richard Rodgers's collaborator for the best part of twenty-five years. Hart always fascinated me, so I grabbed every opportunity to talk to people who had known him. The more I did so the more I realized that Larry Hart had not been just a lyricist but a percipient man of the theatre with ideas a long way ahead of his time.

By about the middle of 1973 I had amassed enough hours of tape on Larry Hart to believe that I had something of the essence of the man and, indeed, his part in the story of the development of the musical theatre in America. I began to think of writing the first biography of Hart, only to discover that his sister-in-law, Dorothy, was already at work on a memoir of Larry, using all the family photographs and such pitifully few mementos as remained from his life and career. I turned over as much of my material to Mrs Hart as was of use to her and switched instead to writing a series of radio programmes for the BBC, telling the whole story of Richard Rodgers's life: his first career with Hart, his second with Hammerstein and his third alone.

The story was bigger, funnier and infinitely more interesting when told in the words of the people who had been there while it was happening, and the radio programmes could only skim the surface. I soon realized that it would be impossible to tell any part of his story without telling all of it. Thus the story of Rodgers and Hammerstein, which this book nominally is, must also be that of Rodgers and Hart, of Oscar Hammerstein, Otto Harbach, Rudolf Friml, Sigmund Romberg and, of course, Jerome Kern. If that has given the book a wider view than originally anticipated, I venture to hope that it has made it no less interesting.

The incredibly successful partnership of Rodgers and Hammerstein dominated the musical stage for more than twenty years, as no other, before or since. After *Oklahoma!* had kicked musical comedy convention out of the window, nothing was ever the same again. With that show and the ones that followed, *Carousel, Allegro, South Pacific, The King and I, Me and Juliet, State Fair, Pipe Dream, Cinderella* and *The Sound of Music*, standards were set against which all other musicals were measured. It is no accident that during the Rodgers and Hammerstein years many other composers for the Broadway stage produced their best work: Frank Loesser (*Guys and Dolls*), Cole Porter (*Kiss Me, Kate*), Irving Berlin (*Annie Get Your Gun*), Lerner and Loewe (*My Fair Lady*), Sondheim and Bernstein (*West Side Story*), Burton Lane (*Finian's Rainbow*), Adler and Ross (*Damn Yankees*) and Jule Styne (*Gypsy*).

I have tried to recapture some of the excitement of the way it was when it was happening, when nobody ever knew if the show was going to be a flop or a hit, the days when it all went well and the days when nothing went right, as told by the people who were there at the time. They include George Abbott, Larry Adler, Lucinda Ballard, Irving Berlin, Sammy Cahn, Jan Clayton, Agnes de Mille, Howard Dietz, Mary Ellis, David Ewen, Theodore C. Fetter, Dorothy Fields, Helen Ford, George Ford, John Green, William Hammerstein, Rex Harrison, Dorothy Hart, Hildegarde Halliday, Gene Kelly, Joshua Logan, Rouben Mamoulian, Mary Martin, Samuel Marx, Jessie Matthews, Edith Meiser, Mabel Mercer, James Michener, Alice Regensburg, Arthur Schwartz, Vivienne Segal, Kurt Singer, Alec Wilder, Max Wilk and, most important of all, Richard Rodgers. It is to him and to them all that this book is respectfully dedicated.

June 1977   FREDERICK NOLAN

Contents

ACKNOWLEDGMENTS	4
PREFACE	5
LIST OF ILLUSTRATIONS	8
1 *Away We Go!*	11
2 Oscar	33
3 Dick and Larry	65
4 About as far as they can go!	119
5 The *South Pacific* years	144
6 Broadway's miracle men	163
7 Only human	177
8 So long, farewell	206
9 Finale	226
NOTES AND SOURCES	236
CHRONOLOGY	242
BIBLIOGRAPHY	265
INDEX	267

Illustrations

Rodgers and Hart at a rehearsal of *By Jupiter* 12
Victoria Schools, June Allyson and Nancy Walker in *Best Foot Forward* 13
A scene from *Green Grow the Lilacs* 18
'The surrey with the fringe on top' 21
Alfred Drake in the original stage version of *Oklahoma!* 23
Joseph Buloff and Celeste Holm in *Oklahoma!* 23
Rodgers and Hammerstein rehearsing *Away We Go!* 25
The poster for the New York opening of *Oklahoma!* 27
Oklahoma! The principals 29
Oklahoma! The dance in the Skidmore barn 30–1
Oscar Hammerstein I 34
Oscar Greeley Clendenning Hammerstein 38
Otto Harbach 41
Vincent Youmans 43
Rudolf Friml 45
Mary Ellis in *Rose Marie* 46
Victor Herbert 47
Ernest Truex in *Very Good Eddie* 48
Alice Dovey in *Very Good Eddie* 49
Jerome Kern 51
Sigmund Romberg 52
The stage version of *Show Boat* 55
Florenz Ziegfeld 56
'Can't help lovin' dat man' from the 1936 movie of *Show Boat* 58
Oscar Hammerstein and Dorothy Blanchard Hammerstein 60
Oscar Hammerstein outside MGM's Music Department 60
Kern and Hammerstein rehearsing *Music in the Air* 62
Otto Harbach and Jerome Kern filming in Hollywood 63
The Hart home at 59 West 119th Street, Manhattan 67
Lorenz Hart at twenty-three 71
Arthur Schwartz 73

'The Bombay Bombashay' from *Poor Little Ritz Girl*   74
Rodgers and Hart pretending to write 'Manhattan'   76
Lew Fields rehearsing *A Connecticut Yankee*   84
Ben Lyon and Una Munson in *The Hot Heiress*   90
Rouben Mamoulian   92
Maurice Chevalier in *Love Me Tonight*   94
How Hollywood prefers to see its song-writers   97
Setting up a scene for *Mississippi*   99
Irving Berlin, Tom Drake and Mickey Rooney between shots of
   Words and Music   99
Bing Crosby in *Mississippi*   100
A rehearsal of *Babes in Arms*   104
George M. Cohan   106
Dick and Larry in 1940   110
Gene Kelly, Leila Ernst and Vivienne Segal in *Pal Joey*   111
June Havoc with singing waiters in *Pal Joey*   112
Gene Kelly and girls in *Pal Joey*   114
Vivienne Segal   116
Rodgers and Hammerstein, Incorporated   121
Dick, Oscar and their two Dorothys   123
A scene from the 1921 production of *Liliom*   125
Jeanne Crain and Dana Andrews in *State Fair*   127
Rodgers runs through the score of *Carousel*   130
The opening scene of the stage version of *Carousel*   132
The opening sequence of the movie of *Carousel*   132
'If I loved you' (*Carousel*, the movie)   133
Herbert, Dorothy and Joseph Fields   135
Richard Rodgers with Ethel Merman and Irving Berlin   138
The opening sequence of *Allegro*   142
Roberta Jonay and John Battles in *Allegro*   143
The principals of *South Pacific* discuss the play   147
Rehearsing the Thanksgiving show in *South Pacific*   150
Ezio Pinza and Mary Martin: 'Some Enchanted Evening'   150
'There is nothing like a dame'   153
'Happy talk'   154
'I'm gonna wash that man right out of my hair'   155
The final scene of *South Pacific*   157
Mitzi Gaynor sings 'I'm in love with a wonderful guy'   158
Mitzi Gaynor singing 'Honey bun'   158
John Kerr, Mitzi Gaynor and Oscar Hammerstein during the
   filming of *South Pacific*   161

Joshua Logan and Oscar Hammerstein on location for *South
    Pacific*   162
Yul Brynner on stage in *The King and I*   165
Gertrude Lawrence and Yul Brynner in *The King and I*   168
Celeste Holm and Yul Brynner   168
Yul Brynner in the movie of *The King and I*   171
The banqueting hall in the King's Palace   171
Yul Brynner and Deborah Kerr in the movie of *The King and I*   172
Oscar Hammerstein   178
Richard Rodgers conducting   181
Dick and Oscar at work in the Ritz, Boston   183
Joan McCracken and Bill Hayes in *Me and Juliet*   186
Isabel Bigley, Joan McCracken, Bill Hayes and Ray Walston in *Me
    and Juliet*   186
Rodgers and Hammerstein receiving the Alexander Hamilton
    Award   190
Judy Tyler and Helen Traubel in *Pipe Dream*   195
Auditions for *The Flower Drum Song*   199
Richard Rodgers and Joseph Fields at rehearsals of *The Flower Drum
    Song*   199
Richard Rodgers, Gene Kelly and others rehearsing *The Flower
    Drum Song*   200
Richard Rodgers, Gene Kelly, Miyoshi Umeki, Pat Suzuki and
    others   202
Joseph Fields, Rodgers, Hammerstein and Gene Kelly   202
Oscar Hammerstein working on a lyric during rehearsals of *The
    Flower Drum Song*   204
Oscar in his workroom at Highland Farm   208
Theodore Bikel and Mary Martin in *The Sound of Music*   210
Dancing the 'Laendler'   213
Mary Martin and the children   215
Julie Andrews sings 'My favourite things' to the children   215
Christopher Plummer sings 'Edelweiss' in the movie of *The Sound of
    Music*   219
Julie Andrews as 'Maria'   219
Julie Andrews and Christopher Plummer   222
Roger Dann and Jean Bayliss in the London production of *The
    Sound of Music*   222
Richard Rodgers: a recent photograph   231

1. Away we go!

'On Broadway they all know we're stagestruck.'
Oscar Hammerstein II

On 23 July 1942 *The New York Times* reported that the Theatre Guild was planning to produce a musical adaptation of Lynn Riggs's play of 1931, *Green Grow the Lilacs*, with a book by Oscar Hammerstein II and music and lyrics by Richard Rodgers and Lorenz Hart. The brief announcement omitted two very important additional items of information. The first was that the Theatre Guild, then run by Lawrence Langner and Theresa Helburn, was teetering on the brink of insolvency; the second that Rodgers's song-writing partner of twenty-five years no longer had the will or desire to work—and especially not on this project. According to Arthur Schwartz, Hart told Rodgers that the play was corny, that it wasn't their style, and that it wouldn't be any good. Moreover, he didn't want to do another show so soon after their latest hit, *By Jupiter*. In fact Larry Hart did not want to work at all. He wanted to go to Mexico on vacation with his sinister friend and agent, Milton 'Doc' Bender.

From the very beginning Larry Hart had been a difficult partner for Dick Rodgers: 'a partner, a best friend and a constant source of irritation', as the composer put it. Unquestionably the most brilliant lyric writer of his own or indeed any succeeding generation, Larry Hart was also unstable, erratic, a fitful worker and a homosexual trying to solve his problems at the bottom of a bottle. Rodgers found himself in the unenviable position of being not only Hart's collaborator but also his guardian and nurse. There is no doubt that few of their later shows would ever have been written had not Rodgers spent an increasing amount of his time finding Hart and then persuading him to work, easing him through as many hours of creativity as were possible before his craving for the bottle became too intense.

To insiders perhaps, the break-up of the song-writing team of Rodgers and Hart was inevitable. As Larry's sister-in-law Dorothy Hart observed, the remarkable thing was not that they finally split up. It was that they stayed together for so long in a business not noted for long and exclusive partnerships. From 1940 onwards, Rodgers, more than anyone, was aware of his partner's problems and even more aware of how those problems affected him. They forced him to consider what he would do when Larry finally became unable to work. He was still a young man—not yet forty—with a family and a home and a profession, and he did not want to lose any of them. He was successful and

Taken at a rehearsal of *By Jupiter*, this gives some idea of the problems Richard Rodgers (*l.*) had working with Lorenz Hart (*r.*). TMC

Best Foot Forward (1942). The lady who looks like Judy Garland is Victoria Schools (centre) but it really is June Allyson on the left and Nancy Walker (lately maid to Macmillan and Wife) on the right. TMC

prolific, and there would be, no doubt, any number of lyricists happy to team up with him. By the middle of 1941, he knew his days with Larry as his collaborator were numbered. He decided to talk it over with an old friend, a wise and benign man, and a great lyricist who had known both Larry and Dick Rodgers since their college days: Oscar Hammerstein.

> Much as I regretted it, there was nothing I could do about it. I couldn't stop working myself just because Larry couldn't be worked with. I had tremendous faith in Oscar. Oscar had had a bad time of it for many years, but I knew beyond argument about his enormous talent, and felt that if something did happen to Larry, this was the logical direction for me to move in. I was in Philadelphia with a show that George Abbott and I produced together called *Best Foot Forward*. Just to give you an idea how far this thing had progressed with Larry, I wouldn't put my name on the show as co-producer because things were so sensitive. I didn't want to call attention to the fact that I was working away from Larry because I thought that would be harmful.[1]

Over lunch at Hammerstein's farm in Doylestown, not far from Philadelphia, Rodgers unburdened himself of his fears concerning Larry Hart and the future of their partnership. Hammerstein listened without speaking, then advised Rodgers to go on working with Hart as long as Hart was able to work: he knew that if Dick walked away it would kill Larry. 'If the time ever comes that he can't work, call me,' Oscar said. 'I'll even go a step further. If you and Larry are in the middle of a job and he can't finish it, I'll finish it for him and no one but the two of us need ever know.'

Relieved, but perhaps still unsure, Rodgers returned to New York. Hammerstein was everything everyone said he was, and more, but Hammerstein had been associated with nothing but flops for a decade. According to Samuel Marx, Rodgers then talked to Ira Gershwin.

> Ira told me about Dick calling him up to have dinner. It was a dinner set up by Louis Dreyfus, Max Dreyfus's son. Dick talked about the problems he was having with Larry and sort of hinted that he had to make a change. He never asked point blank but always sort of talked around it. And Ira, who was committing a slow suicide after the death of George (and which he is still at work on) turned him down.

By Jupiter was a traumatic experience for Rodgers, who produced the show in conjunction with Dwight Deere Wiman. Not only did he have his usual problems in finding Larry, whose drinking, staying out all night and disappearances were increasing to an alarming degree, but he now had to contend with a co-producer almost equally as adept at disappearing, albeit for totally different reasons. Wiman was a man much more devoted to extra-theatre activities than to his duties as a producer. He once kept Rodgers, who is almost maniacally punctual, and a prospective backer waiting for more than an hour, a breach of manners which, in a producer, Rodgers describes as 'roughly akin to self-immolation'.

Rodgers had hoped initially that Larry Hart's enthusiasm for *By Jupiter*—a musical based on the play *The Warrior's Husband* by Julian F. Thompson and starring Ray Bolger, Constance Moore, Benay Venuta and Vera-Ellen—would keep him relatively sober, if only temporarily. Hart was less dependable than ever before. Finding him lying in his apartment in a semi-coma, Rodgers had Larry admitted to Doctor's Hospital, and they completed the score there. However, as soon as Larry hit the street again, he started hitting the bottle. He disappeared for three days during the Boston tryouts and, all in all, made life hell for his partner. Joshua Logan, who directed the play, remembered Dick Rodgers's reactions.

> He came to me and said, 'Josh, I can't go through this any more. I just haven't got it in me.' He told me that he and Larry had been offered *Green Grow the Lilacs* but Larry didn't want to do it. He had talked to Larry, and I think Larry must have felt, must have known how Dick felt. Then Dick said to me, 'What would you think if I worked with Oscar Hammerstein?' And I said, 'Oh, my God, marvellous, it would be wonderful.'

Rodgers was now forced to play his last card: He told Hart, 'If you walk out on me now, I'm going to do the show with someone else.'

'Do you have someone in mind?' Hart asked.

Rodgers told him he had: Oscar Hammerstein. Without ever looking him in the eyes, Hart told Rodgers he couldn't have picked a better man. 'I don't know why you've put up with me all these years,' he said. 'The best thing for you is to forget about me.'

With that he got up and left the boardroom of Chappell & Co., where they had met. Rodgers simply did not know what to do. He had worked with Larry Hart exclusively for more than twenty-five years. He did not know if he could work successfully with Oscar Hammerstein, or anyone else for that matter. All he could think of was that a long and wonderful partnership had just walked out of the door. He got up to go and tell his music publisher, Max Dreyfus, but before he got as far as the door, he was crying like a baby.

Hart's decision was irrevocable. He went off to Mexico City and, true to Rodgers's prediction, he had to be brought home on a stretcher. His departure left the composer no choice. Rodgers went to the Theatre

Guild and told them he wanted to do the score with Oscar Hammerstein. They agreed—not that they were in any position to do much else. The musical adaptation of the Lynn Riggs's play was just about the Guild's last chance, and the odds that were stacked against it were formidable indeed. The show was budgeted at $83,000, of which the Guild had not a penny. Rodgers and his new partner were faced with the prospect of having to raise all of it themselves. At first, the lack of funds did not worry them; they had a half-century of experience between them, a string of great successes behind them.

They met for the first time to discuss the show at the Barberry Room, a place redolent of literary and theatrical history. It had begun life as the restaurant of the Berkshire Hotel, just across the street from the CBS Building on 52nd Street. The owner, George Backer, made it a private club at the request of critic and columnist Alexander Woollcott, bringing in Norman Bel Geddes to design the room. It was long and narrow, with a very high ceiling from which stars appeared to twinkle. The largest mirror in the world was constructed to cover one wall and compensate for the lack of width. This enormous blue mirror and the plush armchairs which were installed gave the place an unforgettable ambience. When he first saw it, Harold Ross, editor of *The New Yorker*, remarked that it would make a terrific swimming pool once they put the water in. The club, which Woollcott dubbed The Elbow Room, did not last six months. A man named Moriarty took over, and turned it into a public restaurant, the Barberry Room.

It cannot have been a very festive luncheon. As far as either of the two men knew, they might never earn a dollar more than the nominal hundreds which the Theatre Guild had advanced them on signing the contract. Nevertheless they decided to go ahead and purchase from MGM an option for the film rights which that company had taken, and which they could pick up for $50,000 two weeks after the première of the new musical. (They took over the rights in four days.) Nobody they knew agreed with them. One or two came right out and said they were crazy to do a cowboy show, as Rodgers recalled.

> There wasn't anything enormously attractive about the idea. And then on top of that Oscar and I were working together for the first time. Who knew whether this combination would work or not? They were sure in my case that it wouldn't, because I'd had all those years with Hart and suddenly came the split. They knew that I had to fail.[2]

In the summer of 1941, Dick and Dorothy Rodgers had bought a new home, a fifteen-room, five-bath Colonial house in a six-acre plot, one of the most attractive features of which was a massive oak tree with a ninety-foot spread. It was beneath this tree that Rodgers and Hammerstein began to work on the show which would eventually become *Oklahoma!* There were to be many, many such sessions until they were completely familiar with each other's ideas and outlook as well as with the formal content of the show itself.

> What happened between Oscar and me was almost chemical. Put the right components together and an explosion takes place. Oscar and I hit it off from the day we started discussing the show. For one thing, I needed a little calm in my life after twenty-three hectic years. When Oscar would say I'll meet you at two-thirty, he was *there* at two-thirty. That had never happened to me before.[3]

A further advantage to both was the fact that each could work to his preferred method. Rodgers had always composed his melodies first, adapting himself to the wayward ways of Larry Hart. Larry had to have something to work on and the music provided it, although Rodgers would have preferred to set finished lyrics to music. Oscar's experience was the very opposite. His inclination had always been to write the lyrics first, but working with such composers as Rudolf Friml, Herbert Stothart, Vincent Youmans and Jerome Kern, he had sublimated that preference. The reversion to preferred methods brought about several important changes both in the songs and in how they fitted into the show.

Almost from the beginning of his career, Oscar Hammerstein had been dedicated to the idea of bringing seriousness to the musical stage. He was impassioned by the thought of finding something which was neither operetta nor escapism, something which had purpose and coherence, something that was unmistakably American, rather than European, in tradition. He had done his share of shoddy shows which were no more than nitwitted plots upon which to hang a random collection of songs and novelty numbers. He had made a giant step towards realizing his dream when he and Jerry Kern collaborated on *Show Boat*. He had lost his shirt on a few experiments of his own. He brought all that experience, all that passion, to his discussions with Dick Rodgers, and, as Rodgers said, the result was almost chemical.

They concluded that in this show, the play would dictate the techniques and not vice versa. They agreed that the only risky thing to do in the theatre was not to take risks. They decided that the integration of music and text should be paramount, and that the lyrics could and should determine the form of the song. They discussed moods, textures, construction. And breaking rules.

Tradition dictated that the curtain on every musical should rise on

A scene from the Theatre Guild's original production of Lynn
Riggs's *Green Grow the Lilacs*—not really all that far from *Oklahoma!*
TMC

a big, star-spangled production number, a crowded stage full of colour,
dancing and song. Yet *Green Grow the Lilacs* was a simple, unpretentious
story which defied them to open with extravaganza. There was no pre-
cedent, and so they did the only possible thing: they decided to set
one. Which in turn led to other problems. Musical comedy demanded,
nay, insisted on, a chorus line. Yet the play offered no opportunity for
a chorus until half way through the first act, an unheard-of delay in
'bringing on the girls'. Musical comedy had never tolerated so vil-
lainous a character as Jeeter (who became Jud Fry), or a murder. Yet
Riggs's play contained both, and both must stay, Hammerstein said.

> We both realized that such a course was experimental, amounting almost
> to a breach of an implied contract with a musical comedy audience. I cannot
> say truthfully that we were worried by the risk. Once we had made the
> decisions everything seemed to work right and we had the inner confidence
> people feel when they have adopted the direct and honest approach to a
> problem.[4]

Rodgers agreed; and Oscar set to work. The first task was to write
a song with which to open the show, one which would set the tone and
mood for everything that followed. For inspiration, he went to Lynn

Riggs's stage directions. He recalled reading them and thinking what a pity it was that the audience could not do so, for if they could, they would slip easily into the mood of the story. Riggs had described a radiant summer morning, 'the kind of morning which, enveloping the shapes of earth—men, cattle in the meadow, blades of the young corn— makes them seem to exist now for the first time, their images giving off a visible golden emanation . . .' From there it was but a short step to the decision to embody that description in the lyric. The bright golden haze, the meadow, the cattle, the corn were already there. Hammerstein translated them into the simple phraseology of the cowboy, Curly, who would sing them, even going so far as to write at first that the corn was as high as a cow-pony's eye. The lyric took him three weeks to write, one whole week of which was spent agonizing over whether to start the first two lines with the word 'Oh'.

He and Rodgers had long since agreed that in all the songs they would try to capture the essential quality of the character or mood. Oscar's intention was, to use his own words, 'to sock the audience where it lives'. He used simple words because he believed a song was not the place to demonstrate his erudition—a viewpoint profoundly dissimilar to that of Lorenz Hart—and said that each line in a lyric should be the continuation of the one before, or the introduction of a new thought. 'To stay in character the lyric must never let go of the listener for a single instant. It's like fishing. A little slack in the line and they're off the hook.' So, three weeks later, he handed his completed lyric to Rodgers, and was astounded when the composer completed his melody in ten minutes. 'When Oscar handed me the lyric and I read it for the first time, I was a little sick with joy because it was so lovely and so right,' Rodgers said. 'It took nothing to write it. I was so elated that the music came almost as quickly as the time elapsed in writing it down.'

Quite a remarkable reaction from a man who is said to dislike poetry when it is not married to song. Yet stories like this one, although perfectly true, are sometimes a source of irritation to Rodgers. Although it seems amazing that he 'wrote' 'Oh, what a beautiful morning' in ten minutes, it is not when one remembers that Rodgers is first and foremost a craftsman of the theatrical song and the theatrical song alone. Unlike most of his fellow song-writers, he has hardly ever written a song that was unrelated to a specific stage or screenplay. He looks upon his songs as the given musical solution to a specific dramatic problem.

> No melodies are running around in my head. A song almost never occurs to me spontaneously. What I have to say is essentially musical, but it isn't

simply melody for melody's sake. My big involvement is with the characters. I must know how they feel and then I can give them a song to express it. A friend once asked me how long it took to compose the whole score of *Oklahoma!* I said, 'What do you mean, flying time or elapsed time?' Counting everything, overture, ballet music, all the songs, the most I could make it come to was five hours—flying time. But the total elapsed time covered months of discussion and planning, starting with the overall conception and then getting down to specific questions like how to bring the chorus onstage and whether to end this or that scene with dialogue or music. So, before you can say 'Oh, what a beautiful morning' was written in ten minutes, you have to know a little about semantics. By the time Oscar gave me the lyrics and I sat down to the actual business of writing the notes ... these things had all been decided. I have to do an awful lot of thinking ... before I even dream of doing actual notes. I think that the moment of creation should be a spontaneous one, though. I think possibly the results are better if it comes in a rush.[5]

Perhaps an even better example of how closely, and yet how differently, Oscar worked with Lynn Riggs's text is the song 'The surrey with the fringe on top'. This song is what is known in the trade as a 'charm' song. Almost as difficult to create as a comedy number, a charm song is used to establish motive and, as importantly, to make the audience love the characters singing it. In the original *Green Grow the Lilacs*, Lynn Riggs's dialogue went as follows:

> CURLY: A bran' new surrey with a fringe on the top four inches long—and yeller! And two white horses a-rarin' an' faunchin' to go! You'd shore ride like a queen settin' up in *that* carriage! Feel like you had a gold crown set on yer head, 'th diamonds in it as big as goose eggs.
> LAUREY: Look out, you'll be astin' me in a minute!
> CURLY: I ain't astin' you, I'm *tellin'* you! An' thisyere rig has got four fine side curtains, case of rain. And isinglass winders to look out of! And a red and green lamp set on the dashboard winkin' like a lightnin' bug!

and then later

> CURLY: Don't you wish they *was* such a rig, though? Nen you could go to the party and do a hoedown till mornin' if you was a mind to. Nen drive home 'th the sun a-peekin' at you over the ridge, purty and fine.[6]

The raw material for the song is already there; but it needed Hammerstein's lyrical and theatrical genius to turn it into one, and then Rodgers's perfect melody, indicating the clop-clop of the horses, the chicks and ducks and geese scurrying. There are the isinglass windows you can roll right down in case of a change in the weather, the two bright sidelights winking and blinking, and the sun swimming on the rim of the hill. Deceptively simple and, of course, actually anything but.

Oklahoma! (Magna/20th Century Fox, 1955; dir. Fred Zinneman.) Curly (Gordon MacRae) tells Laurey (Shirley Jones) how it will be when he takes her out in 'The surrey with the fringe on top', one of the best sequences in the film. RICHARD ROGERS AND THE ESTATE OF OSCAR HAMMERSTEIN, COURTESY NFA.

What was, and is, remarkable about the score of *Oklahoma!* is that with perhaps one exception, the principal song 'People will say we're in love', none of the melodies bears even a slight family resemblance to the songs Rodgers wrote with Larry Hart. 'Many a new day' with its rippling opening triplets, 'Out of my dreams', 'I cain't say no' and the disturbing, dramatic 'Lonely room' (which occasioned Lynn Riggs to remark, upon hearing it for the first time, that it would probably scare the hell out of the audience) are totally different to anything which preceded them in Rodgers's catalogue. For all that, they are indisputably Rodgers's songs. He is often asked whether the change in lyricists made a profound change in his writing, and, as often, answers no. 'There was no change in my music, none at all. There was a difference because of the way Oscar wrote, the subjects we became involved in—they required a different kind of music. And I had been brought up that way, to make my music fit the text, for a show or a movie or whatever.'

Before long, Hammerstein had a working outline and Rodgers had written enough songs for them to begin trying to interest prospective backers. The big producers would not touch it with a ten-foot pole, and it was not difficult to see why. Apart from Rodgers, none of the principals involved had much to commend them as an investment. Langner and Helburn could hardly dispute the fact that the Theatre Guild was unable to finance its own production. The director was to be Rouben Mamoulian, who had not done a Broadway show for seven years and even that show, *Porgy and Bess*, had been a critical rather than a financial success. The choreographer was Cecil B. de Mille's niece Agnes, a former member of the *Ballets Russes de Monte Carlo*. She had done some work on Aaron Copland's ballet *Rodeo*, but precious little else. Terry Helburn had suggested Shirley Temple for the rôle of Laurey, and Groucho Marx for the part of the leering peddler, Ali Hakim. Rodgers and Hammerstein, backed by Mamoulian, held out for singers and actors who would be right for the parts, regardless of whether or not their names had box-office appeal. Innovative, perhaps, and courageous, certainly; but not the stuff to attract an $83,000 investment. Do another show with Larry Hart, Rodgers was urged. Give us another *By Jupiter*, another *Boys from Syracuse*, but not, for God's sake, a musical about which of two cowboys gets to take a farmer's daughter to a box social.

These reactions forced Dick Rodgers and Oscar Hammerstein into what must have been one of the most humiliating experiences of their lives. With half a century of hits behind them, a formidable record of writing successfully for both stage and screen, they were reduced to working the 'penthouse circuit' cap in hand, trying to raise money for the show. It was no fun at all, as Hammerstein recalled. 'It was hard to finance, all right. We didn't have any stars, and those who were putting up money for plays felt you had to have stars. Dick and I would go from penthouse to penthouse giving auditions. Terry Helburn would narrate the story. Dick would play and I would sing 'Pore Jud is dead'. We weren't hugely successful.'[7]

Auditions had begun in the autumn of 1942. Alfred Drake, who had won the part of the cowboy hero, Curly, had been a Rodgers and Hart discovery in *Babes in Arms* in 1938. Since then he had appeared in shows as diverse as Shakespeare's *As You Like It* and revues like *One for the Money* and *Two for the Show*. Oscar Hammerstein had tried to persuade a bright newcomer to the Broadway scene called Mary Martin to take

Alfred Drake, who played Curly in the original stage version of *Oklahoma!* but later turned down the part of the King in *The King and I*. TMC

Ali Hakim (Joseph Buloff) and Ado Annie (Celeste Holm). He invites her to come upstairs with him at the hotel. 'Upstairs,' he says, 'is Paradise!' 'Oh,' says Annie. 'I thought they was just bedrooms.' TMC

the rôle of Laurey, the heroine, but she turned them down. The part went to a young singer who had been in one of Oscar's disasters, a 1941 show with music by Sigmund Romberg called *Sunny River* which had foundered after six weeks. Her name was Joan Roberts, and in her autobiography, *Never Alone*, she recalled that when she auditioned, Dick was withdrawn, as though deeply preoccupied. Oscar on the other hand was, she said, pleasantly talkative and gave the impression of not having problems of any kind.

They had problems, however, and plenty of them. Even when they augmented their auditions with the singers, the process of raising the money remained totally unreliable and painfully slow. Often they would provide an evening of music and story for the beautiful people in their glittering palaces—and raise not a penny.

Theresa Helburn went to MGM and offered them fifty per cent of the profits of the show for a $75,000 investment. MGM turned her down. Through Max Gordon, the producer, the Guild approached the forceful, leather-tongued Harry Cohn, head of Columbia Pictures, and got him to attend an audition at Steinway Hall. Cohn loved it and promised to put up the money MGM had refused. For a few days, everyone thought their troubles were over, but Columbia Pictures' board of directors disagreed with Cohn. The offer was withdrawn, although Cohn did invest $15,000 of his own money. Seeing the hardheaded Cohn put that kind of money into the show persuaded Max Gordon also to invest. *Away We Go!* had at last become a viable theatrical project, and just in time. Oscar Hammerstein had been tempted to withdraw from the show by the offer of a juicy two-year Hollywood contract dangled in front of his eyes by Arthur Freed. Even Rodgers nursed the secret hope that an Army Air Force commission might take the problems of the show out of his hands.

More problems? Yes, even more. Rouben Mamoulian was interpreting his contract, which gave him 'a free hand', to the literal letter. Temperament, and tempers, were running high. Agnes de Mille and the director were at daggers drawn. His version is that when he told her she was choreographing as if for ballet, and there would be no room for the kind of ballet she was devising on the stage, she screamed that he was ruining her and took her grievances to Dick Rodgers, calling Mamoulian a sour bitch and an even greater tyrant than her uncle. Agnes de Mille recalled that Mamoulian had tantrums when he learned that Dick and Oscar had seen the costume and set designs before he had. She also remembers how the last of the money was raised. Terry Helburn went to see S. N. Behrman, a playwright who had won great

Richard Rodgers and Oscar Hammerstein II during a rehearsal of
Away We Go! and looking a lot more relaxed than they had any
right to be. TMC

acclaim with plays produced by the Guild.

'Sam,' she said, 'you've got to take $20,000 of this, because the Guild
has done so much for you.'

And he said, 'But, Terry, that's blackmail.'

'Yes,' she said. 'It is.'

By the time rehearsals were finished, Mamoulian had become the
villain of the piece. Nobody would talk to him, not even Oscar, who
had been the one who most seemed to understand what Mamoulian
was trying to achieve. The first tryout of *Away We Go!* was scheduled
for the Shubert Theatre at New Haven, Connecticut, on 11 March
1943, and, as usual, interested theatrical people from New York came
up to see it. These savants returned there, after seeing what was little
more than a hastily patched-up version of what the final show would
look like, and spread the savage *bon mot*, allegedly coined by Mike Todd,

'No girls, no gags, no good.' The fact that the verdict ignored the encouraging reaction of the New Haven audience was irrelevant. As La Rochefoucald observed, the misfortune of one's best friends is not always displeasing.

At the end of the first performance of 'Helburn's Folly', another of the less-than-kind sobriquets given to the show, everyone was convinced it was going to be a disastrous flop. Mamoulian recalls that there was a post-mortem at two in the morning and that the general consensus was that the whole ragbag would have to be completely restaged. The director held out, and finally convinced them that he was right. He did so by swearing that if he was wrong, he would never ever direct a stage production again.

Dick and Oscar were far too much men of the theatre to disregard an affirmation of such faith and strength. They plunged into frantic sessions of rewriting before the show moved to Boston for the second stage of its tryouts. More humour and action were written in, for both were sorely needed. A song 'Boys and girls like you and me' was excised, and a three-minute dancing sequence was taken out to be replaced by a rousing choral number. Terry Helburn had expressed regret that there was no song about the land itself in the show, and her idle remark, made while sharing a taxi with Oscar Hammerstein, had stuck in the lyricist's mind. From it burgeoned the song which finally gave the show its name: 'Oklahoma!' Whether or not Oscar was aware of or daunted by the fact that there were already well over a hundred songs with the same title is not recorded. The decision was taken to rechristen the show, but since all the programmes for Boston had already been printed, they decided to save the new title for New York. On 15 March, still called *Away We Go!*, the show opened in Boston.

The Boston experience was so rewarding to both men that thereafter they made it a point to stage all the pre-Broadway tryouts of their plays in that city. They found the constructive and sympathetic attitude of the critics—Elinor Hughes of the *Herald*, Cyrus Durgin of the *Globe* and, most notably, Elliott Norton of the *Post*—invaluable. They fell in love with the Ritz Hotel, and with the city itself. Rodgers has since been quoted as saying he wouldn't open anything, not even a can of tomatoes, anywhere else but in Boston.

The Boston critics predictably found fault with the length of the show—over-running is common with new shows in tryout, and *Away We Go!* was no exception. But the music, the lyrics and the dancing drew rave notices. The backstage disasters—lead dancer Marc Platt sprained two toes in one of the dances, another girl sprained her arm,

The poster for the New York opening of *Oklahoma!* Not exactly informative. TMC

and several of the cast actually appeared wearing heavy applications of greasepaint to disguise the fact that they had German measles— weren't even noticed. Even so, *Away We Go!* was not quite a roaring success. There was competition from a new Vernon Duke musical star- ring Mary Martin, called *Dancing in the Streets*.[8] Business was brisk according to reports, but by no means brisk enough to ensure a sellout for the New York opening.

Oklahoma!, with the additional exclamation point added at the in- sistence of Lawrence Langner, who was afraid that audiences might think the show was about dustbowls and Okie farmers, opened in New York on 31 March 1943 at the St James's Theatre. The curtain went up on an uncluttered stage to reveal a woman churning butter on the porch of a farm. Offstage, a young man's voice sang, in waltz-time, of the bright golden haze on the meadow and the corn as high as an elephant's eye. The first-night audience was stunned, amazed, de- lighted, staggered. From that first few bars of music the show was a hit. Both Rodgers and Hammerstein knew it. 'The audience responded to everything,' Rodgers said. 'Not only could I see it and hear it, I could feel it.' Hammerstein agreed. 'The glow was like the light from a thousand lanterns,' he said. 'You could *feel* the glow, it was that bright.'

The curtain came down to a thunderous ovation. Up in the box he had reserved, Larry Hart cheered and stamped and shouted 'bravo!' It must have been heartbreaking for him to realize, and he must have realized, that his partner had finally achieved without him everything for which they had been working together for so long, but Larry Hart was not capable of envy or malice. He was proud of Rodgers, and he pushed his way through the crowd at the after-show party in Sardi's restaurant and threw his arms around his partner, grinning from ear to ear. He told Rodgers he had never had a better evening at the theatre in his life. 'This thing will run longer than *Blossom Time*,' he predicted, and he was right. Significantly, he did not stay. This was Rodgers and Hammerstein's success, not his.

There was to be a party for the members of the cast and production at the elegant Fifth Avenue apartment of Jules Glaenzer, the president of Cartier's, who was a legendary host to the brightest stars of Broadway. The idea was that they would await the reviews of the New York critics, for New York newspapers, then as now, were on sale in the early hours of the morning whose date they bore. They all confirmed Larry Hart's opinion. There was not a single holdout. *The New York Times*'s Lewis Nichols, substituting for Brooks Atkinson, who was still in the Services, said 'Wonderful is the nearest adjective'. Burns Mantle of the *Daily News* called *Oklahoma!* 'the most thoroughly attractive American musical since *Show Boat*'. Wolcott Gibbs of *The New Yorker* confessed he had 'nothing but the greatest affection for everyone in it', and that his gratitude was 'practically boundless'. Every reviewer praised the show in the most glowing terms, and as they came in, Glaenzer rushed across to congratulate Rodgers and to press a celebratory drink on him. Rodgers says he had no difficulty in refusing. 'I want to remember every second of this night,' he said. 'I'm not going to touch a drop!'

How sweet success was! Soothing balm indeed for those humiliating nights on the penthouse circuit, those ghastly weeks of raising the backing dollar by painful hundred dollars, those months when he, Oscar and Rouben Mamoulian had alone kept up the morale of the entire company. He was, as he had always been, a steadfast believer in the fact that luck plays only a small part in success, but not even Rodgers or his partner could have foreseen how big a success *Oklahoma!* would become. They had a hit, they knew. What they did not know was that they had a phenomenon.

Oklahoma! The principals: Will Parker (Lee Dixon), Ado Annie (Celeste Holm), Curly (Alfred Drake), Laurey (Joan Roberts), Ali Hakim (Joseph Buloff, kneeling) and Aunt Eller (Betty Garde) TMC

It has been fashionable to say that one of the important elements in the success of *Oklahoma!* was that it appeared in 1943, a grim period in World War II when both America and Britain were reeling as Germany and Japan battered them into retreat after retreat. Certainly that might explain the warmth with which its lyrical escapism was greeted at the première; but *Oklahoma!* transcended every and any musical show which had been written up to that time. It ran for five years and nine weeks, an astonishing 2,212 performances. No musical had ever approached that figure.[9] The story did not end with the New York run, either. Two days after the show closed, touring companies took it to seventy cities over the following year. The national company, formed in 1943, played the show for a further five years, appearing in more than two hundred and fifty cities. By 1950, the national company had

Oklahoma! The dance in the Skidmore barn. Aunt Eller (Betty Garde) in the spotted dress, fourth from left; Will Parker (Lee Dixon) in the check jacket waving his hat, and Ado Annie (Celeste Holm) to his left, both arms raised. TMC

played more than 3,000 times in every one of the (then) forty-eight States. Other companies took *Oklahoma!* to Germany, to South Africa, to Denmark, to Sweden, to Australia. At London's Drury Lane Theatre, the show broke the 287-year-old long-run record of that establishment, and achieved the second longest run in London's theatrical history: three and a half years.

In its first decade, *Oklahoma!* produced profits of more than five million dollars for its original backers. The reluctant Sam Behrman's $20,000 eventually produced a return of six and a half million dollars. Richard Rodgers and Oscar Hammerstein became millionaires. The Theatre Guild pocketed four million dollars. A one per cent investment costing $1,500 back in the dark days of New Haven was now worth $50,000.

To this astonishing performance record must be added the honours heaped upon the show. In 1944 *Oklahoma!* received a special citation from the Pulitzer Prize Committee. The show also helped inaugurate a practice which has since become standard in the recording industry, the 'original cast' album. Jack Kapp of Decca approached the partners and proposed that Decca issue records on which the actual cast, conductor and theatre orchestra would perform the songs exactly as they did onstage. 'It was the most exciting concept we'd ever heard of,' Rodgers said. 'Naturally, we consented.' The record set of *Oklahoma!* sold more than a million copies, and this was *before* the advent of the long-playing record, which did not arrive on the scene until 1948. It would also become a launching pad for the careers of a large number of actors and actresses, many of whom were unknown when they first appeared in it. Among them were Celeste Holm, Alfred Drake, Shelley Winters, Howard Keel, Florence Henderson, Isabel Bigley, Iva Withers and Howard da Silva.

Oklahoma! has been revived very frequently, and always successfully, and Rodgers makes no bones about his delight in its having become an American classic. It needs little imagination to guess how he and Oscar Hammerstein must have felt when they met for lunch on the day after the première. On their way, they decided to stroll around to the St James's Theatre and see how business was, following the rave reviews. To their astonishment, they encountered bedlam. Crowds were pushing and fighting to get to the box office. There was even a policeman trying to keep order, Rodgers recalled. He turned to Oscar and asked whether he would like to go some place quiet and talk, or whether he'd prefer to go to Sardi's and show off.

'Hell, let's go to Sardi's and show off,' Oscar said. And they did.

2. Oscar

'His work tended to make people think of him as an
unsophisticated, platitudinous hick, when in fact he was a highly
intelligent, strongly principled and philosophical man.'
Stephen Sondheim

He studied law originally, but there was never much more than a pious
hope that he would become a lawyer. His father, William, was a theatre
manager, his uncle Arthur a Broadway producer. His grandfather, after
whom he was named, was a former cigar maker turned opera impresario. Small wonder, then, that Oscar Greeley Clendenning Hammerstein became an ardent lover of the theatre and remained one all his
life. He said he never really knew his paternal grandfather well. That
top-hatted, Prince Albert-coated, striped-trousered figure with the
goatee and the big cigar was always too busy to spend much time with
his grandson. Oscar always said that the longest time he spent with
the old boy was a visit to his deathbed, but then Oscar had a mordant
sense of humour.

It was in 1906, when young Oscar was eleven years old, that Oscar
Hammerstein I decided to challenge the supremacy of the aristocratic
Metropolitan Opera by building his own Opera House on West 34th
Street and presenting there such modern operas as *Louise*, *Thaïs*, and
Le Jongleur de Notre Dame, works hitherto excluded from the rigidly
classical repertoire of the Met. He imported such talents as Mary
Garden, Tetrazzini, Dalmores, Bonci and Renaud, who had been un-
able to get a hearing at the Met. Fired by his success, Oscar built
another Opera House, this time in Philadelphia, waging war upon the

Oscar Hammerstein I. As well as building opera houses,
theatres and apartment houses and suing Florenz Ziegfeld, he also
found time to invent cigar-making machines, nursing bottles,
men's suspenders and inkwells. LFG

Met's supremacy with a gusto that forced both that organization and
his own into heavy losses. Finally, to remove his competition, the
Metropolitan Opera paid Hammerstein one million dollars for his
undertaking not to produce opera in the city for a decade. He was once
asked if there was a lot of money in the opera business.

'Yes,' he said. 'Mine.'

Oscar Hammerstein II—he preferred using the suffix to the cumber-
some middle names with which he had been lumbered—was born in
an apartment on 135th Street in New York on 12 July 1895. When
he was four years of age the family decided to move down to 125th

Street so that Oscar's mother, always in delicate health, could live in the apartment directly above that of her father, James Nimmo. Oscar's newly-arrived infant brother Reginald placed heavy demands on the frail woman, and it was decided that Oscar would move downstairs and stay with the old man, an arrangement which lasted for three years. Although Oscar continued to share meals with his family, his maternal grandfather became his friend and confidant. Nimmo would give his grandson milk punch laced with whisky in the mornings and then they would walk across to Mount Morris Park nearby so the old man could sketch—his specialty was foliage. At the top of the hill in the park stood a bell tower whose bell was rung daily by an old gent who climbed up the spiral staircase and tolled it by hand. James Nimmo told his grandson that the bellringer was the Devil, and Oscar believed him so implicitly that he was never again afraid of the Devil, because he'd seen him and knew he was a harmless old coot who rang the bell in the park; the same park, incidentally, that young Dick Rodgers would play in a few years later.

Oscar recalled that one of the most vivid memories of his life was a visit as a four-year-old to the Victoria Theatre, that cathedral of vaudeville on 42nd Street built by grandfather Oscar in his pre-opera days and now managed by Oscar's father. Watching the show from a box, the boy was so affected by the lights and the colours and the music (and especially Frank Fogarty singing 'You can't bunko me') that he broke out in a cold sweat and felt faint. When he got home he was so sick he had to be put to bed. But it was the sickness of excitement, an excitement which was to remain with him as long as he lived. 'The fact is,' he was to say many times, 'that I am almost foolishly in love with the stage. The mere sight of a bare stage sends pains up and down my back.' After attending Public School No. 9 in Manhattan (he received a report card which confirmed he was a good boy, and kept it all his life) he was sent to the Hamilton Institute, a private school on Central Park West. His first story, *The Adventures of a Penny*, was published in that school's magazine when he was twelve. He also edited the magazine at his summer camp in Highmount, New York State.

Oscar's literary and theatrical proclivities notwithstanding, his father (his mother died in 1910) insisted that the stage was far too perilous a profession and enrolled Oscar in the law school at Columbia University—perhaps the worst thing he could have done if he wanted to deflect Oscar from theatrical and literary life. For from the turn of the century and to the beginning of the First Word War, Columbia University and the area around it, known as Morningside Heights, was one of the most astonishing seedbeds of talent in America. Oscar's class-mates and fellow students included Morris Ryskind, among whose later credits would be the libretto of the George and Ira Gershwin show *Of Thee I Sing*, the first musical ever to win a Pulitzer Prize. There was Bennett Cerf, a raconteur, writer and wit who would found the publish-ing empire of Random House. There was Herman Mankiewicz, who would create the scenarios for many notable motion pictures, including *Citizen Kane*; and his brother Joe, a future writer and director of such films as *All About Eve*. There was a freckle-faced youngster with a shock of red hair. His name was Howard Dietz, and he would one day some-how marry the tasks of being MGM's publicity supremo, and writing lyrics to the music of Arthur Schwartz. There was gnomish Larry Hart, his partnership with Rodgers still a few years away, profiting from his fluent German by translating foreign plays. There was Max Lincoln Schuster, another embryo publisher, and Mortimer Rodgers, older brother of the tyro composer, who would become a distinguished doc-tor. There was Herman Axelrod, father of playwright George. Milton Berle played on the streets of Morningside Heights. Other friends included the three children of Lew Fields, a former comedian of great renown who had turned producer: Herbert, Dorothy and Joseph would all make their mark in the theatrical world.

Many of this exalted gaggle of talents spent their spare time—and, one suspects, a lot of time not 'spare' at all—writing poetry, lyrics, sketches, plays, columns, newspaper items or short articles. The thing was to get your name in print and the most 'in' of all 'in' things was to get something accepted by 'The Conning Tower', a column or 'colyum' as its originator called it, which appeared regularly opposite the editorial pages in the *New York World*, signed simply 'FPA'. Insiders knew that 'FPA' was Franklin P. Adams, who specialized in light verse and quips much appreciated by the intelligentsia. His standards were very high, and contributors strove for the honour of being in his column, especially at the top of the 'tower' of type. Adams himself spent most of his days playing pool at the Players' Club in Gramercy Park, donat-ing a watch once a year to the contributor whom he considered had sent in the best piece. Not a bad way to run a 'colyum' at that; perhaps his use of the word 'conning' was ahead of its time. At any rate he attracted some rare talents, all of them using the convention of a pseudonym. Morris Ryskind was 'Morrie'. Deems Taylor was 'Smeed' and Herman Mankiewicz 'Mank'. Howard Dietz acknowledged his own 'Freckles'. Oscar was in heady company indeed, and soon plunged into writing himself.

In his junior year he appeared in the 1915 Varsity Show as a long-haired poet à la Bunthorne (the same year that Larry Hart did a befrocked take-off of Mary Pickford, 'skipping and bouncing like an electrified gnome'). The following year, Oscar wrote an additional scene for *Peace Pirates*, the author of which was Herman Mankiewicz. He also did a blackface routine and a comedy dance in a leopard skin. In 1917, after transferring to Law School, he helped write that year's show, *Home James*, and appeared in one scene as a French waiter with the likely name of Dubonnet. The rest of the text was by Herman Axelrod.

Oscar took a part-time job as a process server for a law firm, and later worked in their offices. His salary was five dollars a week, which would have made things tough had he not also had fifty dollars a week coming in from securities given to him by his father. Even so, it wasn't enough to get married on. Oscar was in love, and so he asked his employers for a rise; they refused. He always felt that if they had not done so, he might very well have stayed on and become a lawyer. As it was, he went to see his Uncle Arthur, who gave him the twenty dollars a week he needed in return for his services as assistant stage manager for the Broadway show *You're in Love*. With a book by Otto Harbach and Ed Clark, and music by Rudolf Friml, the show opened on 6 February 1916 and ran for 167 performances. Oscar shifted scenery, helped with the lighting, cued the actors, and did odd jobs. He loved every moment of it, and was soon able to marry his sweetheart, Myra Finn. By a remarkable coincidence Myra was a cousin of Dick Rodgers's father, Dr William Rodgers.

It was in that same year that Oscar met young Richard for the first time. The Players' Club of Columbia University had presented its eleventh annual show, *Home James*, and

After the Saturday matinee of this same Varsity show, while the ballroom of the Hotel Astor was being cleared for the dancing that followed ... Morty Rodgers came up to me. He had in tow a boy about twelve years old, a smaller and darker version of himself, his kid brother Dick. As we were being introduced I noted, with satisfaction, young Richard's respectful awe in the presence of a college junior whom he had just seen playing one of the chief parts in the Varsity Show. I, too, was conscious of my current glory, and realizing what a treat it must be for the child to meet me, I was my most gracious and courteous self—a man about nineteen trying to be a man about town. Whenever I made this effort I always finished far south of Beau Brummel and much nearer Ichabod Crane.

I saw Dick a few more times that year. Morty brought him up to our fraternity house and I heard him play our bruised and beaten piano. We

Oscar Greeley Clendenning Hammerstein—'Ock' to his friends—
as a young man. 'far south of Beau Brummel and nearer Ichabod
Crane'. TMC

all liked him—a cute kid. In my memory of him during this period, he wore
short pants. He tells me now that by that time he had already put on long
pants. All right, but in my memory he wore short pants. This impression—
or illusion—is never quite absent from my conception of him. Behind the
sometimes too serious face of an extraordinarily talented composer and a
sensationally successful theatrical producer I see a dark-eyed little boy in

short pants. The frequent overlapping of these two pictures is an element in what I consider to be my sound understanding of Dick and my affection for him.[1]

Thus Oscar Hammerstein on his first meeting with Richard Rodgers, as he set it down in the preface to *The Rodgers and Hart Songbook* in 1951. Rodgers's recollection of Oscar at the time is of a tall, skinny fellow with a sweet smile, clear blue eyes, and a somewhat mottled complexion. He also recalls that no immortal phrases were uttered, and insists that he was wearing long pants.

By the following year, Oscar had been promoted to full stage manager on another Rudolf Friml musical produced by Arthur Hammerstein. It starred Ed Wynn ('the perfect fool') and Mae West and was called, perhaps predictably, *Some Time* (as in 'come up and see me, some time,' no doubt). If the score was largely forgettable, the production clocked up a very respectable 283 performances at the Shubert Theatre on West 44th Street. One night during the show's run, Mae took young Oscar to one side and advised him to quit the theatre while he still had the chance. 'You've got too much class to hang around the stage, kid,' she told him.

Next, at Arthur Hammerstein's suggestion, Oscar tried his hand at a play which his uncle promised to bring to New York if it was successful. Oscar completed a four-act tragedy about small-town girls. *The Light* failed after its fifth performance during the New Haven tryouts before an audience of perhaps twenty people, and the play is remembered today chiefly for the memorable (if unscripted) scene in that performance where the *ingénue* bemoaned the fact that everything was falling around her at precisely the same moment as her underwear slid down around her ankles.

Oscar's reaction to this disaster, according to Leland Hayward, was typical. He realized that he was involved with a total failure. He got up, fled from the theatre and sought refuge on a bench in a little park nearby. Cursing luck, Fate, and *ingénues* with slack elastic, he suddenly thought of an idea for another show. He began writing it then and there. In movies, his determined optimism would have been met with instant success, but in real life it was to be two long years before the play Oscar started that day actually opened on Broadway. So it was back to stage managing, still keeping in touch with the Columbia Varsity Shows. He wrote the book and lyrics for the 1918 'War Show' *Ten to Five*, which he also directed. He was on the committee which selected, as the 1920 offering, a show by a new team, Richard Rodgers and Lorenz Hart. Rodgers had entered Columbia in the Fall of 1919, and the committee of the Players' Club (Richard Conried, son of the Metropolitan Opera impresario, Ray Perkins and Oscar Hammerstein) liked the Rodgers and Hart songs but preferred someone else's libretto. The show, a satire on Bolshevism, had been written by Milton Kroop. Dick and Larry adapted their songs accordingly and somehow—he professed not knowing how, unless his membership of the committee had something to do with it—a couple of Oscar's lyrics with Rodgers music were incorporated into the show, *Fly With Me*. (In fact, the songs had been written when Rodgers did his second amateur show for an organization called the Infants Relief Society, *Up Stage and Down*.) Morty Rodgers dragooned a patient of his father's named Benjamin Kaye and also Oscar into doing some lyrics. Kaye wrote 'Can it' while Oscar contributed 'Weaknesses' and 'There's always room for one more'. This is how the best of the two went:

> My heart is an airy castle
> Filled with girls I adore
> My brain is a cloud of memories
> Of peaches galore
> There were Jane and Mollie
> And Ruth and Sue
> Camilla, Kit and Patricia too,
> My heart is filled to the brim with you,
> But there's always room for one more![2]

Such was the quality of the first collaboration of Rodgers and Hammerstein, and notable only for a remarkable similarity of approach on the lyricist's part to this and to a song which would appear in 1958 in *The Flower Drum Song* called 'Gliding through my memoree'.

On 5 January 1920 Arthur Hammerstein presented his nephew's first musical, *Always You*, at the Central Theatre. The score was by Herbert Stothart, the star the delightful Helen Ford (soon to become a stunning success in the first Rodgers and Hart musical, *Dearest Enemy*) but the run of sixty-five performances was somewhat short of sensational. A six-months tour brightened the picture, however, and convinced Arthur Hammerstein that all Oscar needed was experience and guidance. To help him gain it, he introduced his nephew to lyricist-librettist Otto Harbach, a prolific and highly successful writer. Harbach was the writer of some big hit songs: 'Cuddle up a little closer, lovey mine' and 'Every little movement has a meaning of its own', as well as the lyrics for Rudolf Friml's *The Firefly* which included the sensational 'Sympathy'.

Born Otto Hauerbach in Salt Lake City, Utah, on 18 August 1873,

Otto Harbach was a lyricist, librettist or collaborator on such supremely American shows as *No, No, Nanette, Sunny, Roberta,* and *The Desert Song.* He died in 1963 at the ripe old age of eighty-nine.
CP

Harbach had given up teaching English in Washington State and come to New York to study at Columbia University. At the age of twenty-nine he went to work for a newspaper and then in an advertising agency before breaking into the theatre with a show called *Three Twins,* which opened on 15 June 1908 and was an immediate success, closing after a run of 288 performances.

Harbach was more than willing to work with Arthur's nephew (as, in later years, Oscar would work with and encourage a young lyricist-composer named Stephen Sondheim) and the two of them teamed with Herbert Stothart to produce *Tickle Me,* a nonsense about a movie company on location in Tibet. Highly-unlikely characters abounded, and sumptuous set-pieces such as 'The Ceremony of the Sacred Bath' were apparently exactly the right ingredients. In 1920 no one went to see a musical expecting an intellectual evening, and *Tickle Me* went some distance out of its way to avoid providing one. It ran for a very profitable seven months.

Fired with success and enthusiasm, Oscar sat down and wrote three straight flops, one after the other. *Jimmie* ran for seventy-one performances. *Daffy Dill* duplicated that dismal record, and *Queen o' Hearts* managed to do even worse: thirty-nine performances. Not that the failures were entirely Oscar's. His collaborators on *Jimmie* were Harbach and Frank Mandel, on *Daffy Dill* Guy Bolton and, on the third show, Mandel again. Even so, this bitter three-year cycle of failure impressed upon Oscar a truth he never forgot, an adage once quoted to him by his grandfather Oscar to the effect that there was no limit to the number of people who would stay away from a bad show.

In 1923, however, Oscar's luck changed. He and Harbach, with Stothart again providing most of the music, wrote a show called *Wildflower*. An important addition to the musical side of the collaboration was a talented newcomer to the Broadway theatre named Vincent Youmans, a shy young genius whose constant illnesses gave him the undeserved reputation of being cold and distant. He was just twenty-five when he began to work on *Wildflower*, having served in the Navy during the recent war, and then worked his way into the theatre via a welltried path, songplugger for T. B. Harms, the music publishers, and rehearsal pianist—mostly for Victor Herbert operettas—until he was befriended by George Gershwin, who was exactly one day younger than Youmans. Gershwin persuaded producer Alex Aarons to take a chance on Youmans much as he had a year earlier with him. Aarons got Fred Jackson, who had written George's first show, *La La Lucille!*, to write another, *Two Little Girls in Blue*, and hired Youmans as co-composer with Paul Lannin. The lyrics were by 'Arthur Francis' (George's brother Ira was still too shy to come out from behind his pseudonym).

There can be little doubt that Youmans contributed greatly to the score of *Wildflower*. His uncluttered musical ear and youth are apparent in the music, and the show was a big hit. With an Italian setting, with Edith Day as its star—a girl who can inherit her grandfather's fortune only if she keeps her ungovernable temper under control for six months—and with a catchy song called 'La Bambalina' which became very popular, the show was a success and its young authors were on their way.

Vincent Youmans, who wrote *Wildflower* with Oscar Hammerstein but is best remembered for *No, No, Nanette!* and *Hit The Deck*. He died, aged forty-seven, on 5 April 1946, the same age as Larry Hart and just as tragic a loss to the musical. There were more than one hundred and seventy-five unpublished songs among his possessions. ASCAP

Youth was flooding into the musical theatre, bringing to it a sparkle, a gaiety and brashness which would sweep away the old Viennese operetta traditions that were slowly smothering it with sweetness. These young men were audacious and proud of that audacity. Twenty-year-old George Gershwin had led the way in 1919 with *La La Lucille!*. Oscar was twenty-four when he wrote his first musical, *Always You*. Youmans was twenty-one and Ira Gershwin twenty-four when they collaborated on *Two Little Girls in Blue*. Howard Dietz was twenty-eight when he wrote all the lyrics for Jerome Kern's *Dear Sir* in 1924. Two years later his partner-to-be, Arthur Schwartz, encouraged by the twenty-nine-year-old Lorenz Hart, contributed songs to *The Grand Street Follies*. Hart himself was only twenty-five and Richard Rodgers the baby of them all at eighteen when they were represented for the first time on Broadway in 1920's *Poor Little Ritz Girl*.

For all its success (it actually ran longer than *No No Nanette!*) *Wildflower* was just the starting point for Oscar Hammerstein. He was already becoming convinced that there might be a way to create a show with depth and realism in its story, while yet remaining entertaining and as melodically fertile as the 'entertainments for tired businessmen' which were the norm. Meanwhile, he did another show with Youmans called *Mary Jane McKane*, Stothart once more providing additional music and William Cary Duncan collaborating on book and lyrics. It opened on Christmas Day, 1923 and ran for 151 performances, which was good, but not good enough. Youmans went off to try his luck elsewhere, luck which would eventually culminate in 1925's *No No Nanette!*, the archetypal Twenties show. By that time, Oscar and Otto Harbach had a thundering smash hit of their own: *Rose Marie*.

Early in 1924, Arthur Hammerstein—who loved spectacular stage effects and had aspirations towards the Ziegfeld glitter—heard that an ice carnival was held annually in Quebec, and that its climax was the melting down of a huge ice palace. Despite the fact that he had not the remotest idea of how such a spectacle might be effected on stage, or into what kind of story it might be incorporated, Arthur despatched Oscar to Quebec with instructions to check up on the carnival. Oscar dutifully plodded up to the Canadian city, and sadly reported that there was not and never had been any such event in Quebec within living memory. Arthur told him not to worry, but to write some other story set in Canada now he'd been up there and seen it. The result was *Rose Marie*, the only musical ever set in the Canadian Rockies.

While Oscar and Otto Harbach were working on the book, and Rudolf Friml put his score together, Arthur set out to secure the biggest prize of all. He wanted to coax Mary Ellis on to the musical stage. Miss Ellis had but recently quit the Metropolitan Opera for a dramatic career, and made no bones about the fact that she was through with singing. She was appearing with Katherine Cornell and Lowell Sherman in *Casanova* when Arthur Hammerstein asked her to come and see him. 'I was very highbrow, very young, and very ambitious,' she recalled, 'and I didn't want at all to go into what I thought was then the lesser musical world.' At Hammerstein's office, she met Oscar for the first time, 'a very tall, thin young man who jumped out of the chair

Rudolf Friml: he got his start in the theatre when Victor Herbert refused to have anything further to do with a temperamental actress in one of Arthur Hammerstein's shows. CP

and looked at me with the most wonderful eyes I have ever seen— gentle, kind, the inner radiance just poured out of his eyes, which I think was the thing that people remember most about Oscar.'

Oscar told her the outline of the story, *Rose Marie*, and his enthusiasm caught her up in it. 'We were very serious about it,' Miss Ellis remembers. 'Every lyric, every idea. We worked like Trojans.'

Rose Marie was different in many ways to the usual musical. With Dennis King and William Kent in the leads, and with Miss Ellis looking stunningly beautiful—'the peer of any musical show star in this country' according to Arthur Hornblow—the show was head and shoulders above the standard piffle then prevalent on Broadway. Its pioneering attempt to incorporate murder into the story, to integrate the dialogue, lyrics and music so that they became indivisible was not, as anyone who has seen the show knows, completely successful. There were many 'specialty' numbers, interpolations which marred its flow.

Mary Ellis resplendent in her *Rose Marie* wedding outfit. CP

Nevertheless, its authors felt it worthwhile to insert a note in the programme to the effect that the musical numbers were so integral to the action that they would not be listed separately: a clear indication of the direction in which Oscar Hammerstein wanted to go.

Change was in the air. On 24 May 1924 the dean of the operetta tradition, Victor Herbert—he of 'Kiss me again', 'I'm falling in love with someone' and 'A kiss in the dark'—died, aged sixty-five. One of his more enduring legacies to music was his part in founding the American Society of Composers, Authors and Publishers (ASCAP) in 1914 to ensure that its members would receive whatever royalties were due them from the performance of their music. Herbert had brought a case

Victor Herbert (1859–1924). The Dublin-born king of the European operetta, he once played in the orchestra of Johann Strauss's brother Eduard. Jerome Kern and Oscar Hammerstein met at his funeral service. ASCAP

against a New York restaurant called Shanley's, who had played one of his songs, 'Sweethearts' (can live on love alone), without permission. The case went all the way to the Supreme Court, which finally decided in Herbert's favour, thus establishing ASCAP's power.

Oscar Hammerstein I had produced Victor Herbert's musical *Naughty Marietta* ('Ah, sweet mystery of life'), and his namesake grandson attended Herbert's funeral, where he was introduced to Jerome Kern. Kern, then thirty-nine, was rightly revered by every other songwriter in the business, and was at the height of his fame and success as composer of the famous Princess Theatre musicals, which began in the following way.

Around 1915, F. Ray Comstock, owner of the tiny (299 seat) Princess Theatre, was having trouble finding suitable attractions for it. He mentioned his problem to a literary agent named Elizabeth Marbury, who suggested trying musicals. Comstock agreed and hired Bessie Marbury as his co-producer, acceding to her suggestion that they employ Guy Bolton and Jerry Kern to do book, lyrics and music. Kern had been waiting for just such an opportunity. He wanted to do musicals with modern stories, with comic but believable situations but without spectacular casts and scenery. No more *Chocolate Soldiers* and *Merry Widows* with their casts of hundreds. The Princess musicals would have a maximum of thirty in the cast, with only eleven instruments in the orchestra. Not that there was much choice: the tiny stage and orchestra pit allowed no more. By using only two sets they would cut costs even further, making the musicals profitable.

Ernest Truex as Eddie Kettle in Kern's *Very Good Eddie*. CP

Alice Dovey as Elsie Darling in the same show. CP

Far more important to Kern, however, was that for the first time he would have a libretto with which he could introduce his songs logically into the action, instead of hanging them on the plot like socks on a washing line. It is not hard to see why he and Oscar Hammerstein hit it off when they eventually met.

The first Bolton–Kern collaboration was *Nobody Home*, which opened at the Princess on 20 April 1915. The reviews were distinctly encouraging, as was the show's four-month run. On 23 December, the second show, *Very Good Eddie*, opened and became a substantial success, running for 341 performances. At the opening night, Kern encountered an old London friend, Pelham Granville Wodehouse, or 'Plum' as everyone called him. 'Plum' had provided a couple of lyrics for songs Kern had written for a London show *The Beauty of Bath*. They celebrated their reunion by forming a partnership to write musicals with Bolton and lost no time in settling down to them. In 1917 they wrote four shows: *Have a Heart*, *Oh, Boy!*, *Leave it to Jane*, and *Miss 1917*. *Have a Heart* was supposed to have followed *Very Good Eddie* into the Princess, but due to a mix-up it had to be given to another producer, Colonel Henry W. Savage. He must have lived up to his name when Bolton, Wodehouse and Kern put *Oh, Boy!* into the Princess where it became a great success, racking up a terrific run of 463 performances and producing a big Kern hit, 'Till the clouds roll by'. *Have a Heart* staggered out of Savage's Liberty Theatre with only seventy-six performances to its credit.

Love o' Mike, running simultaneously at the Shubert Theatre, hit a total of 192 performances. On 26 August the trio unveiled *Leave it to Jane* which managed a respectable 167 performances. Their next, *Miss 1917*, was a flop,[3] despite a cast which included Lew Fields, Andrew Tombes, and the ravishing Vivienne Segal. One of the most avid fans of all these entertainments was a fifteen-year-old boy named Richard Rodgers, future friend and collaborator of Lew Fields, future composer of songs which would make Vivienne Segal famous.

On 1 February 1918 the triumvirate opened the final Princess Theatre show, *Oh, Lady, Lady!* starring Vivienne Segal. They had seldom written anything better. During the tryouts, a song written for Miss Segal had to be dropped; it was a torch song called 'Along came Bill' which, when its lyric was reworked by Oscar Hammerstein some years later, would prove one of the most enduring of Kern's many hit songs.

The Princess Theatre shows were the first real step towards a truly American musical theatre, even if two of its midwives were English. The three men were celebrated in a well-known poem written by an unknown admirer, often said to have been B. G. 'Buddy' de Sylva; whoever it was, he writes suspiciously like Larry Hart.

> This is the trio of musical fame
> Bolton and Wodehouse and Kern
> Better than anyone else you can name
> Bolton and Wodehouse and Kern
> Nobody knows what on earth they've been bitten by
> All I can say is I mean to get lit an' buy
> Orchestra seats for the next one that's written by
> Bolton and Wodehouse and Kern

Jerome David Kern (1885–1945). He inspired Gershwin and
Rodgers to become composers. Arthur Schwartz dubbed him 'the
daddy of modern musical comedy music'. Sharp-tongued and
quick humoured he 'played the piano with no particular flair'
according to Schwartz. 'In fact what he did to his own tunes at
the piano was sheer murder.' ASCAP

There is something eminently fitting about Kern meeting Hammerstein at the grave of Victor Herbert. The two men had a great deal
in common at the time of their first meeting, for both were, in a way,
at a crossroads in their careers. Kern had had a big success with *Sally*,
a Ziegfeld show starring Marilyn Miller,[4] whose score included 'Look

Sigmund Romberg—'Rommie'—wrote more shows than any other theatrical composer before or since. They include *The Desert Song*, *The Student Prince*, *New Moon*, and *Up in Central Park*. He died in 1951 at the age of sixty-nine. ASCAP

for the silver lining', and two quite decent ones with producer Charles Dillingham, *Good Morning, Dearie* (347 performances) and *Stepping Stones* (241 performances). Just the same, his latest effort with Bolton and Wodehouse, *Sitting Pretty*, was not doing well. Kern was discovering that in spite of his success with the Princess musicals, producers like Dillingham, Ziegfeld and Colonel Savage cared little for his ideas of how musicals should be constructed. They wanted comedy songs, novelty songs, or love songs. What they wanted most of all were 'hit' songs that would bring people to see the shows, and Kern had to go along with them or not work. Dillingham now wanted an ornate vehicle for Marilyn Miller which would capitalize on (and hopefully eclipse) her success in the Ziegfeld show. He had signed Miller, Jack Donahue, Clifton Webb and Cliff 'Ukelele Ike' Edwards, and he gave the job of writing the book and lyrics to Harbach and Hammerstein, with Kern supplying the music. It was to be the beginning of a most fruitful collaboration, one which sometimes included all three, and at others only either Harbach or Hammerstein. *Sunny* was the first. It had a shorter run than *Sally* but a fine score, which included the stirring 'Who?' (stole my heart away). Dillingham hired Kern again to do *The City Chap* with a book by James Montgomery and lyrics by Anne Caldwell. The show was a flop. Oscar and Harbach meanwhile teamed up again with Herbert Stothart on a show produced by Uncle Arthur with some music by George Gershwin, called *Song of the Flame*, which was not successful. In the latter half of 1926 Oscar and Otto Harbach wrote two shows almost back to back. One was *The Wild Rose*, produced by Arthur Hammerstein at the Martin Beck Theatre on 20 October 1926, but despite a score by Rudolf Friml and dances by a bright new choreographer named Busby Berkeley, it flopped. The second show, which was unveiled at the Casino on 30 November, was an instantaneous, a roaring success. It was called *The Desert Song*.

Originally known as *Lady Fair*, *The Desert Song* met with very mixed critical reception upon its first appearance, and it was a full month before it really caught on with theatregoers. Indeed, one critic began his review by saying that the question of how simple-minded the book of a musical comedy could be had been debated (in *The Desert Song*) and that the answer was 'no end!' There is no question of it, the plot creaks, the dialogue is corny, the comedy both unfunny and obtrusive. It is the songs, the florid, sweeping, grandiose songs that make the show work. It is constantly revived, the firm favourite of amateur dramatic societies the world over, a sure-fire guarantee of full houses. Oscar Hammerstein and Otto Harbach provided the perfect match for Sigmund Romberg's music in their words for the title song, and for 'One alone'. The lead part of Margo Bonvalet was played by none other than Vivienne Segal, with Robert Halliday in the part of the Red Shadow.

In the autumn of the same year, Doubleday published Edna Ferber's novel, *Show Boat*, to ecstatic reviews. Reading it, Kern was fired by its possibilities as a musical. Here was what he was looking for, something different, solid, adult and new. He and Oscar Hammerstein had already decided that if the right vehicle came along they would collaborate again. Kern called Oscar, who agreed with him about *Show Boat*, so Kern sat right down and wrote a letter to Edna Ferber saying he would like to turn her novel into a musical. The scandalized Miss Ferber refused point blank.

Undaunted, Kern—a persistent, if impatient man—pursued his idea. When he spotted the author at a first night, he asked critic and columnist Alexander Woollcott—a friend of Miss Ferber's and, like her, a member of the chintzy 'Round Table Club' at the Algonquin Hotel on West 44th Street—to introduce them. Woollcott was a strange duck, but he swooped across the lobby and dragged Miss Ferber across to meet the diminutive Kern. Peering owlishly at her over his spectacles and talking very fast, Kern, with Woollcott's assistance, managed to talk her round.

His enthusiasm was dynamic. Every week, he visited her apartment, bringing the latest songs and singing them for her. 'Make believe' and 'Life upon the wicked stage' and then, at last, the sweeping, sonorous 'Ol' man river'. In her memoirs, *A Peculiar Treasure*, Edna Ferber recalled her reactions on hearing 'Ol' man river' for the first time. 'The music mounted, mounted, and I give you my word my hair stood on end, the tears came to my eyes. I breathed like the heroine in a melodrama. That was music that would outlast Jerome Kern's day and mine.'[5]

The story of *Show Boat* is set on a Mississippi riverboat called the *Cotton Blossom* and its characters are real, three-dimensional human beings. There are the boat's captain, Andy Hawks, and his wife Parthy Ann (pun intended) whose daughter, Magnolia, falls in love with the dashing, but weak, riverboat gambler Gaylord Ravenal. The leading lady aboard the show boat is Julie Laverne, who is cast out because of the taint of Negro blood. There is also the black riverboat worker, Joe, a rôle originally played by Jules Bledsoe, but now invariably identified with Paul Robeson, who had the part in the 1936 film version. His singing of 'Ol' man river' made the song into a near-classic.

Enter Florenz Ziegfeld. He deserves a better book than those which have been written about him, but this cannot be it. He was maniacal, tyrannical, impossible, extravagant, probably the most flamboyant and outrageous theatrical producer of them all. He lived in the manner of a Renaissance prince, spending money he often did not have on lavish, spectacular shows 'glorifying the American girl' which were, with some justification, called 'Follies'. Driving, ruthless, yet utterly charming when he wanted to be, Ziegfeld was an insatiable womanizer whose private life was a disaster. His rivalries were bitter and his revenges cruel. It was to him that Kern and Hammerstein now brought *Show*

Show Boat: the show within the show on board the *Cotton Blossom*. Cap'n Andy Hawks (Charles Winninger) is seated far left. Magnolia (Norma Terris) and Ravenal (Howard Marsh) are onstage in 'The Parson's Bride' giving their all. CP

Boat and asked, begged, him to produce it. Ziegfeld refused; and it was a long time before he relented and agreed to do the show. One of the reasons why he took so long was that he was worried that he might not be able to finance it, although, of course, he did not reveal his concern to Kern or Hammerstein.

Oscar often recounted the story of visiting Ziegfeld's château at Hastings-on-the-Hudson, near New York. He and Kern had finished writing the show and were getting worried that they hadn't heard from the producer. Kern hazarded a guess that Ziggy didn't have any money to do the show, and Oscar wondered how they could find out for sure. 'Well,' said Kern, a man of action who would have picked a fight with a full-grown gorilla on a point of principle, 'let's go and ask him!'

When they got to Ziegfeld's mansion, Ziggy's butler, Sydney (who looked more like a bank president than a butler, according to Oscar), ushered them into the drawing-room. Then a maid in a costume right out of the Follies took them through Ziegfeld's bedroom with its priceless four-poster and beautiful *objets d'art*, and into an immense bath-

Florenz Ziegfeld: he sued grandfather Oscar for 'uncalled-for humiliation' and died owing more than a million dollars. CP

room in which the producer was being shaved by his personal barber, a man with a long white beard who reminded Oscar of King Leopold of Belgium. Shaven and dressed in a brocaded silk dressing gown, Ziegfeld offered them a snack—'pot luck' as he called it—which consisted of cocktails, roast beef, champagne, and turtles specially brought up from Florida. There was a footman behind every chair, and everything exuded wealth. Ziegfeld told them about the sensational business that his new show, *Rio Rita*, was doing in Boston. The talk was pleasant, the food excellent; and at about four in the afternoon Jerry and Oscar waddled out in what Oscar described as a kind of misty contentment and headed back to town. Neither of them had had the courage to ask Ziegfeld whether he had any money. How could you ask a man who lived like that if he was broke?

Ziegfeld was a tyrant, and notoriously bad at handling people—especially song-writers. The preceding year he had outraged the highly-successful team of Rodgers and Hart by interpolating an Irving Berlin song into their score for a show called *Betsy*, and leaving them to find out on opening night that he had done so. They never forgave him. There is also a story that when Irving Berlin had finished his score for one of the early *Ziegfeld Follies*, Ziegfeld insisted that there wasn't a hit in the score and he wanted one, right now. Berlin pleaded that he was written out, and hadn't got another melody in him. Ziegfeld locked him in a room and wouldn't let him out until he came up with a hit song. Berlin obliged with 'A pretty girl is like a melody', which became the anthem of the *Ziegfeld Follies*.

Stories of Ziegfeld's high-handedness are legion, and his relationship with Oscar was uncertain. He had no great admiration for the Hammersteins. Early in his career, he had entered into a bitter and costly rivalry with grandfather Oscar Hammerstein over the professional services of Ziegfeld's discovery (and mistress) Anna Held, a rivalry which culminated in a lawsuit. Both men ultimately abandoned the suit, since neither could afford to pursue it, but Ziegfeld was like the Bourbon courtiers, he forgot nothing and learned nothing. Thus, sketches ridiculing old Oscar frequently found their way into Ziegfeld shows.

In March 1927, while at Palm Beach, he sent a long cable to Kern. He liked Kern's music for *Show Boat*, but he was unhappy with Oscar's book, which he felt was sprawling and disappointing.

I FEEL HAMMERSTEIN NOT KEEN ON MY DOING SHOW BOAT I AM VERY KEEN ON DOING IT ON ACCOUNT OF YOUR MUSIC BUT HAMMERSTEIN BOOK IN PRESENT SHAPE HAS NOT GOT A CHANCE EXCEPT WITH CRITICS BUT THE PUBLIC NO AND I HAVE STOPPED PRODUCING FOR CRITICS AND EMPTY HOUSES I DON'T WANT BOLTON OR ANYONE ELSE IF HAMMERSTEIN CAN AND WILL DO THE WORK IF NOT THEN FOR ALL CONCERNED WE SHOULD HAVE SOMEONE HELP HOW ABOUT DOROTHY DONNELLY OR ANYONE YOU SUGGEST OR HAMMERSTEIN SUGGESTS I AM TOLD HAMMERSTEIN NEVER DID ANYTHING ALONE HIS PRESENT LAYOUT TOO SERIOUS NOT ENOUGH COMEDY AFTER MARRIAGE REMEMBER YOUR LOVE INTEREST IS ELIMINATED NO ONE ON EARTH JERRY KNOWS MUSICAL COMEDY BETTER THAN YOU DO AND YOU YOURSELF TOLD ME YOU WOULD RISK A DOLLAR ON IT IF HAMMERSTEIN WILL FIX THE BOOK I WANT TO DO IT IF HE REFUSES TO CHANGE IT OR ALLOW ANYONE ELSE TO BE CALLED IN IF NECESSARY HE AND YOU RETURN THE ADVANCE AS YOU YOURSELF SUGGESTED YOU WOULD AND LET SOMEONE ELSE DO IT IF HAMMERSTEIN IS READY TO WORK WITH ME TO GET IT RIGHT AND YOU AND HE WILL EXTEND THE TIME TO OCTOBER FIRST LETS DO IT TOGETHER I REALLY WANT TO IF OH IS REASONABLE ALL WE WANT IS SUCCESS ANSWER[6]

Kern and Hammerstein went back to work on the libretto again.
And again. It would be another exhausting nine months before the
show opened. Oscar was philosophical about Ziegfeld's dislike of his
work. He realized that Ziggy had never done a play with a story before,
and that the producer expected that by the time the show opened, all
that 'story stuff' would have been cut out and that what would remain
would be the pretty costumes, the songs, the dances and the comedy.

There were several gruelling weeks of rehearsal at the New Amsterdam Theatre, and then the tryouts began in Washington. The first performance of *Show Boat* ran for four and a quarter hours. Even though
the audience loved it, cuts had to be made. The next day Ziegfeld called
a rehearsal for eleven, made some cuts, watched the matinée, made
them do another rehearsal and then sent the cast on for the evening

Show Boat: the 1936 movie made by Universal. Here Julie (Helen
Morgan) sings 'Can't help lovin' dat man' to Hattie McDaniels
and Irene Dunne, who followed it with an incredible 'shuffle'. CP

performance without their even having eaten. On the night and day before the New York opening, everyone worked for a straight eighteen hours as scenes were changed. Oscar Hammerstein acted as co-director (without credit) to Zeke Colvan. The cast included Charlie Winninger as Cap'n Andy (a rôle he was to repeat in the 1936 film of *Show Boat*), Norma Terris as Magnolia and one of Ziggy's personal discoveries as Julie, a tiny twenty-six-year-old beauty named Helen Morgan. The show opened on 27 December and Ziegfeld was convinced it was going to be a disaster. At the first night he sat on the stairs of the balcony. The big numbers did not draw much applause and Ziegfeld was distraught, cursing the audience for not liking the show. Intermission was no better and the finale worse. People left the theatre as if they were relieved to get out. With gloomy despondency, the authors awaited the verdict of the critics. They might have the largest advance ticket sale of any show to that time, but if they were panned that would not mean a thing. Needless to say, the critics raved. 'The All-American Musical Comedy', as its creators had labelled *Show Boat*, became an enormous hit.

It remains Jerome Kern's most impressive work, as vivid and colourful today as it was fifty years ago. In it, for the first time, all the elements of story, setting, lyrics and music were fused. From the opening chorus, where the white people sing about the *Cotton Blossom*, meaning the show boat, and the negro stevedores sing about the cotton blossom they have to carry on their backs, *Show Boat* was one grand bright musical feast, every song establishing mood and character—Ravenal and Magnolia's duet 'Make believe' and the later 'You are love' indicated the change in their emotions. Julie's 'Can't help lovin' dat man' was echoed by Joe's wife, Queenie, for different reasons. The dancers Frank and Ellie, played by the team of Eva Puck and Sammy White (who had made their mark on the Broadway stage in a Rodgers and Hart show called *The Girl Friend* the year before), had a bright duet called 'I might fall back on you' and a mock lament about 'Life upon the wicked stage'. The third major love duet 'Why do I love you?' had been added during the tryouts, when seven other songs were excised. Hammerstein helped 'Plum' Wodehouse to rework the original lyric, 'Along came Bill/Who's quite the opposite/Of all the men in story books', to the vastly different 'Bill' that everyone knows. And of course, dominating the entire score was the sweeping 'Ol' man river'.

Show Boat ran for 575 performances, and the tour of seven months produced a total run of almost two years. On tour, the part of Magnolia was taken by a youngster named Irene Dunne who played the same

Oscar Hammerstein and Dorothy Blanchard Hammerstein in the late Twenties. He wrote 'You are love' for her and not for *Show Boat*. LFG

Oscar Hammerstein in Hollywood: that's MGM's Music Department, where at one time or another, the greatest song-writers in the world worked. LFG

part when the show was filmed some years later. *Show Boat* became and remains a landmark in the musical theatre. There is no question that it set a standard unmatched until *Porgy and Bess*, introducing techniques that would be perfected many years later by Richard Rodgers and the very same Oscar Hammerstein.

Oscar hit a winning streak with *Show Boat*. He and Kern planned to follow it with a musical based on du Bose Heyward's *Porgy* starring Al Jolson, but after considerable heartsearching the author chose George and Ira Gershwin and the Theatre Guild instead. Uncle Arthur already had a Hammerstein–Harbach play called *Golden Dawn* in his own theatre by the time the Kern–Hammerstein musical opened, but the music of Emmerich Kalman and Herbert Stothart was no match for Kern's. *Golden Dawn* ran a respectable 184 performances. It was almost a year after the opening of *Show Boat* before Oscar—with Uncle Arthur again producing and brother Reginald directing—brought a new show, *Good Boy*, to town. His collaborators were Harbach and Henry Myers,[7] a close friend of Larry Hart's. The music was by Harry Ruby and Bert Kalmar, with additional songs by Herbert Stothart, the dances again by young Buzz Berkeley, and *Good Boy* totted up a very satisfactory 253-performance run. This, however, was totally eclipsed by a Romberg musical on which Oscar had collaborated and which opened a scant six days before *Good Boy*. Full-bloodedly back in the operetta tradition (books like *Show Boat* did not come along every season) it was called *The New Moon*. Its songs included 'Stouthearted men', 'Wanting you', and 'Softly, as in a morning sunrise'. Despite the queries of unromantic souls who asked if there was any other kind of sunrise, the show was enormously popular, as were all its songs, even 'One kiss' for all its startling resemblance to Vincent Youmans's 'No, no, Nanette'. *The New Moon* eventually ran for 518 performances, not many fewer than *Show Boat*.

Oscar Hammerstein II had further triumphs ahead of him. In 1929, he collaborated with Kern on *Sweet Adeline*, starring Helen Morgan, who made their song 'Why was I born?' very much her own. Oscar was also trying out his hand as a director of his own work when the opportunity arose, but each time he did so, it seemed, the show failed for one reason or another. One such was *Rainbow* written with Vincent Youmans. So was *Free for All*, for which Charles Whiting provided a score.

Teamed again with Kern, Oscar improved his somewhat spotty record with a hit show *Music in the Air*. 'I've told ev'ry little star' and 'The song is you' were added to his already impressive catalogue. There

Jerome Kern and Oscar Hammerstein II in the orchestra pit of the Alvin Theatre during rehearsals of *Music in the Air* (1932). It shows how easily song-writers could act out their 'rôle' at the drop of a camera shutter. CP

was another hit show with Romberg, *May Wine*, but this one was nothing like the success *The Desert Song* had been, any more than *Music in the Air* emulated *Show Boat*.

The hard times of the Depression, the years following the stock market crash of 1929, were beginning to make themselves felt by this time, and it became progressively harder to get producers to back shows or people to buy tickets for them. Many of the leading Broadway composers and librettists saw the writing on the wall, and headed out to the land of milk and honey—Hollywood. Many of them went because of the extraordinary amounts of money that were said to be paid to successful writers. Most, however, went out because movies were a vital new medium, and besides, that was where the musicals were being made. There was also no disadvantage in being paid on the nail instead of having to wait to find out whether your show was a hit or a flop. For many, Hollywood was a frustrating and unhappy experience;

others ate it up with a spoon. Richard Rodgers hated the place. The Gershwins loved it and settled there. Some writers loathed the producers, who barred them from the sets where their work was being filmed, and the management, who banished them to draughty little cubbyholes and told them to get busy writing masterpieces.

Oscar, according to Sam Marx, went out to work at MGM with Sigmund Romberg on a musical for Evelyn Laye called *The Night is Young*, and a proposed Jeanette MacDonald–Nelson Eddy film with Kern providing the music, *Champagne and Orchids*. It never reached the screen, although both score and script were finished. Marx recalled a good example of Oscar's dry wit. There was a stag party one evening at the home of a playwright, a little man who insisted on doing all the cooking and serving personally.

> Oscar was there, and a whole bunch of us, the writer crowd from MGM. They ragged the hell out of that poor little guy. Donald Ogden Stewart tasted the wine and said 'Oh, God, if you'd only invited Jesus he could turn this into wine!' And later, after a truly sumptuous meal, Oscar stood up with a glass of brandy and said 'How will this go on an empty stomach?'

Jerome Kern and Oscar Hammerstein were teamed finally not at MGM but at Paramount, where they wrote a score which included 'The folks who live on the hill' (that rhyme 'Our veranda will command a ...' always bothered Oscar) and 'Can I forget you?' for *High,*

Not intrepid African explorers: just Otto Harbach (*l.*) and Jerome Kern checking camera angles in Hollywood in the Thirties, when making movies was a bit more of an adventure than it is today. CP

Wide and Handsome. Oscar did the original story and screenplay as well as the lyrics.

Oscar's star was waning, however, and his career went into the doldrums. Although he had a hand in the Astaire–Rogers movie *The Story of Vernon and Irene Castle* in 1938, his Hollywood record was hardly scintillating.[8] By the late Thirties, he was rapidly getting the reputation of a has-been. A new 1939 Broadway show with Kern, *Very Warm for May*, failed despite a lovely score which included 'All the things you are'. Two years later (at the same St James's Theatre at which he would shortly triumph with *Oklahoma*) Oscar wrote (and co-directed with John Murray Anderson) a show called *Sunny River*, with songs by Sigmund Romberg. It ran for thirty-six performances.

Even in this dispiriting time, however, Oscar remained the same— although many years later he admitted that he only kept going through inner conceit. He was forty-six years of age. Thirty of those years had been spent in or around the theatre. He had collaborated with every major theatrical composer in the business—except one. And that one, Richard Rodgers, had come to him when it became apparent that his partnership with Lorenz Hart was drawing to an inevitable close.

So, the following year, Rodgers teamed with Hammerstein to write *Oklahoma!* Its success was so big, its impact so enormous, that both men could have been forgiven if they became over-inflated with the idea of their own genius. But not Oscar Hammerstein. Shortly after the opening of *Oklahoma!* he bought an ad in *Variety* which listed every one of his recent failures: *Very Warm for May* (seven weeks), *Ball at the Savoy* (five weeks), *Three Sisters* (six weeks), *Free for All* (three weeks), *The Gang's All Here* (three weeks), *East Wind* (three weeks) and *Gentleman Unafraid* (three weeks). In typical Hammerstein style, the headline read: I'VE DONE IT BEFORE—AND I CAN DO IT AGAIN!

3. Dick & Larry

Somebody asked Dick Rodgers what was the difference between working with Larry Hart and working with Oscar Hammerstein, and this is what he said: 'When I worked with Larry Hart they used to say, "there goes the little guy with that sonofabitch". When I started to work with Oscar they said, "there goes the big guy with that sonofabitch".'
Arthur Schwartz

Richard Rodgers is a driving perfectionist, a constantly restless innovator and a tough man to do business with, even if all those aspects of his personality have been mellowed considerably by his seventy-five years. He has survived both his lyricists, with whom he produced an astonishing succession of Broadway shows, some of which dramatically altered the traditions of the musical stage. Yet never once has he conformed to any pattern which would allow him to be 'typed' as Gershwin, Porter and Youmans were typed. For all his melodic fertility, his brilliance as a theatrical producer, his enormous contribution to every aspect of the musical, Rodgers as an individual remains an enigma.

He came to the partnership with Oscar Hammerstein, as we have seen, after almost twenty-five years of collaboration with Larry Hart, begun before Rodgers himself was out of school. Rodgers and Hart had constantly broken new ground. *On Your Toes* (1936) was the first Broadway show to make extended use of both ballet and musical interlude—

the famous *Slaughter on 10th Avenue* sequence. In *Babes in Arms* they began to excavate the grave of the traditional line of chorus girls by replacing it with a cast of exuberant sixteen-year-olds. In *Pal Joey*, they broke every rule in the book by having a leading man who was not only a dancer, instead of a singer, but a cheap one, a knave instead of a hero.

It was when his flair for seeing the dramatic and truly new was finally mated with Oscar Hammerstein's enormous range of theatrical experience that the pattern came into perfect place, but no understanding of Rodgers's achievement with Hammerstein is possible without first examining his collaboration with febrile, tragic Larry Hart.

They met for the first time on a Sunday afternoon in 1919. Rodgers was sixteen, Hart twenty-three. The would-be composer already had two quite successful amateur shows to his credit, *One Minute, Please* (presented, during a howling blizzard, at the Plaza Hotel on 29 December 1917); and *Up Stage and Down*, which played one night on 8 March 1918 in the Ballroom of the Waldorf-Astoria. Several members of the Akron Club, a social-athletic group to which Mortimer Rodgers belonged and for whose benefit Dick had written *One Minute, Please* were also in the cast of the second show, among them the son of a paint manufacturer, Philip Leavitt, a classmate of Morty's at Columbia. He liked young Dick's songs so much—he can still sing them, sixty years later—that he decided to try to convince Dick to collaborate with someone permanently, instead of just setting to music any lyric that came along. He knew Lorenz Hart, and had known him since school. Larry, he said, was a lyricist looking for a composer, and would like to meet Dick.[1] Leavitt took Rodgers to the Hart house at 59 West 119th Street, and Larry answered the door himself. He was dressed that Sunday afternoon in tuxedo trousers, carpet slippers and some kind of shirt. He needed a shave. And he was one of the shortest men Rodgers had ever seen, barely five feet tall, with hands and feet like those of a child. His head was too large for the small body, so that it gave him a gnome-like appearance.

Rodgers and Hart hit it off famously. Hart was eking out a living translating the lyrics of German operettas for the Shuberts, the theatrical producing firm. They were not just translations, but adaptations, although Hart was paid practically nothing for his work. They talked, and talked and talked. Rodgers discovered that Hart was a man with a vast cultural background and worldly airs. He had been to Europe, he drank, he smoked big cigars, he was cynically witty, and he had deeply felt and forcefully expressed opinions about the musical theatre.

His feeling for the basic ideas of musical shows were different from anyone else's. He felt they ought to tackle subjects· that at that time hadn't been touched at all. He talked about interior rhyming schemes, and female endings, things I knew nothing at all about. He attacked writers who would not take advantage of the chances there were in the theatre to explore hitherto unexplored territory. I played him some of my songs and he liked them as much as I liked his ideas.

59 West 119th Street, Manhattan. Now deep in Harlem, this was the Hart home, where Dick first met Larry in 1919. AC

They agreed to try collaborating, and throughout the late spring and summer of that year, wrote song after song together. Rodgers soon learned that 'work' with Larry meant starting towards midday, because Larry would still be getting over the night before; and ending towards late afternoon, by which time the man had taken a drink, the drink had taken a drink, and the drink had taken the man. It was a pattern which would remain constant through the next twenty years before the final, precipitate decline.

The enthusiastic Phil Leavitt now paved the way for them to see a producer, the famous Lew Fields. At one time half of the celebrated vaudeville comedy team, Weber and Fields, Lew Fields had turned to producing his own shows—and often starring in them. At the Field's summer place in Far Rockaway, Rodgers was introduced to the entire Fields clan. Lew Fields had four children: Joseph, the eldest; Herbert; the willowy, dark-eyed Dorothy; and Frances.

Rodgers played some of the songs he had written and was gratified—not to say stunned—when Lew Fields said he liked one of the songs, 'Any old place with you', so much that he would buy it and put it into his current show, *A Lonely Romeo*. He was as good as his word; and on 26 August 1919 Eve Lynn and Alan Hale (later to be Errol Flynn's sidekick in many a Warner Bros. swashbuckler) launched the professional career of Rodgers and Hart. It was a jaunty enough little number, all about honeymooning in such diverse places as old Virginia and Abyssinia, promising that the singer would 'court you, gal, in dreamy Portugal' and swearing that he would go 'to hell for ya, or Philadelphia'.

Thus Richard Rodgers became the first and certainly the last sixteen-year-old to land a song in a fully-fledged Broadway show. He had his career, his partner, his collaborator, his best friend, his source of constant irritation. Larry was just as enthusiastic as he. What could stand in their way now?

Richard Charles Rodgers was the second son of William and Mamie Rodgers. He was born in their rented summer house on Brandreth Avenue at Hammels Station, near Arverne, Long Island, on 28 June 1902. When Dick was two and his brother Mortimer (born 13 January 1898) five, the Rodgers family moved to the home of Mamie Rodgers's parents, Rachel and Jacob Levy, a five-storey brownstone at 3 West 120th Street. William Rodgers was a doctor, and so the entire ground floor was turned into a consulting room, waiting room and office suite.

Mortimer seems to have wanted to become a doctor from the start;

he eventually became director of gynaecology at Lenox Hill Hospital. His brother took an almost equally direct line towards his chosen career: music. He was picking out fragments of melodies with two fingers at four years of age, and at six, playing fluently—if by ear— with both hands. Formal piano lessons were unsuccessful. Dick's parents were inveterate theatregoers, their taste running to musicals and operettas. In those days, the complete score of the show was always sold in the theatre foyer, and Dr Rodgers invariably purchased one. At home, Mrs Rodgers would seat herself at the Steinway and play, while her husband sang the songs, from *Mademoiselle Modiste*, or *The Chocolate Soldier*, until little Richard, with his infallible musical ear, would know them by heart. Whereupon he would clamber up on the piano stool and try to play them himself. At twelve, he was spending hours daily at the keyboard; at summer camp, for instance, Samuel Marx recalled that Dick would be indoors playing the piano for hours when all the other kids were out swimming or playing games. When he was fourteen, Dick composed a song called 'Campfire days' which celebrated the joys of Camp Wigwam, Harrison, Maine. He spent his allowance on seats for Saturday matinées, especially the ·Princess Theatre shows by Bolton, Wodehouse and Kern, his idol. 'I remember sitting in the balcony at a show of Kern's called *Love o' Mike*. It was a failure but I listened to the score and I said to myself, "I have to be able to write like this." It was very important to me. I know Kern was the impetus for the whole thing, it was what got me going.'

In that same year, the year he met Oscar Hammerstein for the first time, Dick's first song, a novelty number with lyrics by James Dyrenforth called 'Auto Show Girl', was copyrighted. That Fall he wrote his first complete score, the Akron Club's *One Minute, Please*. Shortly thereafter, Philip Leavitt introduced him to Larry Hart.

Like Dick's, Larry Hart's family was middle class, but their fortunes were much more erratic, and their lifestyle the diametric opposite of the disciplined, almost severe household in which Rodgers grew up. Larry's parents, Max and Frieda Hart, had come to America from Hamburg, and both spoke English with thick German intonations. In addition, the rotund and diminutive Hart senior had a lisp. He called himself a 'promoter'; many of his commercial ventures were on the dubious side of the street.

Lorenz Milton Hart was born on 2 May 1895 in the Hart apartment on 106th Street, off Second Avenue. Two years later a second son, Teddy, arrived. In 1904 the Harts acquired the brownstone on West 119th Street where Max Hart ran a lavish and open house, to which he invited cronies and showbusiness people. The Harts often went to bed and left the parties running down below, for when Max Hart was 'flush' only the best would do. There were other times when Frieda Hart would have to pawn her jewellery to keep up the *ménage*, which consisted of a chauffeur, a footman, two housemaids and Rosie the cook. It was hardly surprising, in view of all this, that Larry Hart grew up without any real respect for money or respectability.

The Hart family claimed to be descended from the German poet Heinrich Heine, although Larry's sister-in-law, Dorothy Hart, insists that 'he couldn't have cared less about all that stuff'. Nevertheless, it was only in Larry that genius flowered, and it is hard to believe that the genius came from his father, a coarse, loud-mouthed man seemingly impervious to culture even if he had trained himself in business and the law, or from his genteel, tiny, strict mother.

He was precocious from the very beginning, writing his first verses at the age of eight or nine. Max Hart would frequently get the boy out of bed to recite his poetry for visitors; one evening, Lillian Russell was among them. Max encouraged the youngster to drink, so that by the time he was in his late teens, Larry already had an unhealthy appetite for alcohol. At summer camp, they called him 'Shakespeare' Hart, because of his penchant for packing his clothing trunk with books instead of sweaters and shirts and sneakers; they also called him 'Dirtyneck' Hart for more obvious reasons.

Except for a brief sojourn at De Witt Clinton High School in New York, Larry was privately educated: at Weingart's Institute on 120th Street, and at Columbia Grammar School. He entered Columbia University in 1913 after a European holiday with his family, transferring to the school of journalism after a year although he had no intention of becoming a newspaperman. He was a member of the group which contributed verse and vignettes to 'The Conning Tower' but he was to major—as he himself put it—in Varsity Shows. He left Columbia in 1917 without a degree, impatient to get started in the theatre. He worked as a counsellor at Brant Lake Camp, putting on the camp shows every fortnight. That he already had a reputation as a writer is demonstrated by the fact that Billy Rose, a song-writer who was branching out into the impresario business, would come up to the camp and go out on the lake in a rowboat with Larry. There Larry would write or suggest ways of writing lyrics for Billy Rose's songs (Rose already had 'Me and my shadow', 'That old gang of mine' and 'Barney google' to his credit) and at the end of the day, Billy would give Larry a $100 bill. Larry never got any credit or any royalty for anything Rose used.

Lorenz Milton Hart at the age of twenty-three. He had just produced his first play, *The Blond Beast* by Henry Myers. It flopped. AC

Max Hart used a different lawyer for every new promotion. There were, according to one of them, two reasons for this. First, the new lawyer would not know what the lawyer preceding him had done or been asked to do. Second, he would also not know that Max Hart had not paid the fees of the earlier attorney, either. One such newcomer to the Hart circle was Arthur Schwartz. Max Hart never paid him, but at least Arthur got to meet Larry Hart,[2] and together they wrote a show for the kids at Brant Lake Camp. It was about a dreamy boy who didn't much care for the athletic life, and Larry came up with a lyric which went:

> I love to lie awake in bed
> Right after taps I pull the flaps above my head
> I let the moon shine on my pillow
> O, what a light those moonbeams shed
> I feel so happy I could cry
> And tears are born within the corner of my eye
> To be at home with Ma was never like this
> I could live forever like this
> I love to lie awake awhile
> And go to sleep with a smile

Schwartz put it to music, along with a couple of others that included 'Down at the lake' (Only lazy seniors frown at the lake). Many years later he would remember that tune when he gave it to Clifton Webb to sing in *The Little Show* of 1929. With a new lyric by Larry's classmate Howard Dietz, it became 'I guess I'll have to change my plan'.

At the time when they worked together at Brant Lake, Arthur Schwartz was hopeful that he and Larry Hart could strike up a permanent collaboration, but Larry explained that he already had a partner, Dick Rodgers. Until they got a break, he said, he could make a living translating plays. He was confident that the break was just around the corner—after all, hadn't the great Lew Fields already interpolated one of their songs into his show?

In September 1919, Dick Rodgers entered Columbia University as a freshman. He and Larry collaborated with Larry's chum Milton Bender on 'an atrocious musical comedy' (their own subtitle) called *You'd Be Surprised*. The musical director was Lew Fields, and the cast included his daughter, Dorothy. Among the songs was one about 'poor bisected, disconnected Mary Queen of Scots' with a lyric by Herb Fields, and a cute one by Dick and Larry called 'Don't love me like Othello' (I'm much too young to die). Oscar Hammerstein was represented as well, with a Rodgers melody to his song 'That boy of mine'. The show was again for the benefit of the Akron Club, and as usual played a one-night engagement in the ballroom of the Plaza Hotel on 6 March 1920. Eighteen days later, the Columbia University Players presented *Fly With Me*, the 1920 Varsity Show, for which Oscar Hammerstein's three songs (including 'Always room for one more') were lifted from the score of *Twinkling Eyes*, and Rodgers and Hart re-used 'Don't love me like Othello'. Most important of all in that year, however, was the fact that Lew Fields found himself with a problem.

Arthur Schwartz in his Schwartz and Dietz days. He also wrote 'How can I ever be alone?' and 'Tennessee fish fry' with Oscar Hammerstein, not to mention 'I know my girl by her perfume' with Lorenz Hart. ASCAP

He had hired two song-writers to do a score for a new show he was producing, *Poor Little Ritz Girl*, and he was desperately unhappy with their work. He came to the Columbia Varsity Show and, since he already knew Rodgers and Hart, put it to them that he might use some of their songs in his show, and some new ones if they would write them. Rodgers was stunned, Hart overjoyed. They didn't yet know that Fields was in a bind; they honestly believed he was hiring them because he thought they were terrific. *Poor Little Ritz Girl* was due to begin its Boston tryouts on 28 May. Fields told the boys he could not pay them as high a fee as 'known' names, neglecting to add that the real reason was that he had to pay off the other team as well. It didn't matter; Dick and Larry would probably have written the score for nothing.

Donald Kerr and Elise Bonwit doing 'The Bombay Bombashay'—
one of the songs Rodgers and Hart didn't write for Lew Fields's
1920 show *Poor Little Ritz Girl*. CP

They set to work eagerly, providing songs for the slender story of an
unsophisticated Southern girl who comes to New York to dance in the
chorus of a show, and rents the apartment of a wealthy young bachelor,
with the appropriately embarrassing results when he returns to town
unexpectedly. Dick and Larry wrote fifteen songs for the show, among
them a rewritten version of 'Don't love me like Othello' called 'You
can't fool your dreams'—an early foray by Larry Hart into that unexplored territory he had been talking about, with Freudian undertones
like, 'You tell me what you're dreaming, I'll tell you whom you love.'

Fields, meanwhile, got cold feet. He was ready to take the show to
New York but he did not think it was strong enough. There were
swingeing changes in the casting. A new musical director, Charles

Previn, was hired. Worst of all for Rodgers and Hart, Fields cut their score to bits to make room for eight numbers by Sigmund Romberg and Alex Gerber.[3]

The show opened on Broadway on 27 July 1920, and ran for 119 performances, but Rodgers never forgot the misery with which he watched it, the disappointment of being what he called 'a badly-bruised conquering hero'. Nevertheless, the reviews were surprisingly good; the show ran for three months, which was considered very satisfactory at a time when a six-month run was a resounding hit. It was even more remarkable considering the competition it had. There was a Kern musical, *Night Boat*, and Fanny Brice and W. C. Fields in the latest *Ziegfeld Follies*. The Gershwins had contributed a score to *George White's Scandals*, the second of that ilk. There was also the Hammerstein–Harbach–Stothart show *Tickle Me* and the vastly successful *Irene*, with its huge hit 'Alice Blue Gown'. On the face of it, therefore, Rodgers and Hart could have been said to have started with a success. What faced them now—and would for five years—was a desert of amateur shows, unsuccessful auditions, and complete failure.

The following year, after writing the 1921 Varsity Show for Columbia (with Oscar Hammerstein helping to stage the book, dances by Herb Fields, and lyrics by Larry Hart) Rodgers quit the college and enrolled at the Institute of Musical Art at 122nd Street and Claremont Avenue, now the renowned Juilliard School. The next three years were the happiest ones of Rodgers's student life. In addition, there were year-end shows there, and he wrote one for each of his years at the school: *Jazz à la Carte*, *Say it with Jazz*, and *A Danish Yankee in King Tut's Court*, the latter having its genesis in Mark Twain and the recently-discovered Egyptian Pharaoh's tomb.

Herb Fields and Larry Hart had come up with an idea for a show which they called *Winkle Town*, but they could not get the book right. They went to an old friend, Oscar Hammerstein, just enjoying the success of *Wildflower*, and Oscar agreed to collaborate, so much did he like the book and the score, one of whose songs was a pretty little schottische praising the delights of 'Manhattan'. Rodgers took the whole thing to Lawrence Schwab, a new producer who was teaming up with writer Frank Mandel to do a musical. Schwab confessed to not knowing enough about music to be able to make a decent judgement, and asked Rodgers to play them for his friend, the powerful Max Dreyfus, head of the publishing house of T. B. Harms Inc.[4] Dreyfus was Kern's publisher, Gershwin's and Youmans's. Rodgers was understandably elated by the chance to audition for Dreyfus, but even when he played

Rodgers and Hart pretending to write 'Manhattan' in a 1929 two-reeler called *Masters of Melody*. CP

'Manhattan' Dreyfus shook his head. He told Schwab the score had nothing of value in it, and suggested he listen to the work of another composer on the Dreyfus books, Vincent Youmans. Rodgers slunk out; he was beginning to get downhearted at being told that his songs were 'too collegiate' and that he had better change his style or quit the business. As it turned out, Vincent Youmans didn't get the Schwab–Mandel assignment, either; it went to George and Ira Gershwin, already establishing themselves as a top song-writing team.

The boys now decided to collaborate on a straight play, using the unlikely nom-de-plume of Herbert Richard Lorenz. First called *The Jazz King* and then *Henky*, it eventually got into the Ritz Theatre in New York on 13 May 1924 as *The Melody Man* and staggered along for fifty-six performances before dropping dead. It had two entirely forgettable songs, 'I'd love to poison Ivy' and 'Moonlight Mama', and the play's only theatrical distinction turned out to be that it gave his first Broadway part to a young actor named Fred Bickel, who was easily persuaded to change his name to the more mellifluous Fredric March.

Walking down Lexington Avenue one day, Larry Hart spotted a plaque on the wall of a house which once belonged to Robert Murray, who gave his name to the district below and east of Grand Central Station. Larry became intrigued by the plaque, which commemorated a little-known event of the War of Independence:

> Howe, with Clinton, Tryon and a few others, went to the house of Robert Murray, on Murray Hill, for Refreshment and Rest. With Pleasant Conversations and a Profusion of Cake and Wine, the good Whig lady detained the gallant Britons almost two hours, Quite Long Enough for the bulk of Putnam's division of four thousand men to leave the city and escape to the heights of Harlem by the Bloomingdale Road, with the loss of only a few soldiers.

Larry saw this as a fertile piece of ground in which to plant a musical and turned the idea over to Herbert Fields, who added a subplot about a romance between Mrs Murray's niece, Betsy Burke, and a British officer, Sir John Copeland. The trio dubbed it *Dear Enemy* and took it to Herb's father, who promptly turned it down. Other producers were equally discouraging—who wanted a musical about the Revolution, for Godsakes?—so the trio resorted to other dodges. Herb ambushed Helen Ford in the lobby of the Algonquin Hotel; her husband George was a producer, maybe if she liked it he would raise the money to do the show. Helen, who had just had a success in *The Gingham Girl*, liked what there was of the book—they had no second act—very much. She promised to try and interest her husband and also John Murray Anderson, the director, whom she knew. The upshot of that meeting at the Algonquin was that she spent a solid year with Dick, Larry and Herb, doing auditions at the drop of a hat for anybody, moneymen or cloak-and-suiters on Seventh Avenue. 'I stuck with it for two reasons,' she said. 'The first was that I didn't have a job. The second was that I knew this would make a star of me, I knew it.'

Not just yet, however. Broadway was bursting at the seams with hit musicals that year: Friml's *Rose Marie*, Romberg's *Student Prince*, Irving Berlin's fourth successful *Music Box Revue*. There was another *Ziegfeld Follies*, another Gershwin hit—and a big one—called *Lady Be Good!* starring Fred and Adele Astaire. Vincent Youmans's *No, No, Nanette!*, trying out in Chicago, was said to be sure to become the hottest ticket in town.

Rodgers confesses now that this was one of the worst periods in his life. He knew that Larry Hart was beginning to lose hope; Herb Fields also. He decided that he had better give some thought to the advice producers had so freely given him and get out of the music business altogether. A friend introduced him to a Mr Marvin, who was in the babies' underwear business, and who was looking for a young man to take the weight of his one-man business off his shoulders. He offered Rodgers fifty dollars a week to start, which was exactly fifty dollars a week more than Rodgers was earning. Dick went home, promising to think it over.

That night he got a call from Benjamin Kaye, a patient of his father's who had·written a couple of lyrics for Akron Club shows which Dick had scored. Kaye was working with the understudies of the Theatre Guild, putting on a show to raise money for tapestries to hang in the Guild's new theatre. Would Dick be interested in writing the music? If so, he would ask two members of the cast and committee, Romney Brent and Edith Meiser, to come and talk it over with him. Rodgers agreed; as it turned out, the date they selected conflicted with Brent's previously arranged date with the lovely Oriental movie star, Anna May Wong. Brent wasn't about to pass up a date with a movie star in order to talk to an unknown musician, so Edith Meiser went to see Rodgers alone. 'I walked into this very elegant apartment and it had an enormous foyer with an enormous grand piano. Dick was there, and he said "Well, I'll play you a few things I've done for the Varsity Shows up at Columbia", and I wasn't terribly impressed, to tell you the truth. Then he played "Manhattan"—and I flipped!'

Edith Meiser excitedly told her committee that she had found their composer, fully expecting to write the lyrics to the songs herself. When they began working, Rodgers diffidently said that he usually worked with Larry Hart, and wondered whether they would mind if Larry tried a few ideas. Miffed, Miss Meiser agreed, and Rodgers broached the idea to Larry. Hart wasn't keen to do the show at all. The strange co-incidence of Theatre Guild, enthusiastic Rodgers and reluctant Hart is almost bizarre, but there is no question that Larry was against doing the show. To begin with, it was a revue, not a book show; secondly, it would play only two performances, and those on a Sunday; third, the budget was at best inadequate; and in the fourth place, he was sick and tired of the amateur grind that put no money in the bank in the first place. Rodgers talked him around, however, and Edith Meiser remembers how, when the first lyrics began to take shape, she had the good sense to know that she was outclassed—'but way out-classed!'

They were young, irreverent, enthusiastic and bright, the pets of the theatre world. Edith Meiser remembered Hart's charisma, particularly, how everyone loved him. 'We were fond of Dick, but Larry was *adored*,' she said.

The revue was entitled *The Garrick Gaieties*, and the two performances were scheduled for the afternoon and evening of 17 May 1925. Orchestra seats were $2.20, balcony $1.65 or $1.10. The programme notes proclaimed that the revue's progenitors had neither principals nor principles and proceeded to prove it by lampooning everything in sight— Michael Arlen's novel *The Green Hat* (The Green Derby), Sidney Howard's hit play *They Knew What They Wanted* (They didn't know what they were getting) and so on. A song performed by Betty Starbuck, Libby Holman and June Cochrane, 'Ladies of the box office', neatly skewered such skewerable types as a Follies showgirl, Mary Pickford, and Sadie Thompson, the heroine of *Rain*. Right after this frolic, Sterling Hayden and June Cochrane did Rodgers's favourite song from the ill-fated *Winkle Town* 'in one'—that is to say, before an unadorned curtain behind which the scenery was being moved. The audience responded with delight to Larry Hart's felicitous pairing of Manhattan, the Bronx and Staten Island too, of going to Coney and eating boloney, or to Yonkers where true love conquers. If one song could have been said to be the hit of the show, it was 'Manhattan'.

The matinée audience gave them a standing ovation. Rodgers remembers Larry Hart running backstage shouting 'It's gonna run a year, it's gonna run a year!' The evening performance was greeted just as enthusiastically, and the verdict of the critics was nothing short of delirious. Rodgers and Hart had a hit, but one which had already closed before it really got started. There was only one thing to do and they did it. They went to the Theatre Guild management and persuaded them to approach Alfred Lunt and Lynn Fontanne, whose play *The Guardsman* was the Garrick's current attraction, and ask them whether they would be averse to ending the play's run and allowing *The Garrick Gaieties* to take its place. Their *chutzpah* paid off. *The Guardsman* was closed and, on 8 June, *The Garrick Gaieties* began a regular theatrical run. Some sketches were dropped, and a new song, 'Sentimental me' (and poor romantic you), was added. For the first time Dick and Larry were actually earning money regularly from their work.[5] Gone were Larry's thoughts of returning to the translation of more blasted operettas, gone forever Dick's career in the baby clothes business.

Dear Enemy had also become a 'live' proposition, now that Rodgers and Hart were no longer unknowns. Helen Ford was still doggedly pursuing support for the play, and came up with a man named Robert Jackson, with whom her husband George had gone to Dartmouth. Jackson had just made a million selling out his chain of stores in Canada, and he was easily persuaded to invest in the show. He took Dick, Larry, Herb and Helen on a mad whirl of the Manhattan night spots while George Ford, nominated producer, arranged for them to try out the show at the Colonial Theatre in Akron, Ohio. George Ford was managing a stock company, and had connexions throughout the country; his uncle had been the Harry Ford in whose Washington theatre President Abraham Lincoln was assassinated in 1865. With George Ford's brother directing, and the cast provided by the stock company whose home the Colonial Theatre was, they rehearsed for a week. Encouraged by the audience response to their one-night performance on 20 July, the triumvirate brought the show back to New York, where John Murray Anderson, free now of the commitment which had prevented his directing earlier (and perhaps encouraged by the fact that they had finance), agreed to direct the show. They tried out in Baltimore; Helen Ford remembers that it was so hot that the beautiful Revolutionary War costumes were soaking wet with perspiration. They opened at the Knickerbocker Theatre in New York on 18 September with the new title *Dearest Enemy*. Show, star and songs won plenty of praise. Helen Ford—'the little flowerpot' as Herb called her—had been right; *Dearest Enemy* made her a star, due in part to her then-outrageous entry clad only in a barrel. Thanks to Anderson, the settings were visually charming and apposite. The songs were neat, witty and just naughty enough to charm, as in 'War is war' when the young ladies learn that the British are coming, and sing 'Hooray, we're going to be compromised!' and then add, philosophically, 'war is war!'. The undoubted hit of the score was 'Here in my arms', which by clever alternation of the lyrics was at one stage a duet for Betsy and her British lover ('Here in your arms, it's adorable') and then a solo lament when he went off to war ('It's deplorable that you are never there'). There was a rousing patriotic finale (devised by George and Harry Ford) in which Washington appeared. *Dearest Enemy* settled down for a run of nearly a year at the Knickerbocker, a success indeed for the newcomers.

There was also a moment of sweet revenge for Rodgers. He received a call from Max Dreyfus of T. B. Harms, asking peevishly why he had taken the music of *The Garrick Gaieties* to one of Dreyfus's competitors, and inviting him to join Harms with the score of *Dearest Enemy* and all his and Larry's future work, at a royalty of three cents a copy. Rodgers managed to refrain from reminding Dreyfus that he had dismissed most of the songs in *Garrick Gaieties*, including 'Manhattan', as of no value at that traumatic interview.

Suddenly Rodgers and Hart were in demand, and Rodgers plunged into work as though it were water, pushing Larry Hart to produce song after song after song lyric to match his abundant outpouring of melody. In 1926 Rodgers and Hart had five musicals playing on Broadway, and another in London; as if this were not enough they also wrote songs for a Billy Rose revue called *The Fifth Avenue Follies*.

Dearest Enemy was still playing to packed houses when Dick, Larry and Herb brought *The Girl Friend* to New York on 17 March. Produced by Lew Fields and centring on the then-topical theme of six-day bicycle races, the show contained not only the title song and a clever ditty called 'The damsel who done all the dirt' but also the durable, lilting 'Blue room'. The show reinforced the claim of Rodgers and Hart to being the brightest, freshest song-writing talents on Broadway, and due note was taken of Hart's sophisticated, witty way with a lyric. Robert Benchley, writing in *Life* magazine (not the picture magazine, but the one best remembered because Benchley was its critic), remarked that Hart's lyrics showed unmistakable signs of the writer's having given personal thought to them. 'Considerably more,' said Abel Green in *Variety*, 'is anticipated from Rodgers and Hart.' The boys did their best not to disappoint.

Two months later they unveiled a second edition of *The Garrick Gaieties*, their score studded with charming songs. 'Sleepyhead' (which had been cut from the score of *The Girl Friend*) and 'What's the use of talking?' are little sung these days, but 'Mountain greenery' is as popular now as it became that half century ago.

They were approached now by the English actor Jack Hulbert, who was planning to produce a play called *Lido Lady* starring himself and his wife, Cicely Courtneidge. He wanted songs in it: Rodgers and Hart songs. It took the partners little time to decide that since the show was to be set in Venice, they ought to take a trip to Europe to do some research before heading for London to rehearse the show in the autumn. They sailed on an Italian ship, the *Conte Biancamano*, whose name Larry Hart rolled around his tongue, pretending he was speaking Italian. They went to Naples and Sorrento. In Venice they met Noel Coward and a young fellow with delicate features and large, soft eyes called Cole Porter who lived in the palazzo where Robert Browning died. Porter was young, rich and homosexual, and already had done a couple of unsuccessful Broadway scores. Nothing had come of them, so he composed mainly for the entertainment of his friends.

From Venice the partners went by train to Paris and on to London, where they added songs to the already-written libretto, one of them being 'Here in my arms'. The show was successful, if undistinguished; the song-writers more than a little disenchanted with their producer. Hulbert treated them distantly—he refers to them in his autobiography as 'our American college boys'—and they set sail for home as soon as the score was complete. The ship was the *Majestic* and among its passengers were Benjamin Feiner, his wife and daughter. Their son Ben was a great buddy of Dick's, and he lost no time in looking them up. He lost even less time in making the acquaintance of the lovely Dorothy Feiner, whom he married in 1930.

Dick and Larry were soon deep in the throes of Herb Field's newest idea, a show built around the dream fantasies of its heroine, Peggy Ann. Since the theme was (to say the least of it) unusual for a musical, the boys decided to go the whole hog. There was no opening chorus as such—in fact, for the first fifteen minutes there was no singing or dancing at all. The finale was not a rousing medley of the show's songs but a slow comedy dance, nearer ballet than the usual 'routine' and indicative of the direction in which Dick and Larry were pointing. Rodgers's music and Hart's lyrics were as unusual as the show, which opened at the Vanderbilt, home of many of the great Rodgers and Hart shows, on 27 December after two weeks in Philadelphia. Its cast was headed by Helen Ford and there were some other familiar names aboard: Edith Meiser, Betty Starbuck, and Lulu McConnell, the original Poor Little Ritz Girl. The songs were ingenious: 'A tree in the park' was the hit at the time, although 'Where's that rainbow'? has weathered the years better.

The night following the opening of *Peggy Ann*, Florenz Ziegfeld's new show, *Betsy*, opened at the New Amsterdam. It was a disaster. Rodgers and Hart's first collaboration with the Great Ziegfeld was one long unhappy tale of woe culminating, as we saw earlier, in his hiring Irving Berlin to write a 'hit' for the show—which Berlin obligingly provided. Certainly nothing of Dick and Larry's was notable, except a darkly pessimistic song revealing the other side of Hart's mercurial character and called 'This funny world' (makes fun of the things you strive for). *Betsy* lasted only five weeks and put a very large dent in Ziegfeld's bank account.

Between May 1925 and December 1926 Rodgers and Hart turned out the astonishing number of six Broadway musicals, one revue, and a London show. They decided there was only one thing to do now, and that was improve on the record. A call from C. B. Cochran in London provided them with an excuse to do another tour of Europe before going there to work on the score for a revue Cochran was putting on, called *One Dam' Thing After Another*. In Paris, Rodgers remembers, he and Larry were seeing the sights with two girls, Rita Hayden and Ruth Warner, whom they knew from New York. Suddenly a car came out of a side street and missed their taxi by inches.

> One of the girls said 'Oh, my heart stood still!' and Larry said 'Say, that'd make a great title for a song'. I called him a dirty name for thinking about work instead of the fact that we'd been almost killed. And the next thing I knew we were in London working on a show and I found in my little black notebook the words 'My heart stood still'. Finally I placed the words and remembered the incident. I knew that he'd been right, there was a good title there, and I wrote a tune for it. Larry came into the room and I said 'I've got a tune for your lyric' and he said 'What lyric is that?' I said 'My heart stood still.' 'Never heard it before in my life,' he said. I said 'They're your words, it's my tune, and I think we've got a song.' And sure enough, we did.

As well as providing an example of Rodgers's penchant for understatement, the story of how 'My heart stood still' was written gives an insight into how Dick and Larry worked. The songs usually began with Rodgers providing a melody, or working with an idea for a title which Larry had given him.

One Dam' Thing After Another starred Jessie Matthews and Sonny Hale, soon to be the cynosure of all eyes because of their rules-be-damned romance. Hale was married to the actress Evelyn Laye, who sued for divorce amid banner headlines a year or so later. The show's success was only moderate, but is notable for other reasons. One is that the pianist was Leslie Hutchinson, who as 'Hutch' became one of Britain's most beloved radio and nightclub pianists; the other is that among the chorus girls was a beauty named Sheilah Grahame, who later became Scott Fitzgerald's mistress, a Hollywood gossip columnist, and a writer.

A fun show—and what fun to hobnob with London society! Rodgers met the Prince of Wales, the d'Erlangers, the Guinnesses, 'royalty' of the Mayfair set. Larry Hart had different predilections and rarely attended parties, especially ones as fancy as those thrown by the d'Erlangers. Back in New York, he and Dick kicked ideas around with Herb Fields, turning finally to one they had shelved five or six years earlier, when they had approached Charles Tressler Lark, executor of the Mark Twain estate, for permission to turn Twain's novel *A Connecticut Yankee in the Court of King Arthur* into a musical. Lark had given them the rights free, but they'd never got the show together, not even in the amateur production called *A Danish Yankee in King Tut's Court*. Their option had lapsed and now when they went back to the lawyer, things were

Lew Fields directing a rehearsal of *A Connecticut Yankee*. TMC

changed. Rodgers, Hart and Fields were not unknowns any more. They were being spoken of as the natural successors to Bolton, Wodehouse and Kern, and Mr Lark made sure that the Twain estate got a royalty. Herb tried to get his father interested in producing, but Lew turned him down, saying it would not make a good musical. The trio persisted, and when they completed the book in which the Yankee, 'Sir Boss', comes to jazz up Camelot on a percentage basis, Fields changed his mind. *A Connecticut Yankee* went into rehearsal in the summer of 1927, and the boys had lots of fun with the plot, which has Sir Boss introducing King Arthur to such inventions as telephone, radio, efficiency experts and other 'benefits' of the twentieth century. The King gradually begins to talk like President Coolidge, Merlin like Damon Runyon, his speech a mixture of Olde English and Broadway slang ('Methinks yon damsel is a lovely broad'). The knights are reduced to carrying sandwich boards, 'a hell of a job for a knight', with advertising slogans proclaiming 'I would fain walk a furlong for a Camel' and the merits of a show called *Ye Hibernian Rose of Abie*. To beef up the score, Rodgers decided to add 'My heart stood still' which was now a big hit in London.

Several other producers, notably Ziegfeld and Dillingham, had already heard of it and were anxious to buy it for one of their shows. Rodgers got them all off his back by saying he'd already slated it for *Yankee* and paid Cochran $5000 to get it back, probably the best bargain struck for a song since Ed Christy of Christy's Minstrels paid Stephen Foster $50 for the rights of 'Old folks at home'.

A Connecticut Yankee opened at the Vanderbilt on 3 November 1927. It was a happy show; indeed Rodgers had had only one disagreement with his producer during the whole thing. During rehearsals at the Walnut Street Theatre in Philedlphia, Lew Fields wanted to cut out a song because he was sure that the audience would not understand Hart's cute Olde-English/American slang lyrics. Rodgers put his foot down, insisting on keeping it. 'I was stupid,' he recalls with a grin. 'I liked it.' Fields relented and the song, 'Thou swell', stayed in.

'Thou swell' was only one of many delights. Larry Hart had concocted lyrics that made everything else on Broadway look infantile, and even if the book wasn't everything it could have been—Herb Fields tended to rely a great deal on well-tried 'routines' and situations from his father's enormous files—the score was a miracle of originality. There was a cute tongue-in-cheek love song called 'I feel at home with you' in which Sir Galahad serenades his lady by telling her that neither of them is too bright, which is why he feels that way. In 'On a desert island with thee' Hart had even rhymed 'nonce' and 'honi soit qui mal y pense', erudition heretofore unheard of in a Broadway show. Add 'My heart stood still' and it's easy to see why the show was a thundering hit—418 performances on Broadway and a year and four months on the road. (It failed, however, to survive the Atlantic crossing.)

Despite their having kept their hit song from him, Charles Dillingham still wanted Dick and Larry to score his new show, to star Bea Lillie, Jack Whiting, Clifton Webb and Irene Dunne. The book, by Guy Bolton and the song-writing team of Kalmar and Ruby, who also wrote librettos, was at best, so-so. Some of the lines, as Bea Lillie remarked in her autobiography, had obviously been imported at great expense from the British Museum. *She's my Baby* folded after seventy-one performances. By the following April, the old trio—perhaps quartet, since the show was produced by Lew Fields—were back together. Herb Fields had just had a big success writing a show about the Navy called *Hit the Deck!* (with Vincent Youmans's music). What more natural than to do another about the Marines and call it *Present Arms*? Only one of the show's songs became a standard, but it was a good one: 'You took advantage of me'. It was succeeded at the Mansfield

Theatre by another Rodgers–Hart–Field show, *Chee Chee*. Despite the fact that it was probably their most interesting experiment in theatrical terms thus far, *Chee Chee* was a dreadful failure. It was a one-joke show, Helen Ford remembered, and that a joke in extremely bad taste. 'Even the cast was dumb,' she said. The critics were bored or pained or disgusted; all of them missed the point, which was the note printed in the theatre programme to the effect that 'the musical numbers, some of them very short, are so interwoven with the story that it would be confusing for the audience to peruse a complete list'. There were several attractive songs, but none caught the fancy of audience, or public. 'Dear, oh dear', 'Moon of my delight' and 'I must love you' (a reworking of which would appear as 'Send for me' in *Simple Simon*) were the best of the bunch.

Rodgers knew how to take failure as well as success; neither changed his positive attitude to life. He was twenty-seven, a good-looking, stockily-built young man with centre-parted hair who looked, according to one newspaper reporter, like an amalgam of Noël Coward and George Raft. He dressed then as he does now, like a conservative banker. He had a terrace apartment at the Lombardy Hotel on East 56th Street, where his next-door neighbour was Edna Ferber. He was earning about a thousand dollars a week; he had plenty of time for pretty girls—he has always adored the company of beautiful women—and his new automobile. His biggest problem—apart from coping with his own success, which he seems always to have done with aplomb—was, as usual, the effervescent, irrational little man who wrote his lyrics. Dick loved Larry, but there were times when their differences resulted in flaring arguments and bitter words. Rodgers was methodical, systematic, organized. Hart was everything else. Only one thing remained constant in his approach to his work, according to his partner. He hated doing it, and loved it when it was done.

To get Larry to work, Rodgers had to bully, plead, order or trick him into it. But by definition, Dick's problems with Larry were Larry's problems with Dick. Larry wrote lyrics like a flash, the most intricate, clever lines falling off the point of his pencil seemingly without effort. Rodgers has told a story about seeing him write lyrics in a noisy rehearsal hall, with the dancers thundering away on the stage and the principals shouting out their lines. 'In half an hour, he fashioned something with so many interior rhymes, so many tricky phrases and so many healthy chuckles in it that I just couldn't believe he'd written it that evening.' 'He would go into another room and come back with a lyric in no time,' George Abbott says. So while his partner fumed and fretted, Larry would be off somewhere 'having fun'—his euphemism for getting crocked. He'd done his lyrics; that was that. Rodgers, however, had to remain with the show and take the stick when revisions were needed, new choruses had to be added, songs cut and new ones substituted. Then it was always 'Where's Larry'? And it was his job to find him.

Larry was always on the town. His haunts were not the ritzy clubs but the Eighth Avenue bars around 44th and 45th Streets, where the young actors hung out. His constant companion was Milton Bender, the detestable dentist, a showbiz groupie whom everyone said was Larry's procurer.[6] Larry was the easiest touch on Broadway. Dorothy Hart recalls he once walked into a barbershop and as he left, grandly announced that he was going to pay for everyone else's haircut and shaves, too. An actor he knew borrowed $500 from him 'to buy the option on a play' but actually used the money to get his girl friend an abortion. Larry hooted with glee when he found out how he'd been conned. He thought it was a great trick.

One of the best descriptions of Larry Hart was written by Oscar Hammerstein.

> I think of him always as skipping and bouncing. In all the time I knew him, I never saw him walk slowly. I never saw his face in repose. I never heard him chuckle quietly. He laughed loudly and easily at other people's jokes and his own too. His large eyes danced, and his head would wag. He was alert and dynamic and fun to be with.[7]

But not so much fun to work with, Rodgers pointed out.

When the immovable object of his unwillingness to change came up against the irresistible force of my own drive for perfection, the noise could be heard all over the city. Our fights over words were furious, blasphemous, and frequent, but we both knew that we were arguing academically, and not personally.[7]

Dorothy Hart said Larry had a terrible temper. He would jump up and down, scream and shout and tear his thinning hair. Rodgers's temper was more the 'slow burning' kind, but he was and can still be implacable when it concerns his music or his shows. Josh Logan pointed out that Dick was a sensational editor of Larry's words, and certainly, whatever the tribulations both of them underwent, the results were superb.

The boys ended 1928 on an optimistic note. Just before Christmas, producers Alex Aarons and Vinton Freedley hired them to do the score for a story by Owen Davis called *Loving Ann*. It reached Broadway on 11 March 1929, and audiences at the new Alvin Theatre, built in 1927 by the producers and named for the first syllables of their Christian names, found they were in for another of those Long Island 'tennis anyone'? stories. *Spring Is Here*, as the show was now called, contained a clever lyric and verse for a song titled 'Yours sincerely' which solved two problems simultaneously: it connected the three sides of the eternal triangle in the plot, and—since he could not sing—it could be recited by the leading man. *Spring Is Here* is notable, however, for one of Rodgers and Hart's most famous creations: 'With a song in my heart', the melody of which came to Rodgers during the elation he felt in the hours following his first trip in an airplane. More shows of varying quality followed. *Heads Up!* for Aarons and Freedley; *Simple Simon*, starring the great Ed Wynn, and produced by Florenz Ziegfeld early in 1930. And why, after their mortifying experiences with Ziggy, did the song-writers elect to work for him again? There was one very simple reason: the failure of the New York stock market in October 1929. Money, to put it mildly, was nervous. For another, if another was needed, Rodgers had just become engaged to his sweetheart, Dorothy Feiner. They were married on 5 March 1930 at the Feiner apartment, 270 Park Avenue. Larry Hart and Herb Fields were ushers, Morty Rodgers, Dick's best man. They honeymooned in Europe, dined with the Mountbattens in London, and lived in a borrowed house at 10 York Terrace. Later, Larry Hart joined them to work with Dick on the score of a new Cochrane show starring Jessie Matthews called *Ever Green*. They all went to the first night of their friend Noël Coward's *Private Lives*. They met the Duke of Kent. They heard that 'Ten cents a dance', a last-minute addition to the score of *Simple Simon*, was a hit in New York. It had come about in a curious manner. The leading lady was prone to taking one drink too many, and Ziegfeld fired her during the Boston tryout. He replaced her with a young singer who had been making a bit of a name for herself in a show called *The 9.15 Revue*. He stamped in to see Dick and Larry, whom—as was his wont with songwriters—he bullied. He had already cut several songs including one called 'Dancing on the ceiling' and he told them that he was fed up with their clever stuff. 'Everything you fellows write is fancy,' he said. 'I want you to write me an ordinary song. You hear? Just an ordinary song.' So Rodgers and Hart went back to the Ritz-Carlton and wrote 'Ten cents a dance'. Ruth Etting got the song, and when the show came to New York she stopped it cold every night.

Something else was in the air: the movie musical. A couple of Rodgers and Hart shows got to the screen in one truncated form or another by 1930, but the demand for good songs—stimulated in 1928 by the enormous success of the all-talking, all-singing *Broadway Melody* was insatiable. Hollywood made Dick, Larry, and Herb Fields an offer they could not refuse, and as soon as they could, they headed west on the Super Chief. All three of them were highly enthusiastic about the prospects ahead of them; indeed, Rodgers went out of his way to toss garlands at his new employers, the brothers Warner. In a long interview with the magazine, *Cinema*, he explains fully not only his own feelings, but the ideas he, Larry, and Herb had for writing movie musicals.

> We had all sorts of ominous warnings before we came out here. All the routine fables about stars who ate peas with their knives and producers who couldn't read or write. We were good and scared. Herb and Larry got here first. When they saw how wrong the advance reports had been, they had Jack Warner frame me. The first day in, I went to the studio to meet Mr Warner. He was just like the producers in the funny stories. He sprawled over the table and said 'Well, now you're here, you got to get to work. And I don't vant none of your highbrow songmaking. Musik vit guts ve got to have—songs vit real sendiment like 'Stein song' and 'Vit tears in my eyes I'm dencing'. It turned out the whole thing had been a put up joke arranged by Jack Warner with the others . . . My God, offices with Oriental rugs and studio cars at your disposal, and people to carry your papers so you won't strain yourself . . . Our supervisor never interferes and we have almost carte blanche. They gave us the cast we wanted; they've put every facility at our disposal, given us intelligent co-operation. These gags about Hollywood slavedrivers must be myths.

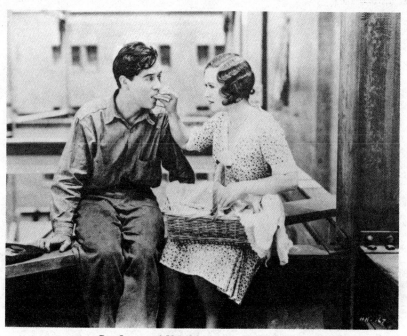

Ben Lyon and Una Munson in *The Hot Heiress* (First National,
1931). It wasn't so hot: maybe because of undying gems like
'Nobody loves a riveter like his mother'. NFA

They weren't, as Rodgers and Hart would all too shortly discover,
for their honeymoon with Hollywood would be but a short one. Nevertheless, fired by their first project, screenplayed by Herb Fields and
called *The Hot Heiress*, Rodgers outlined the way they planned to write
for it.

In the theatre, musical comedy is framed in footlights and its honest artifici-
ality is charming in itself. But the screen is too personal for that. There are
no footlights, nothing between the audience and the people talking inti-
mately on the screen. On the stage no one is jarred if the ingénue suddenly
goes into a tap dance. But on the screen her earlier actions have been too
believable to allow for this.

The dialogue, the action and the story progression are kept in quick
tempo. As for the songs, the point is not that they be logically 'planted'.
The very planting of the number is false. The heroine kidnapped by Arabs
and in the middle of the desert singing an aria to the accompaniment of
a fifty piece orchestra is ridiculous. Most important in songs for the screen
is their relevance. We are not making them numerous. They are seldom
reprised. And they are all definitely connected with the story, pertinent to
the actors and the action. We ease into them in the dialogue, so that before

you know it, the characters are speaking lyrics and their gradual entry into the song appears very logical.[8]

The Hot Heiress contained three songs. One other was cut before the release of the film, which was a fragile thing not helped at all by songs like 'Nobody loves a riveter' and the cutsey-pie 'You're the Cats' which was so unlike Larry and Dick as to stir doubts that they actually wrote it.

The score completed, they crossed the continent and the Atlantic to do some extra work on Cochrane's show *Ever Green*, which was due to begin its out-of-town engagement at the Kings Theatre, Glasgow that October. The juxtaposition of Larry Hart and Glasgow in October is a little hard to conceive of, but he and Dick were there, worried sick by the late arrival of a huge revolving stage which Larry had suggested would facilitate the many scene changes in the show. The turntable arrived three days before the show was due to open, and didn't work. Panic. Half the cast had colds or bronchitis. Finally, they got things working, with much revision and—according to the show's star, Jessie Matthews—much bullying by Rodgers. 'It's strange,' she said. 'He didn't seem to understand artistes at all'.

They got the show to London and opened it on 3 December and, perhaps to their surprise, drew extremely good notices. Special mention was made of 'Dancing on the ceiling', the song Ziegfeld had ditched during the tryouts of *Simple Simon* because it was too fancy.

Dick and Larry were not able to stay in London to savour their success, nice though it must have been after the failure of their first movie. They were already involved in a new show for producers Schwab and Mandel—the same Lawrence Schwab to whom Rodgers had once taken *Winkle Town*, the same Frank Mandel who had once collaborated with Oscar Hammerstein—which utilized some of their experiences in California. Staged by Monty Woolley, a chum of Cole Porter's, *America's Sweetheart* starred a pert newcomer, named Harriette Lake, making her Broadway debut. Talking to Samuel Marx many years later, the little girl from Valley City, North Dakota, who was to be offered a movie contract on the strength of her performance in *America's Sweetheart* and change her name to Ann Sothern, remembered that Rodgers was very stern, and scared her half to death. He didn't want her in the play; she remained only at Schwab's insistence. Harriette, whom one of the critics described as 'a lovely synthesis, one part Ginger Rogers, one part Ethel Merman', was a big hit, although the show was only a mild success. It added two more gems to the memorable contents of the Rodgers and Hart song book, 'I've got five dollars' and 'We'll be the same', and it had one other distinction: it was the last full collaboration between Herb Fields and Rodgers and Hart. Rodgers has always insisted that there was no falling out between them; yet it seems considerably more than likely that he and Larry were aware of the fact that the weakest part of their collaboration with Herb Fields were his books. He was a 'formula' writer who tended to rely on the tried-and-true, the old-but-reliable routines of the early musical. Dick and Larry were beginning to see that formulae must be avoided at all costs, something they demonstrated with panache in their next project.

Rouben Mamoulian: true originator of the integrated musical. CP

Warners had torn up their contract after *The Hot Heiress* flopped, but the following year Paramount offered Dick and Larry a contract to write a score for a new musical movie to star Jeanette MacDonald and Maurice Chevalier. Called *Love Me Tonight*, it was originally to have been directed by George Cukor, but he was dropped without explanation and replaced by Rouben Mamoulian. Larry Hart wrote about their experience on the movie some years later in *The New York Times*, one of his very rare declarations on the subject of his craft.

> The first thing we did was to study pictures, not on the sound set but in the cutting room. Then, with Chevalier and Rouben Mamoulian, we developed for the first time dialogue with a sort of phony little half rhyme, with a little music under it cut to the situation. We also put a portable soundtrack in an open field with an orchestra. We had a doctor coming to Jeanette MacDonald's room and the sing-song conversation went something like this:
> Now, my dear, remove your dress.
> My what?
> Your dress.
> Is it necessary?
> Very.
> It isn't rhyme, it isn't anything like it; but it's screen talk and it isn't difficult if you know the medium. I'm a great believer in conversational rhythm. I think in terms of rhythmic dialogue. It's so easy, you can talk naturally. It's like peas rolling off a knife. Take the great screen actors and actresses, Bette Davis, Eddie Robinson, Jimmy Cagney, Spencer Tracy. They all talk in rhythm. And rhythm and movement are the life of the screen.[9]

Love Me Tonight was unquestionably the best movie score ever written by Rodgers and Hart. Its songs were fresh and lilting: 'Mimi', 'Isn't it romantic?' and 'Lover', as well as the title song, were beautifully inter-woven into the dialogue and action. In the opening sequence of the film Maurice sings 'Isn't it romantic?' in his tailor's shop, performing it as a jaunty, optimistic tune which is picked up by one of his customers, then a taxi driver, then a man on a train, then some soldiers riding through the countryside (they thunder it out as a rousing march) and finally, via some gypsy musicians, to Jeanette, dreaming of love in her chateau. There were typically cheeky Hart puns in the song 'Lover' which Jeanette MacDonald sang as she drove her carriage recklessly through the forest, at one moment serenading her lover and at the next admonishing her horses. 'Like two lovers rolling in the— hey!' was one of the more felicitous examples of how Larry got his lines past the censor. Light-years ahead of its time, *Love Me Tonight* demonstrates clearly Rouben Mamoulian's dedication to the integration of song, lyric and dialogue, indicates how much of the technique—which

he would use some years later when he directed Gershwin's *Porgy and Bess*—he brought to *Oklahoma!* when the time came (and how little credit he has been given for it).

Paramount picked up Dick's and Larry's option, and offered them *The Phantom President*, starring the original Yankee Doodle Dandy, George M. Cohan. Dick, Dorothy and their daughter Mary moved out to Beverly Hills, where Larry stayed with them until he found a house of his own on North Bedford Drive. There he installed his widowed mother, and became a paid-up member of the gay fringe in the movie colony, throwing huge manners-be-damned parties (he once invited the entire Olympic swimming team) and generally living it up. *The Phantom President*, however, was an unhappy experience for everyone. Cohan, who had written many successful shows and such hit songs as 'Mary's a grand old name' and the World War I anthem, 'Over There', thought Dick and Larry upstarts, and referred to them slightingly as Gilbert and Sullivan. He took no cognizance of the fact that in Broadway terms he was very much a has-been; as a former director, writer, composer and producer he felt he ought to have been running the show and didn't take it kindly when he was not too gently told he was not. When he left Hollywood Cohan told an interviewer, 'If I had to choose between Hollywood and Atlanta, I'd take Leavenworth.'

Dick and Larry tried again for integration, for the kind of interweaving of dialogue and music that had been so successful in *Love Me Tonight*, but director Norman Taurog was less sympathetic than Mamoulian, and *The Phantom President* was not a success.

Nevertheless, they were offered a job by United Artists, a film to star Al Jolson. Jolson had been the star of the first talking picture, *The Jazz Singer*, but his career was on the wane (although, like Cohan, Jolson was not about to face up to that unpleasant fact). Larry Hart was excited and awed to be working with Jolson, who had always been one of his idols (he did a passable imitation of The Singing Fool, according to his sister-in-law, Dorothy Hart). Rodgers was impressed by the fact that the authors of the screenplay were Ben Hecht and Sam Behrman, two very highly-paid writers. Behrman, of course, was the reluctant playwright who was dragooned into backing *Oklahoma!* some years on. Ben Hecht was the one who coined that immortal reply to the statement of one disgruntled writer that the moguls of Hollywood had no taste and that working for them was hell. 'Yeah,' said Hecht, 'and all they give us for it is a lousy fortune.'

Hallelujah, I'm a bum (genteelly altered to *Hallelujah, I'm a tramp* for British consumption) was a fragile story about unemployed men, vic-

Maurice Chevalier sings 'I'm an Apache' in *Love Me Tonight* (Paramount, 1932, dir. Rouben Mamoulian). He and co-star Jeanette MacDonald got along about as well as Jekyll and Hyde. NFA

tims of the Depression, living in a Central Park shantytown in New York. For it, Dick and Larry went the whole way with their rhythmic dialogue, working so closely with the writers that it is almost impossible to separate the 'talking dialogue' from the 'singing dialogue'. Many of the 'songs' are almost recitative, and nearer to Gluck than movie music. Dick and Larry played minuscule parts in the film, as a photographer and bank teller respectively. It was their second appearance on-screen. In 1929 they had taken part in a two-reeler called *Masters of Melody* in which they 'acted out' the writing of such songs as 'Manhattan', 'The Girl Friend', 'Blue Room' and 'Here in my arms'. It was pretty bad; perhaps that was why they were permitted no dialogue by director Lewis Milestone when they appeared in *Hallelujah*.

Much as they enjoyed working on it, however, this Rodgers and Hart experiment did not work at the box office, and they found a new home at Metro-Goldwyn-Mayer, where the last tycoon, Irving Thalberg, was head of production. Thalberg had been very impressed by *Love Me Tonight* and offered Dick and Larry a choice of assignments. One was a musical version of a Thorne Smith novel. The other was a fantasy, a Hungarian play about a man who marries an angel. They chose the play and set to work with a young writer named Moss Hart (later to collaborate so successfully with George S. Kaufman and to crown his career by becoming the director of *My Fair Lady*). He was not related to Larry Hart.

Louis B. Mayer, head of MGM, planned *I Married an Angel* as a starring vehicle for Jeanette MacDonald, and had lured the Iron Butterfly away from Paramount for just that purpose. With the screenplay and the score complete, Mayer cancelled the project. It seemed someone had told him that the Catholic church would object to the idea of someone going to bed with an angel.

So, for a year, Dick and Larry served out their terms of what Rodgers calls 'soft labour' at MGM. A song 'That's the rhythm of the day' was interpolated into a Joan Crawford-Clark Gable movie *Dancing Lady*, sung by Nelson Eddy as if his very life depended upon it, which it may well have done at that time. Another song, 'That's love' was sung by Anna Sten in Sam Goldwyn's *Nana*. They were assigned to a Jean Harlow movie which MGM's publicity chief, Howard Dietz—the same Howard Dietz who composed with Arthur Schwartz—had dreamed up. It was to be called *Hollywood Party* and it would star every comedian and comedienne on the MGM lot with lots of 'guest' spots for the big names and a score by Rodgers and Hart. Harlow, they discovered, had a range of three notes, and so they wrote her a song called 'Prayer'

How Hollywood prefers to see its song-writers. A still from
MGM's *Words and Music* (1948), a purported film biography of
Rodgers and Hart. Marshall Thompson (Herbert Fields) looks
wary, Tom Drake (Richard Rodgers) tries for the same expression
the real Rodgers often wore, and Mickey Rooney (Larry Hart)
goes on chewing the scenery up just as he always did. NFA

which she would sing as a stenographer wailing, 'Oh, Lord, if you're
not busy up there ... be nice and make me a star.' *Hollywood Party*
turned into a nightmare. Harlow never came near it, the song was
dropped, and before the movie was finished, it had songs not only by
Dick and Larry, but by Nacio Herb Brown and Arthur Freed, Walter
Donaldson, Gus Kahn, and Dietz himself. Rodgers felt disconnected
from his work. He was playing tennis and wasting time, living what
he later referred to as the life of a retired banker. He began to loathe
Hollywood, loathe the conditions in which they worked. Sam Marx,
who was MGM's story editor then, remembered their office: 'They had
a little cubbyhole that was just big enough for a small, a very small,
grand piano. At least the company was prepared to go that far and
gave them a grand and not a battered upright. So they had a grand
piano and they had a piano stool. There may have been a chair. They
had nothing else.'

Now Dick and Larry were asked to come up with something for a
nightclub sequence in a Gable–Loy–Powell thriller called *Manhattan*

Melodrama, which may be remembered as being the last movie watched by John Dillinger, Public Enemy Number One, before the G-men gunned him down outside the Biograph Theatre in Chicago. It will not be remembered at all for a song called 'The bad in every man' which a blackfaced Shirley Ross sang in a tatty 'Harlem' scene. The song was a rehash of the Harlow tune, and just as unsuccessful. Then one day, Jack Robbins, MGM's music publisher, met Dick and Larry, as Arthur Schwartz recalls.

> He heard the melody and the lyric and said the tune is great but that lyric of course is not commercial, you ought to write a commercial lyric for it. And Larry was offended by this, because he wrote his songs to fit the scenes in which they were called for, and he said 'What do you mean, commercial, what do you mean? It should be something like "Blue moon" I suppose you think? And Robbins said, 'Yeah, "Blue moon".'

In its third incarnation, 'Blue Moon' became a great success, one of the very few songs Dick and Larry ever wrote outside a score. Hart never liked it.

Totally disenchanted, Dick and Larry were dealt a further blow by an item in O. O. McIntyre's column that asked rhetorically—McIntyre knew where they were—what ever had become of Rodgers and Hart? Their reaction can be gauged by an item from the *Hollywood Reporter* of 10 December 1933, the day Mary Pickford filed for divorce from Douglas Fairbanks.

> Richard Rodgers and Lorenz Hart ironed out their MGM difficulties and withdrew the resignation they handed in just before they hopped off on two weeks vacation. The song-writing team was dissatisfied with the assignments they had been receiving and felt they could not do themselves or the studio justice with them. The team will write the musical score and additional music for the Lehar operetta *Merry Widow* on their return.

The Merry Widow turned out to be yet another unhappy experience. Rodgers found there was no additional music for him to write, and he had no clear idea of how he could be expected to improve on Lehar anyway. So the assignment ended with Larry (with some assistance from Gus Kahn) writing new lyrics for some of the old songs, notably 'Paris in the spring', 'Vilia' and the title waltz. In February 1934, after what the Reporter described as 'plenty of arguments and bickering one way and another,' MGM set Jeanette MacDonald to play the widow opposite Maurice Chevalier, a choice which that worthy opposed to the last ditch but 'had to bow to the logic of the situation as was outlined by both Irving Thalberg and Ernst Lubitsch'. What was that about Hollywood slavedrivers, Dick?

Director Edward Sutherland and cameraman Charles Lang setting up a scene for Paramount's *Mississippi* (1935). No prizes for spotting W. C. Fields, but a bonus point if you can name the scowling kibitzer in the top hat (Paul Hurst). NFA

Irving Berlin, in town to check out *Easter Parade* at MGM, looks in on Tom Drake and Mickey Rooney in their Rodgers and Hart rôles for *Words and Music*. He's probably laughing because even he can play the piano better than Tom Drake. NFA

Bing Crosby in *Mississippi* (Paramount, 1935, dir. Edward
Sutherland). Would you buy a used song from this man? NFA

The boys had been back east and seen the parlous state of the Broadway stage. There was one Kern show, a *Music Box Revue* by Irving Berlin, and the last of the *Ziegfeld Follies*. (Ziegfeld had died on 22 July 1932). Lew Fields was no longer producing; Mandel and Schwab had split up; so had Aarons and Freedley. The Theatre Guild was tied up with *Porgy and Bess*. Only the Shuberts were still putting on shows. Between March and June of that year not one musical opened on Broadway. So Dick and Larry returned to their velvet-lined rut and went to work on a Paramount epic starring Bing Crosby, Joan Bennett and W. C. Fields called *Mississippi*. With typical obtuseness Paramount credited Rodgers and Hart on screen with Stephen Foster's 'Old folks at home'. Even so, the Crosby renditions of 'Easy to remember', 'Soon' and 'Down by the river' were considerably more successful than anything else Dick and Larry had done latterly.

Mississippi was their Hollywood swan song; they went back to Hollywood only twice after that, and on their own terms. Rodgers's dislike of the place grew stronger as the years went by until, by the time he worked with Oscar Hammerstein, he would not deign to go near the place. 'We were enormously unhappy there,' he said in later years. 'They didn't understand us, and we didn't understand them. There was no meeting of minds at all.'

Things were getting better on Broadway, but they were far from bright. For a year after they got back Dick and Larry had a lean time of it. They auditioned a story for Lee Shubert which they had dreamed up in Hollywood when they heard that RKO were looking for vehicles to star Fred Astaire and Ginger Rogers. They called it *On Your Toes* and they told Astaire about it and played him a couple of the songs. He turned it down, afraid his public would not accept him in a rôle in which he did not wear top hat and tails. So the opportunity to audition, even for the stone-hearted Shuberts, was not to be turned down. Rodgers went up to Shubert's apartment (his office was too small to hold a piano) and began to play the score while Larry Hart, who had no voice at all ('He had a voice like a raven,' Rodgers says) began to sing. By the third number Hart was doing his best to bellow and Rodgers had the loud pedal on the floor, all to no avail. Lee Shubert had fallen fast asleep. He took an option on the show, anyway; but proceeded to keep Dick and Larry dangling. Rodgers was anxious to get back to work—even Larry was. Their Hollywood money was dwindling rapidly, and Dick now had a second daughter, Linda, who had arrived on 5 March 1935, coincidentally her parents' fifth wedding anniversary.

Meanwhile Billy Rose, Larry's old lyric-writing friend and now a Broadway producer, had hired Ben Hecht and Charlie MacArthur to write 'the biggest musical extravaganza in the history of the world'. Part circus, part musical, it would be staged in New York's biggest theatre, the Hippodrome on 44th Street and Sixth Avenue. He had gutted the interior of the theatre and turned it into, almost literally, a three ring circus. He had hired Jimmy Durante, Paul Whiteman and his orchestra, and actress Gloria Grafton. Now he wanted a score— by Rodgers and Hart. *Jumbo* as the show was called, rehearsed all through the summer of 1935 as Billy Rose frantically tried to raise more money to keep up with the amount he was spending. Meanwhile everybody and his aunt dropped in on the rehearsals. The Broadway joke was that the impresario was not going to open *Jumbo* until everyone in New York had seen it. However, after many vicissitudes, *Jumbo* opened on Thanksgiving Day, 1935. With 'Little girl blue' and 'My romance', with 'The most beautiful girl in the world' and 'Over and over again' Rodgers hit a new vein of melody and Hart his best bittersweet style. Although *Jumbo* was far too ponderous an investment ever to make money, it ran well into 1936, by which time Dick and Larry had taken the lapsed option of *On Your Toes* away from the Shuberts and given it to Dwight Deere Wiman, a producer with whom they were to share a string of memorable hit shows. They brought in director George Abbott, who had worked with them on *Jumbo* to get experience in staging a musical. In a 57th Street rehearsal loft, Larry Hart met the former principal choreographer of the Ballets Russes, George Balanchine, who had come to America a few years earlier, and persuaded him to choreograph the show. Jo Mielziner designed the settings and Irene Sharaff the costumes. If the book wasn't Tolstoy, the score was distilled Rodgers and Hart. *On Your Toes* marks the beginning of a tremendously productive time for the two men. It opened on 11 April 1936 at the Imperial Theatre in New York, and ended with a run of 315 performances. Its most enduring success was 'There's a small hotel', originally written for *Jumbo* and never used, but the score was full of felicities. 'Too good for the average man' poked its thumb in the eye of the fads and fancies of the wealthy: psychoanalysis, birth control, caviar, and so on. Hart's outrageous rhymes—matching 'stick to' with 'in flagrante delictu' for example—were pure delight, and Rodgers caviar and so on. Hart's outrageous rhymes—matching 'stick to' with indigestion), the moving lament, 'Glad to be unhappy', 'Quiet night'

and the title song are vintage, if now sadly-neglected, Rodgers and Hart, but *On Your Toes* was remarkable in one other aspect. For the very first time, ballet was used in a musical comedy both as spectacle and to advance the story itself. The music Rodgers wrote for this scene, the finale of the show, has become a near-classic. It was, of course, 'Slaughter on Tenth Avenue'.

Rodgers and Hart had never rested on their laurels, and never would. Their only formula, they said, was to have no formula, their only rule never to follow what they had just done with the mixture as before. On 14 April of the following year, they unveiled *Babes in Arms*, and, once again, they threw away the rule-book. The cast was led by real kids—the lead girl singers were seventeen and fifteen respectively—and

Babes in Arms (1937): Singer Mitzi Green gazes adoringly at Dick Rodgers, who is explaining a musical point to pianist Edgar Fairchild (in hat). George Balanchine is seated behind Fairchild and that's Larry Hart's head you can see the back of. Standing, extreme right, is producer Dwight Deere Wiman. CP

not older actors pretending to be kids. The traditional chorus line was tossed out. Scenery and props and costumes were far from elaborate (the whole budget was $55,000) and the story was just a wisp of a thing about the children of vaudeville troupers who put on a show to avoid being sent to a work farm. *Babes in Arms* includes so many great songs that one can only marvel at it: 'Where or when?' and 'The lady is a tramp', 'My funny Valentine' and 'I wish I were in love again', 'Johnny one note' and that wicked lampoon upon the current craze, cowboy songs, 'Way out west' where, according to Larry Hart, 'seldom is heard an intelligent word'. *Babes in Arms* became a solid hit, notching up 289 performances at the Shubert Theatre. A final credit not usually given to the show is that its dancing chorus included a newcomer called Dan Dailey, later the lanky, laconic dancing star of such technicoloured movie spectaculars as *Mother Wore Tights* and *It's Always Fair Weather*.

Despite their unhappy experience with him in Hollywood, Rodgers and Hart agreed to score a show for George M. Cohan written by George S. Kaufman and the same Moss Hart with whom they had worked in Hollywood on the aborted *I Married an Angel*. Kaufman and Hart were the hottest playwrights on Broadway, with the smash hits *Once in a Lifetime* and *You Can't Take It With You* to their credit. Their idea was to write a play in which the actual President, Franklin D. Roosevelt, would be played onstage by Cohan, and (at the time) it caused a tremendous furore, which in turn resulted in *I'd Rather Be Right* having an almost unprecedented advance sale. In fact, it was a pretty harmless spoof, whose action all takes place on one Fourth of July in Central Park. Apart from 'Have you met Miss Jones?' none of its songs is ever heard these days, primarily because most of them were so closely integrated into the story that they are not really performable away from it.

Although *I'd Rather Be Right* was a thumping hit (290 performances) the association with Cohan was no more pleasant than before.[10] In addition, Dick Rodgers was dissatisfied with a financial arrangement which gave Kaufman and Hart eight per cent of the weekly gross while he and Larry got only five. During the tryouts at Ford's Theatre in Baltimore, they were asked to replace one of the songs, 'Everybody loves you'. The new number stopped the show, and Rodgers was delighted. 'Now maybe we can have a few encores,' he said, during a run-through, 'and someone may even remember a couple of bars!' Kaufman was not amused; he did not believe that any show written by him depended for its success on music, for which he had no ear and less regard. He and Rodgers argued, and the argument boiled over with all the other

George Michael Cohan, looking here just as he must have looked
when he told Rodgers and Hart not to take any wooden nickels.
ASCAP

frustrations Dick was suffering—Cohan's cavalier attitude to himself,
Larry, and their songs, Kaufman's indifference, the unfair royalty
shareout and so on. They stood on the pavement outside the theatre
and yelled at each other loudly and at length. In the end, Kaufman
had his way. 'He was bigger, richer and older', Rodgers said, not
admiringly.[11]

The next Rodgers and Hart show was a much happier affair. On
11 May 1938 they brought *I Married an Angel* into the Shubert, a new
show based on the Janos Vaszary play they had rescued from MGM
back in 1933. A brilliant young director named Joshua Logan joined
the 'regulars', producer Wiman, choreographer Balanchine, designer

Mielziner, musical director Gene Salzer, orchestrator Hans Spialek. The star of the show was Vera Zorina, the lovely ballerina who had so brilliantly danced the 'Slaughter on Tenth Avenue' ballet in *On Your Toes*. There was a special part for Vivienne Segal, one they had promised to write for her since they had seen her playing light comedy in California. Dennis King played the banker who marries the angel, Walter Slezak, Charles Walters and Audrey Christie were the other stalwarts who performed such delights as that hilarious send-up of Radio City 'At the Roxy Music Hall', 'Did you ever get stung (where the doctor can't help you?)' the title song, and the sweet cynical piece of advice Vivienne Segal offers the angel, that a woman can get away with almost anything but, she adds, you have to do it with 'A twinkle in your eye'.

'Musical comedy has met its masters!' shouted Brooks Atkinson in *The New York Times*, giving *I Married an Angel* a rousing critical send-off on its 338 performance run. The show was bought for filming soon after the opening by——yes, of course, MGM.

Long before MGM had swallowed its pride, however, Larry and Dick were hard at work on another show. In November of 1938 the boys from Morningside Heights presented *The Boys from Syracuse* (235 performances) an adaptation of *The Comedy of Errors* which owed but one line of its dialogue to Shakespeare.

The show was vintage Rodgers and Hart champagne. George Abbott's complex story of the two sets of twins encouraged Larry Hart to come up with equally complex lyrics to match Rodgers's witty and eminently singable tunes. 'Agamemnon, Achilles, and Ajax,' lamented three warriors, 'we would rather have stayed home and played jacks.' The audience was told what to expect right at the outset, when it was announced that the show was 'a drama of ancient Greece. If it's good enough for Shakespeare, it's good enough for us!' 'You're privileged to miss a row of diatribes by Cicero' the cast told the audience, who loved it and loved the songs ('Falling in love with love' and 'This can't be love' were among them). Richard Watts Jr, writing in the *New York Herald Tribune* said 'If you have been wondering all these years what was wrong with *The Comedy of Errors* it is now possible to tell you. It has been waiting for a score by Rodgers and Hart and direction by George Abbott.' The show's success was doubly satisfying for Larry Hart, for his brother Teddy made a big hit in it.

Six really big successes in precisely half that many years made Dick and Larry Big News, and on 26 September 1938, just a few weeks before *The Boys from Syracuse* began its tryouts in New Haven, they received the ultimate American accolade: their picture appeared on the cover of *Time* magazine. (The only other American song-writer who had ever appeared there was George Gershwin). *Time's* essay made full use of the colourful habits of Larry Hart, 'a tiny, swarthy, cigar-chewing bachelor who at forty-three is getting bald and ... lives with his mother, whom he describes as "a sweet, menacing old lady"'. Rodgers, said *Time*, took the world in his stride; his partner was ever tempted to fume, deprecate, explain, protest—and meet a question with a wisecrack rather than an answer. Rodgers and Hart told the world that they had written the score of *I'd Rather Be Right* in three weeks ('I don't know if it's true, but I do know it's possible,' Rodgers says now), that they didn't think much of the new 'swing' music and preferred their songs played at the tempo in which they had been written—a topic they would turn into song in their next show. *Time* estimated their income at $100,000 a year, a very great deal of money indeed in 1938.

Within a year, Rodgers, Hart and Abbott had another show ready. It was based on a story by George Marion, Jr (who had written some of *Love Me Tonight*) and, although originally conceived as a movie, proved easy to adapt to the stage. Full of fresh-faced kids once again, *Too Many Girls* was a college story unlikely to have strained anyone's intellect, and among its discoveries were Desi Arnaz, Eddie Bracken and Van Johnson. Bracken became a most unlikely wartime star out at Paramount, Van Johnson a teenage idol at MGM. Desi Arnaz, too, was snapped up by the movies, and went out to RKO to film *Too Many Girls*, in which he was teamed with a vivacious redhead named Lucille Ball.[12] So it's fair to say that had Larry Hart and his pal 'Doc' Bender not literally shovelled Arnaz into the cast of the show (Arnaz didn't even know who Rodgers and Hart were) a couple of zillion television viewers would have never sampled the wacky delights of a show called *I Love Lucy*.

Too Many Girls was merry, melodious, mindless and successful. As well as its best-known song, 'I didn't know what time it was', it included a sardonic elbow-in-the-eye for Manhattan called 'Give it back to the Indians' and a song which bewailed the fate of song-writers in the swing era. Bands like Gene Krupa's with drums like thunder were great; 'but the melody is six feet under,' said Dick and Larry in 'I like to recognize the tune'. One or two of the songs in the show are all the work of Richard Rodgers, music and lyrics, because Larry Hart was simply not there to write them. The same problems were to arise with the next show, *Higher and Higher*.

This mishmash arose out of Rodgers and Hart's not unnatural desire to write another starring vehicle for the lovely Vera Zorina, who had been such a hit in *I Married An Angel*. Producer Dwight Deere Wiman hired Joshua Logan to direct, Jo Mielziner to design the sets, and Lucinda Ballard to do costumes, but *Higher and Higher* doggedly refused to come together. Zorina was filming *On Your Toes* in Hollywood and couldn't get away. Logan couldn't do a hell of a lot with the book. Larry didn't like it and retreated to the bottle. *Higher and Higher* sank lower and lower. It was never exactly a flop, but 108 performances was a long way short of success. As Rodgers has said many times since, 'When a trained seal steals the show, you know how bad it is.' Even so, there were some fine songs in the score, including one of Rodgers's prettiest waltzes, 'Nothing but you', and the wistful 'It never entered my mind'. The cast included Shirley Ross and Leif Erickson, he who became the paterfamilias in television's *High Chaparral*; and in the chorus line were two beauties called June Allyson and Vera-Ellen who had a bright future ahead of them at MGM.

Dick and Larry realized that perhaps their change of pace had been a mistake, but they were not in the habit of holding inquests. They were already preparing another show that had grown out of an idea put to Rodgers by the novelist John O'Hara while they were trying out *Too Many Girls* in Boston the preceding year. O'Hara thought that a series of stories he had been writing for *The New Yorker* about a brass-faced master of ceremonies in a cheap night club might be made into a show. Yes, yes and yes again, said Rodgers and Hart, and John

Dick and Larry 8 October 1940. They were already working on
Pal Joey. Compare with Hollywood's idea of them (p. 97). CP

O'Hara started work on what would become *Pal Joey*. They needed
someone special to play the lead, a dancer rather than a singer, someone
who could make the audience like the hero even though they knew
they ought to despise him. They found him playing a small part in
a show called *The Time of Your Life*. His name was Gene Kelly.

With George Abbott directing, they brought *Pal Joey* to the Ethel
Barrymore Theatre on Christmas Day, 1940 with not a few misgivings.
How would the audience react to the idea of a heel as a hero, a society
lady who pays for her boyfriends as his patron, and a not-too-bright
dancer as his girl friend? Vivienne Segal, who played the society lady,
Mrs Prentiss Simpson, remembered that Rodgers was nervous about
some of Larry's more risqué lyrics and wanted her to change them;
Larry as adamantly refused to allow it. Abbott was nervous, not at all
sure that the show wouldn't flop. *Pal Joey* was radical and different,
and—probably—ahead of its time.

In many ways it is the apotheosis of the Rodgers and Hart partnership, unquestionably the most biting, daring thing they wrote together, as good to watch today as it was nearly forty years ago. (It bears practically no resemblance whatsoever to the politely-laundered movie version, by the way). With Leila Ernst as the not-too-smart Linda, Vivienne Segal perfect as the cynical woman who buys her boys and discards them when they become tiresome, *Pal Joey* was something totally new to the Broadway stage. Hard-edged and brittle, it lived in a world Larry Hart knew like the palm of his hand, and everything he wrote for it was sharp, hip and sardonic. Rodgers matched his partner note for word, even achieving the remarkably difficult feat of

Gene Kelly, Leila Ernst and Vivienne Segal as Joey, Linda and Vera in *Pal Joey* (1940). Larry Hart adored Miss Segal above all other women; it's not hard to see why. TMC

Gladys Bumps (June Havoc), the blackmailing chorus girl, with singing waiters (among whom are Van Johnson (r.) and Stanley Donen). Miss Havoc is the original Baby June you remember from *Gypsy*—her sister was Rose Hovick, aka. Gypsy Rose Lee. TMC

writing wonderful 'bad' tunes like 'Chicago', 'That terrific rainbow' and 'The Flower Garden of my Heart' for the nightclub sequences.

Larry loved to get his naughty lyrics past Mrs Grundy. In the song 'Bewitched, bothered and bewildered' for instance, Vivienne Segal sings about losing her heart and not caring. Joey is a laugh, she says, but 'I love it because the laugh's on me'. Innocuous enough; until you know how Larry Hart chortled with delight when he read those lines over the phone to Joshua Logan and explained with glee that they meant Joey was actually *on* Vera Simpson.

Critical reaction to *Pal Joey* was mixed, but mostly good, although Larry was badly wounded by the adverse comments of Brooks Atkinson. 'Although it is expertly done,' Atkinson wrote, 'can you draw sweet water from a foul well?' Gene Kelly recalled that when the review was read over the phone to him, Hart broke down and cried. Raves from Richard Watts Jr ('brilliant, sardonic and strikingly original') and Wolcott Gibbs ('musical comedy took a long step towards maturity') and others were no consolation.

Strangely enough, the legend has sprung up that *Pal Joey* was not a success, which is far from the truth.[13] Although, as Gene Kelly says, the flower-hatted matinée audience stayed away from it in their thousands, *Pal Joey* ran for eleven months, with a three month tour afterwards. It was and it remains a landmark. It demonstrated that a musical could be set in a world completely removed from operetta-land, about people who were not all peaches and cream. Who else but they would have written as pretty a love song as 'I could write a book' and have it sung so cynically, for effect, by the hero-heel? Who else could have created 'Zip', the lament of the intellectual stripper who thinks about Schopenhauer while she is taking off her clothes?

Rodgers was supremely happy, basking in the glow of success, recognition and the wealth that was beginning to come now that he and Larry were sharing in the financial rewards of producing as well as writing their shows. He was doing work he loved to do, he had a lovely wife, two delightful daughters, friends galore.

Hart remained what he had always been, only more so. Success couldn't change Larry, because Larry couldn't change. He had always drunk too much, but now he drank more. He had always stayed out all night, but now he began staying out for two or three nights, or disappearing without explanation. He had always been late for meetings but now he often did not show up at all, or, if he did, Rodgers would take one look at him and know that Larry could no more work than fly. He had always tried to protect Larry from himself, but now Larry was going around with a pretty pernicious crowd, dreary stupid people who were happy to let Larry pick up the bills for their fun, and vacuous blond boys brought along by the sinister Bender.

Gradually the gulf between Dick and Larry had reached irreparable proportions. Drinking far too much, shadowed everywhere by the unpleasant Bender, Larry became so dishevelled that former acquaintances would cross the street to avoid him. Could this unhappy, maudlin,

Gene Kelly was the original *Pal Joey*. When the film was made Frank Sinatra got the part although Harry Cohn wanted Jack Lemmon. TMC

reeling wreck be the same man who, between 1935 and 1942 had written the words for such songs as 'Glad to be unhappy', 'It's got to be love', 'There's a small hotel', 'Have you met Miss Jones?', Spring is here', 'The shortest day of the year', 'Who are you?', 'You're nearer', 'I didn't know what time it was', 'My romance', 'The most beautiful girl in the world', 'It never entered my mind', 'On your toes', 'I could write a book', and 'Bewitched, bothered and bewildered'? It was, all too sadly, it was.

As we have seen, most of *By Jupiter*, the last completely new Rodgers and Hart show, was finished while Larry was 'drying out' at Doctor's

Hospital in New York. It was ironically to be their biggest hit, although the irony must have twisted the knife in Larry Hart's soul, for it was still running when Rodgers and Hammerstein's *Oklahoma!* opened at the St James's Theatre and made such shows as *By Jupiter* obsolete.

On the Easter Sunday after *Oklahoma!* opened, Frieda Hart died, and with her went Larry Hart's last tenuous link with any kind of normal life. He lived alone in the huge duplex apartment at 320 Central Park West, once the scene of loud, never-ending parties to which Paul Whiteman would bring his entire band, carefree dinner parties when nobody knew how many people would arrive. He talked about projects in which he had no real intention of becoming involved, a musical version of a novel called *The Snark Was a Boojum*, a show with a book by Paul Gallico and music by Emmerich Kalman. There were rumours that he was going to work with Kern now that Hammerstein was partnering Rodgers, but nothing came of that, either, nor of an offer from Arthur Freed to team with him on an MGM musical called *Royal Wedding* (which was eventually written by Burton Lane and Alan Jay Lerner). His sister-in-law, Dorothy Hart, spent a great deal of time with Larry during this low period of his life.

> The thing was, he and Dick had reached a point where they had done everything together that they could. All partners sooner or later split up. The remarkable thing was not that they split up but that they ever stayed together for so long. Dick had lost his patience with Larry. I don't blame him, I can't. Larry didn't want to write any more. He didn't know what to do with his life or himself. The break didn't mean anything; he *wanted* the break. His life had come to an end long before he died.

Everyone who knew Larry was saddened by his sudden, drastic decline. Everyone wanted to help but nobody knew what to do. Herbert Fields went to see Dick Rodgers and they came up with the idea of reviving one of Larry's favourite shows, *A Connecticut Yankee*. A revival, they felt, would be better than a completely new show, for Larry would balk at that. If they added a fatter, meatier rôle for Vivienne Segal, whom Larry adored, they might just get him interested. Delicately, they broached the idea to Larry and to their joy and relief he agreed. He brightened up, as if reassured to be working with old friends again. He had always been especially fond of Herb, who was hitting a winning streak with his books for musicals by Cole Porter: *Du Barry was a Lady* and *Panama Hattie* (co-authored with B. G. de Sylva); *Let's Face It* and *Something For the Boys* which he wrote with his sister Dorothy. Herb was part of the gay scene, too, but he always maintained the fiction of his straightness with a string of statuesque chorus girls for whom he bought immensely ostentatious mink coats. They began re-working the original plot of *A Connecticut Yankee* to bring it more up to date. Dick Foran, playing the Yankee, was now a Lieutenant in the Navy, Alice, who is Alisande ('Sandy') in the Camelot sequence became a WAC and so on. Dick persuaded Larry to work at the Rodgers's home in Connecticut, beneath the same tree under which so much of *Oklahoma!* had been conceived. Larry was docile and well-behaved: convalescent, almost. He cut out liquor completely and gave the impression of really trying hard to stay on the wagon. Keeping the best of the original songs, Dick and Larry added 'The Camelot Samba'—the new dance was all the rage—and 'You always love the same girl' plus a song that might very well have been an expression of Larry's deepest personal feelings

Vivienne Segal today: 'Everyone says I was Larry's sweetheart, but I never loved him like that.' AC

at that time. The opening lines of the verse 'You can count your friends on the fingers of your hand, if you're lucky you have two' set the tone, and 'Can't you do a friend a favour' might well be addressed to everyone for whom Larry felt love and affection, everyone who, he felt none the less, rejected him because he was misshapen and ugly. For him to have written such words is tragedy indeed.

The very last song he wrote was as scabrously witty as anything he had ever done. It was called 'To keep my love alive' and Vivienne Segal stopped the show every time she sang it.

Once rehearsals were over, however, Larry fell off the wagon and rolled right back into the gutter. He went back to the clipjoints and the clubs, the bars and the alleys. He had always managed to lose his overcoat and hat when drinking, and now he navigated around Philadelphia during bitter winter weather in a light suit, sowing the seeds of pneumonia. He attended the opening of *A Connecticut Yankee* in New York with the illness already killing him, but nobody knew that.

The night of 17 November 1943 was bitterly cold, with sleet in the wind. Larry was at Delmonico's on Park Avenue, where he had taken a smaller apartment, and he telephoned Helen Ford and invited her to go with him to the première of *Yankee*. She was mortified when she came down the steps into the dining-room of the hotel. Larry was drunk, and his voice carried across the whole room when he announced her slurringly as the most beautiful singer in America. 'It was terrible,' she remembered. 'Larry was with a young couple, a beautiful young man and an actress I recognized vaguely. He was falling-down drunk, and there was no food. He kept on ordering more drinks until finally we got him into a cab and went to the theatre.'

When they arrived at the Martin Beck Theatre, Larry disappeared, and Helen spotted Dorothy Hart. They joined the crowd milling around the ticket window and discovered that no tickets had been set aside for them. Larry, who was nowhere to be seen, had simply assumed he could turn up and ask for as many as he wanted whenever he wanted to. Helen Ford and Dorothy Hart went backstage to see if Larry was there. Instead they met Dick Rodgers.

'Oh, my God!' he blurted, 'is Larry here?'

He sent two men out into the lobby to watch for Larry, but Larry somehow eluded them. When the curtain went up and the lights went down, he was standing in his accustomed place at the back of the theatre. Rather than create a scene they let him be.

Larry was quiet at first, but he gradually grew more agitated and feverish, reciting the lyrics in an undertone that steadily grew more audible. By the time Vivienne Segal got to 'To keep my love alive' in the second scene of the first act, Larry's croaky voice was loud and slurred. The two men whom Rodgers had charged with keeping Larry quiet bundled him out into the lobby, where he began kicking and yelling and creating exactly the kind of scene everyone had been so anxious to avoid. Dorothy Hart rushed out and got Larry into a taxi, taking him to her apartment. When she had him settled down on the couch, she hurried out again to meet her husband Teddy, who was playing at the Imperial Theatre in the Mary Martin musical *One Touch of Venus*. When they got home, Larry was still asleep on the couch, breathing stertorously and perspiring heavily. They left him there, having no inkling that he was critically ill. At four in the morning, Dorothy Hart looked in on her brother-in-law, but he was gone; a check with the doorman revealed that Larry had taken a cab home to Delmonico's.

Two days later he was found there in a coma, and rushed to Doctor's Hospital. There, at 9.30 p.m. on the night of 22 November 1943, while the sirens were wailing 'all clear' after a practice air-raid alert, the gossamer spirit of Larry Hart slipped away from pain. The doctor came out and told the little group of people—including Teddy and Dorothy Hart, Larry's business manager William Kron, Milton Bender, and Dick and Dorothy Rodgers—that it was all over.

'It was inevitable,' Dick Rodgers muttered. 'The way it had to be.'

And perhaps, unknowingly, he was right. The era of Rodgers and Hart was ended.[14] The world in which they had flourished would never be the same again. The Rodgers and Hammerstein years lay ahead; inevitable, the way it had to be.

4. About as far as they can go!

'It is not our intention to die broke if we can help it.'
Richard Rodgers and Oscar Hammerstein II

While his new collaborator was giving his partnership with Lorenz Hart one last try, Oscar Hammerstein went to work on a long-cherished project, a musical based on Bizet's opera *Carmen*. He changed the locale from Spain to the American south, stipulating an all-black cast. And he called the show *Carmen Jones*.

Bizet's melodies and Oscar's lyrics blended beautifully. The 'Toreador's March' became 'Stand up and fight' and the 'Habanera' was speeded up to provide the exciting 'Beat out dat rhythm on the drum'. *Carmen Jones* was vivid and different, and producer Billy Rose was gratified to discover that he had a big hit on his hands (the show ran over five hundred performances and was later filmed). But even before *Carmen Jones* opened in December 1943 Rodgers and Hammerstein were making plans for their next collaboration.

Oscar felt that it should be as 'small' as *Oklahoma!* had been 'big', and one of his ideas was a musical version of Lindsay and Crouse's hit play *Life With Father*. He had known Russel Crouse ever since Crouse's disastrous debut in the playwriting business back in 1931. Crouse collaborated with Morris Ryskind and Oscar on a turkey called *The Gang's All Here!* which provoked one critic to riposte 'What the hell do we care?' The *Life With Father* idea didn't jell, but that did not matter. Rodgers and Hammerstein could and must proceed cautiously. They were to some degree in the position of the man who went to an agent and told him that he concluded his act by committing suicide onstage. 'Oh, yeah?' said the agent, 'And what do you do for an encore?' Indeed, one of his old Hollywood friends had come up with an idea, as Rodgers remembers.

> I had a short dialogue with Sam Goldwyn one night. He was a very funny man and I was very fond of him. But when he saw *Oklahoma!* he phoned me at home and said, 'Would you come down to the theatre, I'd like to see you.' This was at the end of the first act. At the end of the second act I went down to the theatre and stood in the back and he came up with his wife Frances, and they were dewy-eyed. Terribly enthusiastic. And Sam said, 'I have a great idea for you. You know what you ought to do next?'
>
> I said 'What, Sam?'
>
> And he said, 'Shoot yourself!'

Actually, Rodgers has never been bothered by the thought of having to follow his own act. 'You get into the habit of disregarding the problem,' he says, 'and just go ahead and try.'

Meanwhile, he and Hammerstein were setting up a series of other business arrangements, through their lawyer Howard Reinheimer. Between them they laid the foundations for what was to become in a few years one of the most powerful and influential organizations in the American theatre. The basic intention was to put the composers in a position, *vis à vis* their own work, that would have made Ziegfeld envious.

They had already discussed with old Max Dreyfus the idea of becoming their own publishers in affiliation with his company, which had been renamed Chappell & Co. In 1944 Williamson Music Inc., was established (so named because both its proprietors had fathers named William) and a suite of offices was rented at 488 Madison Avenue. A London branch was established at the same time. It would later be run by Jerome Whyte (the former stage manager who had once confided to Rouben Mamoulian that he wouldn't give him ten cents for *Oklahoma!*'s chances in New York). Chappell & Co. agreed to charge Rodgers and Hammerstein a percentage for the use of their offices, staff and distribution facilities, but Williamson Music was and would remain a hundred per cent the property of the two men. It started off by publishing the music of *Oklahoma!*, not a bad start by any standard.

Their second step was to announce that Rodgers & Hammerstein Inc. would also act as producers of other writers' work. A small office in the RKO Building at Rockefeller Centre was opened, dubbed Surrey Enterprises, with Morris Jacobs as its manager. On 19 October 1944 the new organization announced its first venture. It was John van Druten's play *I Remember Mama*, and it was a resounding hit.

Rodgers and Hammerstein, Incorporated. Producers, publishers and composers, available for interviews and photocalls. CHAPPELL & CO.

It is worth digressing for a moment to examine, if briefly, the record of Rodgers and Hammerstein as producers. They presented six straight plays and two musicals, *Annie Get Your Gun* and a revival of *Show Boat*, between 1944 and 1950. The income from these—only two of the plays were failures—together with out-of-town presentations and Hollywood movie deals made for an extremely profitable sideline, which piled even further profit on to the sizeable ones the two men would reap from their own musical productions. In 1951 the magazine *Business Week* estimated the income of the team as around one and a half million dollars a year. By the mid fifties, the firm was grossing well over $15,000,000, by which time it had also bought The Theatre Guild's investment in the early Rodgers and Hammerstein triumphs. Dick and Oscar owned a hundred per cent of everything they wrote, and a good sized piece of everything else.

They set themselves several other guidelines and stuck to them. Anyone wanting motion picture rights in their work had to pay up forty per cent of the profits of the movie, and no haggling. Collaboration with Rodgers & Hammerstein meant that Rodgers & Hammerstein got fifty-one per cent of the credit, and 51 per cent of the billing, not to mention the action. Always publicity-conscious, Dick Rodgers and Oscar Hammerstein set up machinery not just to handle publicity (most shows employ a press agent anyway) but actively to seek it on their behalf. Dick felt that the name of Rodgers and Hammerstein should be kept constantly in front of the public; that it would help to sell tickets. To that end he and Oscar became the most available composer and lyricist in theatrical history. Hundreds of thousands of words were written by, for and about them—their work, their methods, their history, their hopes and their plans. The result of all this was twofold. It required a recognizable and repeatable story with a beginning, middle and foreseeable end, ironing out all the kinks, creases, frays and tears in the material of their lives. The 'factoids' thus created (to use Norman Mailer's immortal word) were thus established as unassailable fact and the sweetness-and-light image of Rodgers and Hammerstein was created and continued.

The second effect of this access to the media was to consolidate the Rodgers and Hammerstein interests, to make them into an empire with Rodgers (Hammerstein to a much lesser degree) at its head. He was no longer a theatrical song-writer with business interests, but a tycoon who happened to write songs. He spent more and more time in an office that has all the charm of a dentist's waiting room; the only concession to his craft was the Steinway grand piano there.

Dick and Oscar came from strikingly similar backgrounds. Both had grown up in the same part of New York, gone to the same schools and summer camps, done Varsity Shows. Both had grandfathers who played a strong part in influencing the boys, both had fathers named William. Both had strong-willed wives named Dorothy who were interior decorators. (Oscar divorced his first wife in 1928 after meeting and falling in love with an Australian-born actress named Dorothy Blanchard aboard the Cunarder *Olympic* in 1927—the same year, by almost-absurd coincidence, that Dick Rodgers met and fell in love with Dorothy Feiner aboard the *Majestic*.)

Dick, Oscar and their two Dorothys in 1959. AC

Both men subscribed to the Puritan Work Ethic: you worked because you worked. Both had the same orderly, disciplined approach to what they did. Both had similar inclinations in their private life, neither smoking nor drinking to excess, favouring early nights rather than late ones. Like the Rodgers family, the Hammersteins maintained two homes. Dick and Dorothy Rodgers had a duplex in the East Seventies, Oscar and Dorothy Hammerstein a town house on East 63rd Street. Rodgers had a country home in Connecticut, Hammerstein a farm in Bucks County, Pennsylvania. They had the same interests, the same friends, the same ambitions. Little wonder that the longer they stayed together the more similar their outlook became. Towards the middle of their partnership, Rodgers was to remark that he and Oscar had an almost telepathic rapport, rather like an old married couple who can almost communicate without speaking.

Their partnership has been made to seem so pre-ordained, in fact, that their initial uncertainty has been forgotten. It is, however, a matter of record that shortly after the opening of *Oklahoma!* Rodgers discovered to his dismay that Oscar Hammerstein was actively discussing a new project whose composer would be Jerome Kern. Rodgers learned that the lawyer involved was his old friend Howard Reinheimer. He went to see Reinheimer, who got Oscar along. Rodgers convinced both of them that it would be a major mistake for he and Oscar to separate.

So, by Christmas of 1944, Dick and Oscar were involved with two big successes, *I Remember Mama* and *Oklahoma!* They were also thinking seriously about their next musical. The idea for it grew out of a weekly luncheon that Dick and Oscar shared with Terry Helburn at Sardi's. They called it 'The Gloat Club' because they spent so much of their time gloating over the success of *Oklahoma!* but they also used these meetings to discuss new ideas. Dick and Oscar always made it a point to ask everyone they knew to come up with ideas for shows. They either already knew or had quickly learned how to listen to everyone, no matter how screwy their ideas might sound, on the off chance that there might be a show in them. Terry Helburn's suggestion that Ferenc Molnar's play *Liliom* might be just such a vehicle certainly sounded as screwy as most.

Liliom had originally been produced by the Theatre Guild in 1921, with Joseph Schildkraut playing the part of Liliom, who is allowed to return to earth sixteen years after his death to do a good deed. He visits his wife Julie and his daughter Louise in the guise of a beggar, but does more harm than good before he is called back to eternity. Originally produced in Budapest in 1909, *Liliom* had been twice translated.

The first version was called *The Daisy* and it was never produced. There is an undying legend that the translation was one of Larry Hart's uncredited adaptations. Since the second version, a translation by Benjamin Glazer which leaned heavily on the first, was the one produced by the Guild, there is wry historical irony in Terry Helburn's having suggested it for a new Rodgers and Hammerstein show.[1] Dick and Oscar had seen the 1940 revival starring Burgess Meredith and Ingrid Bergman as Liliom and Julie, and were convinced that it was impossible to turn the play into a musical. Neither had any feel for the Hungarian locale; additionally, the play had a bitter 'down' ending totally unsuitable for a musical.

Helburn persisted, getting Lawrence Langner to add his weight to her pleas. It didn't have to be set in Hungary, did it? Why not New Orleans? Oscar was just as unhappy with that idea. He had no feel for the Deep South, either, especially the Cajun cadences of New

Liliom (Joseph Schildkraut) ponders his problems in this scene from the 1921 production of *Liliom* by Ferenc Molnar, which was based, some say, on an original adaptation by Lorenz Hart. TMC

Orleans vernacular. Then there were all the other problems. It was well known that Puccini had once approached Molnar asking permission to turn *Liliom* into an opera. Molnar haughtily turned the composer down, saying that he wanted *Liliom* to be remembered as a Molnar play, and not as a Puccini opera. It was agreed, however, that Molnar be approached with the proposition that Rodgers and Hammerstein adapt the work. If he turned them down, nothing was lost.

Meanwhile—perhaps inevitably is again the right word to use—the movies wanted a Rodgers and Hammerstein show for the screen. There was no question of a movie of *Oklahoma!* for years yet—Dick and Oscar had not the slightest intention of killing the golden goose at the St James's Theatre—but 20th Century Fox's Darryl F. Zanuck came up with a good idea. In 1933 Fox had filmed Phil Stong's charming novel *State Fair*, with Will Rogers, Lew Ayres and Janet Gaynor. Wouldn't it make a good musical?

Rodgers and Hammerstein screened the movie and loved it. They agreed to write the score for a remake which would star Jeanne Crain, Dana Andrews, Dick Haymes and Vivian Blaine, but with one proviso in the contract: that neither of them had to work in Hollywood. It must have given both of them a very great deal of pleasure to insert that clause. 'They were so intimidated by the fact that Oscar and I had written *Oklahoma!*' Rodgers said, 'that they made the picture just the way we wrote it, and it turned out to be one of the two first class pictures I ever had in my life.'

State Fair, which was set in Iowa, was filmed in California and written in Pennsylvania. Oscar's screenplay stuck fairly close to the original (Sonia Levien and Paul Green did the adaptation), and his lyrics and Rodgers's music were quite masterful. They wrote eight songs for *State Fair*, (one called 'We will be together' was never used) including the martial opening chorus 'Our State Fair', 'That's for me', 'Isn't it kinda fun', a splendid waltz called 'It's a grand night for singing' and 'It might as well be Spring!'

Since that winsome lament is the only Richard Rodgers song ever to have won an Academy Award, its genesis deserves retelling. One day Oscar telephoned his partner. He was stuck trying to come up with a song for Maggy (Jeanne Crain, whose voice was dubbed by Luanne Hogan) who has got the blues for no good reason. She feels as if she has got spring fever, he told Dick, but that won't work because everyone knows State Fairs are held in the Fall. How would it be if he wrote that she knows it's autumn but, feeling the way she does, it might as well be Spring?

'Oscar' Rodgers said, 'That's exactly it.'

State Fair was the same kind of homey, just-folks story as *Oklahoma!* — which was exactly why Darryl Zanuck wanted it. If just-folks stories were what the public wanted, then that was what they were going to get. For nearly a decade after *Oklahoma!* and *State Fair* there was a boom in movies that looked back nostalgically at an America that probably never was but everybody wished had been. They were sentimental and beautifully mounted: Judy Garland in MGM's *Meet me in St Louis*, Deanna Durbin in Universal's *Can't Help Singing*, its music provided

Jeanne Crain and Dana Andrews in *State Fair* (20th Century Fox, 1945, dir. Walter Lang). Her performance of 'It might as well be Spring' won Rodgers and Hammerstein their only Oscar, but the song was really sung by Luanne Hogan. NFA

by Jerome Kern, Rita Hayworth in *My Gal Sal* and Jeanne Crain again in *Centennial Summer* with music once more by Kern, his hundred and ninth (and sadly, final) score.[2]

Rodgers and Hammerstein had no intention, however, of lingering in the same pastures. On 23 October 1944, the *New York Post* carried a short item with a cynical twist in its tail. 'After fifteen months, all the legal technicalities involved in the production of the musical version of *Liliom* were settled last week. The smallest percentage: eight tenths of one percent go to Ferenc Molnar, who merely wrote the play.'[3] Dick and Oscar were beginning as they meant to continue.

First auditions were scheduled for 22 January 1945 and Rodgers and Hammerstein settled down to adapt the play. It was very difficult to find a way into, Rodgers recalled. They had agreed, quite suddenly, that *Carousel*, as they were going to call the show, should be set in New England and not New Orleans. Liliom had become Billy Bigelow, a 'barker' on a carousel at a fairground, Julie a young girl working at a nearby mill. Billy was hard to make believable, and Oscar was stuck until Dick remembered that they had had the same problem with Joey in *Pal Joey*. Seeking a way to make him understandable to the audience, Dick and Larry had written a sort of soliloquy called 'I'm talking to my pal' which Joey sang to his 'one and only friend'—himself. The song had been cut before the show opened, but perhaps this was the way to explain Billy to the audience? Oscar picked up the idea and ran, coming back quite quickly with the first part of what was to become the famous 'Soliloquy'. At this stage it was called 'My boy Bill' but it gave the writers the key they needed to get into the play. After that, scene after scene suggested itself, and everything began to fall into place except the ending. It proved just as hard to find a way out of the play as it had to find a way in. Molnar's pessimistic ending simply would not do for a musical; they must end on an upbeat. They found the solution by replacing Molnar's ending with a graduation scene, in which Billy's daughter Louise realizes that she is not an outcast if she doesn't want to be one. From that scene the song 'You'll never walk alone' sprang almost naturally.[4]

The show was beginning to take shape, even if Oscar's original opening was unsatisfactory (he had two old people, Mr and Mrs God, sitting in rocking chairs outside their New England cottage) and there were still great chunks of pure Molnar dialogue to be rewritten. Rouben Mamoulian was signed as director, and Agnes de Mille to choreograph. Out in California, Theresa Helburn found a beautiful young singer named Jan Clayton who had made a couple of minor films for MGM.

She brought her East to audition for the part of Julie opposite John Raitt, who had been in a touring company of *Oklahoma!* and was pretty much as unknown as she. Indeed, it was again Rodgers and Hammerstein's deliberate policy to cast unknowns in their musical, or to bring in graduates from earlier ones. Jan Clayton recalled that there was only one member of the cast of *Carousel* who had ever been in a New York show: Jean Casto, who had been in *Pal Joey*. Everyone commiserated with her on being plunged into her 'blood bath'. 'It wasn't, though. We had worked so hard, and we had complete confidence in Dick and Oscar. I had no idea of the troubles they had gone through or how apprehensive they were about the show. The New Haven opening night was—I believe—about a 1.30 a.m. finish, I might be a little wrong.'

Cutting and rewriting every day, they moved to Boston's Colonial Theatre, and opened there on 27 March 1945. Mr and Mrs God were still in the script, but Mamoulian came up with the much more charming and workable idea of the Starkeeper, the nebulous heavenly setting, and the stars hanging out to dry like clothes. The actors and actresses had constantly to learn and relearn their parts, Jan Clayton recalls.

> Oh, those were the most fascinating times in Boston because we had three weeks there and every night we'd play the show, then go back to our hotel, beautiful marvellous Ritz, all go to our rooms, get into our pyjamas and robes, meet in one big room, order the coffee and sandwiches and everything, and memorize our changes for the next day. John Raitt was absolutely phenomenal because he had more changes to begin with, he had so much more to do. He could do that better than anyone else I ever worked with in my life—and stay solid. Because every night there were changes.

Elliott Norton, theatre critic for the *Boston Post*, filed two reports which illustrate the development of *Carousel*—and its problems. The first, written on opening night:

> CAROUSEL HAS FINE MUSIC BUT IT IS RUNNING HALF AN HOUR TOO LONG AND GETS RATHER TEDIOUS. DANCING NOT WHAT IT MIGHT BE AND A MINIMUM OF COMEDY. I DOUBT VERY MUCH WHETHER IT WILL EVER BECOME ANOTHER OKLAHOMA! FOLLOWS TEXT OF LILIOM PRETTY CLOSELY FOR MUCH OF THE EVENING BUT POLICE COURT JUDGE HAS BEEN REPLACED BY AN ELDERLY MAN AND WOMAN, CO-RULERS OF HEAVEN. JOHN RAITT AS LILIOM CHARACTER SINGS WELL BUT LACKS ACTING SKILL. THE PLAY NEVER GETS UNDER YOUR SKIN THE WAY LILIOM DID.

On 11 April, a scant eight days before the New York opening, Norton saw the play again. This time he was much briefer.

> CAROUSEL MUCH IMPROVED BY REVISIONS. FIRST ACT NOW EXCELLENT, SECOND ACT SEEMS TO ME TO DRAG. MUSIC HEARD FOR SECOND TIME SEEMS UNUSUALLY

Dick Rodgers runs through the score of *Carousel* for the cast. TMC

BEAUTIFUL. TWO ENTIRELY NEW SCENES IN PLAY, SEVERAL SHORT SEQUENCES, TWO NEW BALLET SEQUENCES.

Now, as ready as they could be, the entire company had to undergo its most rigorous scrutiny. Ferenc Molnar expressed his desire to see the show. Jan Clayton remembers the occasion very well indeed.

I understood they were all very nervous about his reaction, understandably, they wanted so much for him to like it. So after it was all over, Mr Molnar, who was a charming gentleman, I can tell you, said to the Theatre Guild, to Mr and Mrs Langner and Theresa, 'It's a beautiful thing that you've done with my story. And Mr Hammerstein, your words, what you've done with the book, I'm so pleased. Mr Rodgers, your music made the whole thing.' Then he turned to Rouben Mamoulian who, in case you don't know, smokes cigars about the size of a baseball bat and doesn't use an ashtray—he uses a bucket!—he turned to Mamoo and he said '*But*, Mr Mamoulian!' and everybody's face changed. You can just imagine—Mamoo's heart just plummetted to his feet! 'But, Mr Mamoulian,' Molnar said, 'You smoke too much.'

Richard Rodgers watched the New York opening from a stretcher placed behind some curtains in a box at the Majestic Theatre on 19 April. He had ripped a back muscle carrying his cases from train to taxi (war service had virtually stripped railroad stations of porters) and he was heavily sedated. In his blurred state he was convinced that *Carousel* was laying an egg, but he was entirely wrong. It won the hearts of all the critics, even those who compared it with its predecessor. It was at the start of a two-year run, during which it would win the New York Critics' Award as 'best musical' and the Donaldson Awards in no less than eight categories. In London, it would pack the Drury Lane Theatre for sixteen months.

Although these figures are nowhere near as impressive as those of *Oklahoma!* it was in many ways a more daring and innovative show, and the nearest Rodgers and Hammerstein would ever come to writing an American opera. It is to many their best score, and Rodgers makes no bones about its being his personal favourite.

The score, in fact, deserves closer examination than usual, for it is not always possible to isolate the songs in the way that one normally can. Rodgers had dispensed with the conventional overture, replacing it with a waltz suite that he had originally written for Paul Whiteman, who never performed it. Opening the show with a colourful fairground scene immediately put the audience into the correct mood, time and place. The first scene—'the bench scene'—is almost pure Molnar, but Molnar so cunningly mixed with Hammerstein lyric, so sensitively underscored by Rodgers's music, that it is only after several viewings that the watcher realizes that the whole scene is one extended musical piece. It runs from Carrie's mildly-exasperated 'You're a queer one, Julie Jordan' through to her rapturous description of her new beau 'Mister Snow' whose clothes smell so strongly of fish that when they first met it knocked her flat on the floor of her room. Now that she

Top left
The opening scene of *Carousel*. Julie (Jan Clayton) and Billy (John Raitt) on the carousel, watched suspiciously by Mrs Mullins (Jean Casto, in striped skirt) The setting is, as always, by Jo Mielziner.
TMC

Bottom left
The opening sequence of *Carousel* (20th Century Fox). Worth comparing with the original stage version. The Billy Bigelow part was originally to be played by Frank Sinatra, who walked off the set on the first day of shooting and never came back, never apologized, and never explained. NFA

Above
The 'If I loved you' sequence from *Carousel* (20th Century Fox, 1956; dir. Henry King). The great thing about movies is the authentic locations which make phoney-looking sets obsolete! NFA

loves him, Carrie says, her heart is in her nose, and 'fish is my fav'rite perfume'. There follow short scenes between the girls and Billy, then Billy's employer Mrs Mullins, then Julie's employer and a policeman, all constantly counterpointed by Rodgers's music, thematically under-scoring what the characters onstage are saying and doing. It was Molnar, rather than Oscar, who provided the title for 'If I loved you' *Carousel's* principal love song. Liliom, talking to Julie, says he bets she wouldn't marry a rough fellow like him ... that is, of course, if she loved him. And Julie replies: 'Yes, I would Mr Liliom ... if I loved you.'

There was no big chorus number until the second scene, but it was a cracker when it came: 'June is bustin' out all over' (Oscar having again been inspired by the weather). The charming 'When the children are asleep' is best known for its chorus, but its bright, irreverent verse tends to be regrettably overlooked. The 'Soliloquy' had grown con-siderably from its original concept, Oscar's 'My boy Bill' (his son's name is Bill) to a seven and a half minute narrative of unashamedly operatic dimensions. As the father of two girls, Rodgers had come up with the suggestion that Billy ought at least to consider the fifty-fifty chance that his wife might produce a daughter, and for this segment of the soliloquy (which has eight distinct melodic themes) Oscar added the sentimental 'My little girl'. Dick put a melody to Oscar's lyric which could well stand alone as one of the best he has ever done, but then, everything in *Carousel* was top drawer, melodious, moving, merry, at times even genuinely philosophical, as in Julie's song 'What's the use of wond'rin'?'

Hammerstein always felt that this song's failure away from the play was entirely due to the single word 'talk' with which the song ends. According to Joshua Logan, Oscar knew that he was defying con-vention by making the ending abrupt and hard to sing. His original lines were 'Anywhere he leads you, you will go' rhyming with 'You're his girl and he's your fellow, that's all you need to know'. Nevertheless, he had a perverse desire to do it the hard way, so he substituted 'walk' for 'go' and ended with 'and all the rest is talk'. He was never happy with it.

So, armed with Donaldson awards for best musical, best lyrics, best score, with their director Rouben Mamoulian named best director and Agnes de Mille a winner for dance direction, with John Raitt tapped as best male performer in a musical and Peter Birch as best male dancer, and *Carousel* named best musical of the year by the New York critics, Dick and Oscar had done it again. Now, true to their record of never doing the same thing twice, they did something quite astonishing. They gave a smash hit show to another composer.

Herbert and Dorothy Fields had known both Dick and Oscar since childhood. They had been, as we have seen, collaborating successfully as librettists on Cole Porter musicals, and had just finished work on a show scored by Sigmund Romberg called *Up in Central Park*, which looked like being a big hit. Rodgers takes up the story.

> They came into the office one day and said, 'We have an idea: how would you like to see Ethel Merman playing Annie Oakley?' And the next sentence in the dialogue was us saying to them, 'Go home and write it and we'll produce it.' We may have been involved in something else, I don't know. But I think for that particular subject we felt we could do better than have ourselves as writers.

The 'something else' was obviously *Carousel*, but in retrospect the decision to write neither book nor songs seems a strange one for them

Herbert, Dorothy and Joseph Fields: the best thing that ever came out of Far Rockaway. CP

to have made, unless it was occasioned by the fact that Dorothy Fields, who had written some pretty nifty lyrics herself, expected to do so with *Annie Oakley*.[5] Producers Rodgers and Hammerstein immediately got in touch with Jerome Kern (could that fifteen-year-old boy in the balcony of the Princess Theatre have ever dreamed that one day he would be commissioning the composer he idolized to write a show for him?). Kern was out in Hollywood putting the finishing touches to *Centennial Summer*. Lyricist Leo Robin ('Thanks for the memory', 'Beyond the blue horizon', 'Diamonds are a girl's best friend') had been assigned to work with Kern and was in great awe of the composer. Every day Kern would call him and ask him if he had anything, and Robin found that, far from encouraging him, this made him dry up. Kern started looking for other lyricists, including Johnny Mercer, E. Y. Harburg and Oscar Hammerstein, all of whom contributed lyrics for songs in the movie. Although he does not class them as his best work, Robin's songs 'In love in vain' and 'All through the day' have outlasted all the others.

Kern was delighted to hear from Dick and Oscar, and told them he was coming back East for a revival of *Show Boat*, anyway. He would be happy to work on the new show. Kern arrived in New York early in November, 1945. He had been in the city only three days when he collapsed on Park Avenue just a few blocks from the Rodgers and Hammerstein offices. Suffering from a cerebral haemorrhage, he was taken to Welfare Island charity hospital (the same institution in which Stephen Foster had died) because when he was picked up no one knew who he was. At the hospital, an ASCAP membership card was found in his pockets, and that organization was called. They in turn called Dick and Oscar. The two men rushed to the hospital to find that Kern was in a ward filled with mental cases, drunks and derelicts, some fifty or sixty of them. The doctors and nurses had gathered them together and explained who the new patient was, and asked them not to make any noises or disturbance. Not one man disobeyed. The nurse on duty, Oscar recalled, extended her shift that day to twenty-four hours, and when Kern's wife, Eva, thanked her, said that Kern had given so much pleasure to the world, she thought she would like to give something to him. Two days later, Kern was moved to Doctor's Hospital, where he died on 11 November at 1.10 in the afternoon. Oscar Hammerstein was the only person with him.

The following Monday funeral services were held in the chapel of Ferncliff Crematorium in Hartsdale, New York. Oscar Hammerstein delivered the eulogy, as he had done eight years earlier for George Gershwin.

Once the shock of Kern's death had worn off, Dick and Oscar faced up to the enormous problem of how to replace him. They had told Joshua Logan, who was still in the services, that they wanted him to direct *Annie Oakley* as soon as he got out. Josh called Rodgers one day and learned that the producers had come up with another composer. Logan asked how they'd done it, and Dick said they had made an alphabetical list of every composer they knew. The first name on the list was Irving Berlin. Everybody said there was no point in asking Irving Berlin, because if he was involved, it would have to be his show, his ideas, his money and his songs. In that department, Irving Berlin wrote the rule-book: his control over the minutiae of his own career and output is all-embracing and total.

It was Oscar Hammerstein who said 'Wait a minute! How can a man say no until he's been asked?' So they asked him, and Irving Berlin agreed to do the score. To everyone's relief, Dorothy Fields was just as enthusiastic about Berlin as everyone else, and *Annie Get Your Gun* was on its way.

They held their first conference on a Friday. Berlin said he would like to take the script away for the weekend to see if he could come up with anything. The following Monday morning he bounced into Rodgers's office with three songs: 'Doin' what comes naturally', 'You can't get a man with a gun' and 'There's no business like show business'. Then, with astonishing facility, he added 'They say it's wonderful', 'The girl that I marry' and 'Who do you love, I hope?' Logan remembers that everyone was very enthusiastic about the latter song.

Now Irving has a way of doing his songs, of looking right into your eyes, almost grabbing you by the collar as he sings, as if he wants to get your reaction to every nuance, the moment you think it. If your eyes should get out of focus or whatever, Irving will shake his head and say 'No good, eh? You don't like it, right?' and he's quite likely to toss it out. Well, this day, right after he'd played 'Who do you love, I hope?' he played us the second chorus of 'There's no business like show business'. Now I don't know what we were doing, maybe we were thinking where to put the other song, or discussing something else. Anyway, we'd all raved about how marvellous it was already, we couldn't rave again. Well, to cut a long story short, a few days later Irving was playing the score for Hugh Martin—he likes to get everyone's opinions of his songs, it's as if he really needs that reassurance that they're terrific—and I said, 'Irving, you didn't play "Show Business".' 'No,' he said, 'that's out, I threw it out.' I said 'Whaaaaaat?' 'I threw it out,' he said. 'I could see from your faces the other day you guys didn't like it.'

And that is how the anthem of show business very nearly didn't get

Producer Richard Rodgers with two of the reasons why he considered *Annie Get Your Gun* 'failure-proof'—Ethel Merman and composer Irving Berlin. LFG

into *Annie Get Your Gun*. They spent a very tense and frantic half hour trying to find the lead sheet, which Irving had told a secretary to put away. It was discovered beneath a phone book.

Berlin turned out the score of *Annie* so fast that it was hard to keep up with him. Logan recalled a discussion in Oscar's living-room at the East 63rd Street house, where they decided they needed another song in the second act. The principals, Frank Butler and Annie Oakley, have quarrelled, and Logan felt the situation called for some kind of song. 'A quarrel duet?' Rodgers said. Berlin jumped to his feet, bringing the meeting to a close by saying he had to go and write the song. Logan and his wife Nedda took a cab back to the St Regis Hotel, where they were staying. When they got to their room at the hotel, just a few blocks downtown, the phone was ringing. It was Irving Berlin, who triumphantly sang them 'Anything you can do, I can do better' which he had written in the taxicab on his way back to the office.

Annie Get Your Gun opened at the Imperial Theatre on 16 May 1946 and ran for nearly three years. It took Donaldson Awards in three categories: best female performer in a musical (Ethel Merman) best director (Logan) and best score. Surprisingly, some of the critics didn't think much of the latter; Brooks Atkinson actually referred to it as 'undistinguished'. But then, Jerome Kern once said that the score of *Oklahoma!* was 'condescending'.

There was an important consequence of Dick and Oscar's having been the producers of *Annie Get Your Gun*. Richard Halliday and his wife Mary Martin were at the New Haven opening of the show, and Halliday became convinced that Annie would be a great rôle for Mary. Until then, everyone thought of the girl from Weatherford, Texas, as the 'cute' type, the sex-kitten who'd done a mock striptease in *Leave it to Me* singing Cole Porter's 'My heart belongs to Daddy', the witty goddess of *One Touch of Venus*. Halliday knew better, so at the Langners' Connecticut home he had Mary prove she could belt out a song as well as la Merman. Dick and Oscar were there, weekending with their wives. So were Terry Helburn and Ina Claire. The tradition was that after lunch everyone had to perform. Mary cut loose with 'You can't get a man with a gun' and Dick and Oscar just couldn't get over it. They asked her to open *Annie* in London, but Mary didn't want to do that. Instead she proposed that she take the show on the road.

Rodgers and Hammerstein were amazed but delightedly accepted. It was flying in the face of accepted practice for an established star to go on tour in a rôle that someone else had made famous, but they were becoming accustomed to flying in the face of tradition. Mary Martin went on the road with *Annie Get Your Gun* and made the show her own, although in a different way to Ethel Merman. Anyone who has seen both performers will tell you it is difficult to say which of the two was a better Annie. The show began its tour in Dallas on 3 October 1947. Until it reached San Francisco the following May, Mary Martin would be out of sight but never far from Rodgers and Hammerstein's minds.

Meanwhile they were busy, producing a play by Anita Loos called *Happy Birthday*, written for and starring her friend Helen Hayes, with Joshua Logan directing. It had an unobtrusive little song by Rodgers and Hammerstein called 'I haven't got a worry in the world' which was pretty indicative of the way Dick and Oscar must have been feeling. The play was a hit; it eventually ran for almost a year and a half at the Broadhurst.

Rodgers and Hammerstein's next production was the Norman Krasna play *John Loves Mary*. Krasna, a veteran Hollywood scriptwriter and playwright, is famous as the man who, while working for the foul-mouthed and tyrannical Harry Cohn, legendary boss of Columbia Pictures, dictated a codicil to his will which he then announced to the Press. It stipulated that on his death Krasna be cremated and his ashes thrown in Harry Cohn's face.

John Loves Mary was a slight thing about a young soldier coming back from overseas with a British girl whom he has married so she can come to America with him. He is doing a favour for his friend, her true love, but the friend had thought her dead in an air raid and married someone else. The complications arising from all this and from concealing those complications from the girl's parents resulted in a happy comedy which was destined for success. It opened at the Booth Theatre on 4 February 1947. One of the cast, a little-known actor named Tom Ewell, would eventually become the star of a play (and movie) called *The Seven Year Itch*, written by George Axelrod, son of the man who had written the book for the 1921 Columbia Varsity Show staged by Oscar, with songs by Rodgers and Hart. Sometimes the theatre is a very small world indeed.

During the Boston tryouts of *John Loves Mary* Joshua Logan, directing, felt unhappy about the ending of the second act. Dick and Oscar came up to see the play, agreed that the ending was weak and stayed on trying to come up with something. The more they watched, the less successful they were; after several days, tempers began to fray. Then Logan came up with an idea.

> I said, 'listen, how would it be if we have the father and the mother see the boy out of the house, then go to bed. As soon as they've gone, he comes back in, kisses the girl, and they go into the bedroom—curtain!' Well, you'd have thought I'd suggested they make love onstage. Oscar got up out of his seat, you know, purple! He glared at me, and said 'Anybody who'd make a suggestion like that is a *cad*!' Afterwards, Norman said to me, 'You know, Josh, everyone always told me Oscar was as cool as a cucumber, well, if he is, he's the most belligerent cool cucumber I've ever seen.'

While lightweight and far from 'important' *John Loves Mary* ran for over five hundred performances, making it yet another success for Rodgers and Hammerstein. They were the golden boys. Nothing, it seemed, could go wrong for them.

During this time, Oscar was deeply immersed in something which had been one of his most cherished ambitions to write ever since he could remember: a play which chronicled the life of one man, from his birth to his death. The man would be a doctor, and the play would set out to make some fairly large statements about life and love and ambition and the pursuit of happiness. Oscar put the idea to his partner, and Rodgers, a doctor's son, loved it.

He put a great deal of himself into the play. His son William thinks that Oscar tried to say in it everything he had learned about life. 'Much of the first act was based on his memories of his own childhood,' Hammerstein says. 'He had always been intrigued by it, you know, his mother died when he was twelve. I always felt his songs came out of his feelings about her.'

As Rodgers and Hammerstein developed the story, which was to be called *Allegro*, they became increasingly convinced that once more they were going to be forced to defy conventional techniques. Perhaps, in their earnest desire to do something truly different and important, Dick and Oscar lost sight of their first duty, which was to entertain. As it turned out, *Allegro* was a great deal closer to a morality play than a musical, and the unorthodox techniques they used to stage it—nearly-bare sets, a sort of Greek chorus which comments on the action onstage, and ghosts ('presences' Oscar called them) of characters who have died earlier in the story—militated against a light touch. Joshua Logan confesses that he was 'deeply grateful' when Dick and Oscar told him, apologetically, that they had promised the director's job to Agnes de Mille. He felt that the book was deeply flawed, sentimental and mawkish in parts, and that the score was not one of Rodgers's best. 'I think, too,' he adds, 'that they had had a rough time facing the smash success of Irving Berlin with *Annie Get Your Gun*. They were over-anxious. They wanted to do something sensational and they tried too hard.'

Re-examined today, *Allegro*'s main fault seems to have been that it was ahead of its time, the integration of story and music far too advanced even for audiences now becoming accustomed to musicals which actually had stories (*Brigadoon* and *Finian's Rainbow* are its contemporaries), but its forty-week run was nothing like enough to recoup the huge investment that had been needed to put it on. Cole Porter had once remarked that the changes Rodgers and Hammerstein had effected in musical theatre had made it that much harder for everyone else. By definition, they had also made it that much harder for themselves.

Allegro was to be the last association of Rodgers and Hammerstein

Allegro: the opening sequence in which the hero is born. The ensemble propose 'Joseph Taylor, Jr' as a possible future President of the U.S.A., a rôle Oscar suggested for more than one of his stage 'sons'. LFG

with the Theatre Guild, who brought the show to New York on 10 October 1947. It had undergone drastic changes out of town, and suffered a few small calamities as well. At the New Haven opening there had been a false fire alarm during the second act. Panic was quelled only when Joshua Logan, who was in the audience, got to his feet and ordered the people scrabbling for the exit doors to sit down. When Logan gave orders at the top of his voice, people obeyed. The panic subsided and the performance went on, only to be stopped again when Lisa Kirk fell into the orchestra pit while singing 'The gentleman is a dope'. Two of the musicians hoisted her back on to the stage, where she continued singing as if nothing had happened!

In New York the critics were kind, but divided. The show had been weakened by giving the job of director to a choreographer. Agnes de Mille's dances were fine, but she had handed over to Rodgers and Hammerstein the staging of the songs and dialogue. Neither man had ever aspired to be a Joshua Logan, and so the presentation was uninspired. The sheer size of the production and the unusual staging subtracted what little warmth there was from the story. The songs were unremarkable: 'A fellow needs a girl' and 'You are never away' had brief popularity, but they have not stood the test of time. *Allegro* was a failure although, as Rodgers says, nothing to be ashamed of. It had an advance sale of $700,000. It won Donaldson Awards for best book, best lyrics and best music. Both Dick and Oscar retained their affection for the play, but as Hammerstein ruefully admitted later, 'if the writer's aim is misread it can only be because he hasn't written clearly enough'.

In later interviews, both men philosophically accepted that in *Allegro* they had over-estimated the ability of the audience to identify itself with the leading character. Both also said that it was the only one of their plays which they felt one day they might perhaps rewrite and produce again, but all that was much later. At the time, the failure of *Allegro* got under their skin, as a young author who was to be associated with them on their next venture remembered. 'They were inwardly burning because of the reception accorded to *Allegro*,' James A. Michener said. 'Those fellows were so mad I was fairly confident that they could make a great musical out of the Bronx telephone directory.'

Roberta Jonay as Jennie and John Battles as Joseph Taylor, Jr, who hopes to become a great doctor but somehow or other gets sidetracked because life goes too quickly, too *Allegro*. LFG

5. The South Pacific years

'I had the same feeling about *South Pacific* as I had about *Oklahoma!* and *Annie Get Your Gun*. It was failure-proof.'
Richard Rodgers

The outstanding hit of the 1948 theatrical season was *Mister Roberts*, starring Henry Fonda, William Harrigan, Robert Keith and David Wayne. It was written by Thomas Heggen and Joshua Logan, and Logan directed. While he was preparing the play for Broadway, Logan dined one evening with scenic designer Jo Mielziner, and during dinner Jo's brother Kenneth McKenna joined them. He mentioned to Logan a book which had been submitted to him (he was a story editor at MGM) and which the studio, with its usual unerring judgement, had turned down. The book was called *Tales of the South Pacific*, and McKenna suggested that Logan might find it useful for background material, since *Mister Roberts* was also set in that theatre of war.

It wasn't until Logan was on vacation in Miami prior to the opening of his play that he finally got around to reading James A. Michener's collection of stories. Michener, a former Macmillan editor, had been stationed during the war at Espiritu Santo in the New Hebrides. Over a six-month period in 1945 he set down a series of 'tales', told by a naval officer, about the American servicemen and local inhabitants on an island in the South Pacific. It was rewritten twice before he submitted it to his former employers, who published it in the spring of 1947, and it won the Pulitzer Prize for Literature when those awards were announced at the end of the year.

Logan was particularly impressed with the story called 'Fo' Dolla''
and, to a lesser degree, by another called 'Our heroine'. He was sure
that 'Fo' Dolla'' was a very rich story capable of being adapted into
a play or a musical or a movie, although which he was not sure.

Visiting Logan and his wife Nedda in Miami was Leland Hayward.
Hayward was the top, top theatrical agent, among whose clients were
Fred Astaire, Gene Kelly, Judy Garland, Helen Hayes, Henry Fonda—
'the Toscanini of the telephone', George Axelrod called him. Hayward
was married to the movie star Margaret Sullavan. They had homes
in Hollywood and New York, they owned planes and boats and cars.
Hayward had three hundred pairs of shoes and nearly as many suits,
and he and his wife lived a reckless, disordered life.[1] He was a sharp-
eyed, crafty entrepreneur who rarely missed a trick, and while Logan
was taking an afternoon nap, Hayward picked up *Tales of the South
Pacific* and read it. Logan awoke to find Hayward almost exploding
with excitement.

'Josh,' he said, 'we've got to buy this sonofabitch!'

Logan agreed, even though neither he nor Hayward knew exactly
what they were going to do with the property if they did buy it. All
they knew was that it was terrific and that they had better grab it before
someone else did. Hayward set to work to put a deal together, meanwhile swearing Josh Logan to secrecy—an act not unlike forbidding
a skylark to sing. Logan was far too excited about the book, far
too much a theatre man not to talk about it, and when he ran into
Dick Rodgers at a cocktail party he had to tell him. It wasn't just that
he loved the book, he says; he had felt right from the outset that Rodgers
and Hammerstein would be the only people to talk to if they decided
to do 'Fo' Dolla'' as a musical. Rodgers methodically noted down the
title of the story in his little black notebook, and as promptly forgot
what it referred to.

When *Mister Roberts* tried out in Philadelphia, Oscar Hammerstein
came over from nearby Doylestown to see the show, and Logan asked
him to give him some pointers on anything that was wrong.

> He said, 'I'll tell you all about it, give me a ring tomorrow.' When I called
> him he read me his notes on *Mister Roberts*, which were very helpful, we
> always help each other in any way we possibly can. Then he said, 'Before
> you hang up, have you got any ideas of anything for Dick and me to do?
> We can't find a property that's suitable.' And I said, 'Didn't he tell you
> about *Tales of the South Pacific*?' Oscar said he'd never heard of it, so I told
> him to call Dick and ask him whether he'd read it and what he thought
> of it. So he called Dick, who said, 'Yes, I've read it, Oscar, and it's great,
> but some sonofabitch owns the rights and we can't get them.' Now I'd told

Oscar that we already had the rights and he said to Dick, 'Is the name of that sonofabitch Logan?' And Rodgers said, 'Yes! That's the sonofabitch!'

Now Joshua Logan had to break the news to Leland Hayward, who was 'absolutely, desperately upset' with Logan for letting Rodgers and Hammerstein in on their secret, because he had not yet finalized the deal with Michener. He bitterly told Logan that Rodgers and Hammerstein would have them over a barrel and, sure enough, Dick and Oscar insisted that if they were going to do the show, they wanted fifty-one per cent of the property. 'That gives them final say and us no say, Josh,' Hayward said. 'All this thanks to you.' He was very bitter about it.

Logan said he didn't care what they demanded—a statement he was later to regret—because he so much wanted Dick and Oscar to do the show. Hayward capitulated, without ever forgiving Logan for spilling the beans, and the contracts were signed. In the light of subsequent events, it is interesting to note exactly how dominant Rodgers and Hammerstein were, both in creative and financial matters.

Nine per cent of the gross went to Dick and Oscar, with Logan taking three and the author of the book on which the whole thing was based a mere one per cent. The management's half of the takings was split two to one in favour of Surrey Enterprises, the producing firm owned by Rodgers and Hammerstein. Co-producers Hayward and Logan took the remaining third, which in turn was split two to one between them, Logan taking the larger share. In addition, the stars of the show, Mary Martin and Ezio Pinza, both received seven per cent of the gross, and designer Jo Mielziner a flat $100 a week. These royalties were, of course, over and above whatever return the participants might realize on their investment in the show's $225,000 budget. (A five per cent investment in *South Pacific* would produce a return of $25,000 at the end of its first year.)

These rewards were still, however, a long way in the future. Logan and Hammerstein had some meetings and Oscar told the director that he preferred the story 'Our heroine' as the main theme of the show, possibly, Logan feels, because Oscar identified rather more with the older man in it. 'Our heroine' was about a romance between an expatriate French planter and an American nurse stationed on the island. It was daring stuff for a musical, because Emil de Becque was a middle-aged man, the nurse a much younger woman. Oscar felt that 'Fo' Dolla'', the story of a love-affair between an American lieutenant, Joe Cable, and a native girl, Liat, was stronger. 'He always said you should have a stronger secondary story, because that's the one that hasn't got

The principals of *South Pacific* assemble to discuss the play, or at least look as if they have. *L.* to *r.* Joshua Logan, Rodgers, Hammerstein, Mary Martin and James Michener. AC

all the attention on it, or the stars playing in it, so it's got to be a stronger story in itself,' Logan explained.

Auditions began. Oscar had never had any doubt about whom he wanted to play the part of the Army nurse, Ensign Nellie Forbush from Little Rock, Arkansas, who falls in love with Emil de Becque. Mary Martin was out in California with the touring company of *Annie Get Your Gun* when Dick and Oscar called her.

By this time, I'd practically lost my voice, it had gone down about twelve octaves because of yelling those songs, twenty-two songs a day on matinée days. And Dick said, 'We've just bought a property called *South Pacific* and Ezio Pinza is going to be the male star. Would you come back and listen to the score? We want you to play opposite Pinza in the show, play the part of the Army nurse.'

And I said, 'What do you want, two basses?'

I couldn't conceive of playing opposite an opera star, but they said please, please, come back to New York and listen to it. So we went back East, and went over to Dick's house in Connecticut. There was Dick, and Oscar Hammerstein, and Joshua Logan, and they said, 'Now just listen to three songs, that's all we've written. We have no book yet. But—don't give us your answer for twenty-four hours.' So we heard 'A cockeyed optimist', 'Some enchanted evening' and the twin soliloquies. My husband, Richard, and I went home and we didn't say a word to each other. We sat there and looked at each other, and then we said, 'Do we really have to wait for twenty-four hours? Can't we call them now?' And I said, 'Yes, yes, yes, please, please, please!'

Pinza, who was inspired (and extraordinarily lucky) casting, had come to the show almost accidentally. His agent, Ed Lester, had called Rodgers one day and admitted that he was in a bind. Pinza had quit the Metropolitan Opera with the intention of starring in a musical. The trouble was, Lester said, that there was no suitable musical, and his contract with the mettlesome opera singer had a penalty clause in it which Pinza would have no hesitation in applying. Lester did not want to pay Pinza $25,000 for doing nothing; had Rodgers and Hammerstein anything cooking that might be suitable? Rodgers immediately saw the potential of the handsome, mature, swaggering Pinza in the rôle of the French planter, de Becque. Although they had neither script nor songs, they signed him immediately.

By the time Dick and Oscar contacted Mary Martin in California, they had written some songs, but the book was not even begun. Joshua Logan went to Europe on vacation, expecting to return at the end of the summer to find Oscar's first draft completed.

I had heard one or two songs from the first scene before I left: 'Some enchanted evening' and 'Twin soliloquies'. I asked Dick about the book, whether I could get a copy. And suddenly the truth came out, he'd been covering up until then, he didn't have to face anybody he knew. He said, 'He's stuck, he's absolutely stuck. He can't write. I don't understand it. He's got the first scene written and a little tiny bit of the next scene, but they don't jell.' I said, 'How could that be?' He said, 'Well, he claims to hate the military to such a degree that he's never read anything about the Army, it's always gone past him. He doesn't know the difference between a lieutenant and a captain.'

Rodgers suggested that Joshua Logan might go down to Doylestown and give Oscar some help. After all, Logan had been educated at Culver Military Academy, and had served in the Army Air Force during the war: he knew about the military. Logan called Oscar, and got himself, his wife, and a secretary, Jim Awe, invited down to the

Doylestown farm. He told Oscar that he would bring along a dicta-
phone, and Oscar recoiled from the idea as though it were a snake.
'I'm not very comfortable around machinery,' he protested, 'besides,
I thought we ought to start on a horse and buggy.' Logan looked at
the calendar. They had about six months before the show was due to
begin its tryouts in Boston. 'I think we'd better start on a jet airplane,
Oscar,' he said, 'or we'll never make the date.'

Highland Farm was a working farm, run by Oscar's Norwegian
masseur. Oscar bought it when the masseur threatened to quit his profession to raise prize Black Angus cattle. The masseur got his farm,
Oscar got his cherished daily massage and the Hammerstein brood
got a country house. Logan and Oscar started work as soon as Logan
got there.

> He had these marvellous ideas for solidifying the story, but he really didn't
> know how to write about the military and he was also stuck on Southern
> talk. He seemed to be uncertain; frightened, even.
>
> Well, we started kicking ideas around and the two of us got on fire. We
> used to meet in the afternoon. He'd write lyrics in the morning and I'd
> sleep. Then we'd work all afternoon, dictating, and the two secretaries
> would type the first draft, and then we'd correct it and make a second draft
> with six copies.
>
> We found that we were using not only 'Fo Dolla'' and 'Our heroine'
> but also 'Operation Alligator', the story of the coastwatcher, and 'Boar's
> tooth', which is the one with Billis in it. All of those were brought into the
> story plus an idea that Oscar had had, that they were going to give a Thanks-
> giving show. It went really very well, and we did finish the first draft in
> ten days. And all through this time, when I would come to bed at night,
> my wife would say, 'But aren't you writing it? How could you be making
> all these contributions without being a co-author?' And I said, 'Well, I am
> a co-author, but I just can't ask him to let me be.' She said she didn't see
> why not. She said you couldn't write a man's play for him and expect to
> do it for free. I said, 'Well, he is embarrassed about it, I'm sure, because
> he never brings it up.'

Logan hurried back to New York with the draft, and the question
of co-authorship was left unresolved. There was work to do: auditions,
casting, staging. It was not for a week or so that Logan saw Oscar again,
by which time he was becoming convinced—determined is his word—
that the play was going to win the Pulitzer Prize. Feeling enormously
apprehensive, he told Hammerstein that he wanted a credit as co-
author. 'Oscar was silent for a moment, and then said, "I'm sorry I
didn't offer it to you myself. Of course you can have it. We'll work
out the exact details later." ' They worked on the script for a while,
and Oscar left. Logan and his wife opened a bottle of champagne to

South Pacific rehearsals: Mary Martin in the Thanksgiving show. They used a song called 'Suddenly lucky' which wasn't very. TMC

Ezio Pinza and Mary Martin in *South Pacific* rehearsals: the 'Some enchanted evening' sequence. TMC

celebrate, but their celebration was premature. The next day Oscar appeared again. 'I'm sorry,' he said, 'but I can't do it. I don't think that I should be penalized for not being the author of this show. Everybody expects me to be the author and giving someone else co-author credit would be a great penalty.'

'You can't look me in the face and tell me that I didn't write the major part of this story,' Logan said. 'No, perhaps even more than that,' Oscar replied. 'But Rodgers and Hammerstein cannot and will not share a copyright. It's part of our financial structure.' He went on to enumerate the points that the corporation required, this size of credit for Logan as co-author, that size of credit for Rodgers and Hammerstein as producers. 'Their word was law,' Logan says. 'They were that powerful. And when somebody disobeyed that law, they were punished.' He told Leland Hayward about his talk with Oscar. Hayward shrugged. 'You're at their mercy,' he said.

> The thing was, I wanted to do the show more than anything else in the whole world. And now the whole thing had become terribly ugly to me. All of this, of course, had been dictated by Howard Reinheimer, their lawyer, and Dick Rodgers. I don't, however, think that Oscar was completely blameless. He had a certain amount of steel in him, otherwise he wouldn't have survived the way he did. I suppose, looking back, I could have forced them to share the copyright. Lindsay and Crouse got them to do it later on in *The Sound of Music*.

With the libretto in working shape, the ideas came in thick and fast, and the cast began to take shape. Ezio Pinza and Mary Martin were set as the leads from the start. Juanita Hall, a mulatto singer who had been in the original production of *Show Boat*, was spotted by casting director John Fearnley singing in a show put on by the Stage Manager's Club, auditioned and walked off with the part of Bloody Mary, Liat's mother. The rôle of Liat went to Betta St John, who, as Betty Striegler, had been Bambi Lynn's replacement in *Carousel*. For the part of Lieutenant Cable, they tried to get a young singer named Harold Keel who had led the English production of *Oklahoma!* Unfortunately he had just signed a contract with MGM (he had changed his name to Howard Keel) so the part went to William Tabbert.

Four days before rehearsals began, on 3 February 1949, *The New York Times* carried a succinct announcement that 'In recognition of the extraordinary contribution made by Joshua Logan in the preparation of the first script of *South Pacific*, Rodgers and Hammerstein announce that henceforth he will share credit for the book with Oscar Hammerstein II'. It was grudging recognition of Logan's decisive part in the preparation of the musical; but it was all he was going to get.

Oscar's problems with the script were, however, only one factor among the dozens confronting the partners in staging the show. James Michener recalled the first meeting they had in New York to discuss it.

> Everyone was there, Josh Logan, Leland Hayward, Oscar Hammerstein, Richard Rodgers, Jo Mielziner, all these great names of the theatre. The meeting lasted for about two and a half hours, and they laid out the complete framework for the work they were going to do. During the first two hours, Richard Rodgers did not say one word. At the end of the two hours he turned to me and said, 'Michener, I'd like to ask you one question.' I thought he was entitled to that. He said, 'When I score this music, do I have to use a wailing guitar?' I said, 'In the part of the South Pacific I was in, I never heard such an instrument.'
>
> 'Thank God,' he said, and he said not another word that whole meeting.[2]

In a long article in the *New York Herald Tribune* of 3 April 1949, a few days before the show opened in New York, Rodgers recorded his reservations about scoring *South Pacific*.

> An island in the South Pacific could only mean one thing musically, and that was the sound of a steel guitar or a xylophone, or perhaps a marimba struck with what is known as a soft stick. This is a particularly mushy, decayed sound, one which is entirely abhorrent to me. The idea of having to deal with it for an entire evening was far from enticing ... To my amazement and joy I found that in this part of the South Pacific there was no instrumental music of any kind ... This caused a complete shift in my approach to doing the score ... I realised that I would be allowed to do what I'd always wanted to do by way of construction: give each character the sort of music that went with the particular character rather than the locale in which we found him ... In the whole score there are only two songs that could be considered 'native'. These are sung by a Tonkinese woman and here I made no attempt whatsoever to be authentic or realistic. The music is simply my impression of the woman and her surroundings in the same sense that a painter might give you the impression of a bowl of flowers rather than provide a photographic resemblance.

The two songs were, of course, 'Bali Ha'i' and 'Happy talk'. The first had been in Rodgers's mind almost from the outset when they were discussing the opening of the play. He jotted down the striking three-note opening of the song and played it for Oscar. 'These are the notes which will open the show,' he said, and they do.

Logan and Hammerstein told him that they wanted to do a song about the island, and that the same theme would be marvellous for it. They gave it a working title, 'Here I am', and Oscar got started on it. It took him quite some time to find the key to the song, which came when designer Jo Mielziner was preparing his scenery sketches

South Pacific: Lt Cable (William Tabbert) watches disapprovingly as Luther Billis (Myron McCormick) illustrates just why 'There is nothing like a dame'. In the British company, one of the sailors in this sequence was an unknown called Sean Connery. TMC

South Pacific: Bloody Mary (Juanita Hall) sells Lt Cable (William Tabbert) on the delights of 'Happy talk' with her daughter, Liat (Betta St John). Oscar nearly threw the song out because he didn't think there was any way to stage it. TMC

for the show. For the third scene of Act One, he needed a backdrop with a picture of the island. As he painted it, he became dissatisfied: the island did not have enough mystery about it. Dipping his brush into some water, Mielziner blurred the top of the island, making it look as if it were surrounded by mist. He called Logan. 'Come on down and have a look at Bali Ha'i', he said. When Logan saw the painting he called Oscar. Hammerstein took one look at it and the words 'my head sticking up from a low-flying cloud' came to him. The lyric came very quickly after that, but not as quickly as Rodgers's melody. He wrote that in about ten minutes flat, reputedly over coffee at Joshua Logan's apartment. He didn't even need to go to the piano.

New songs were coming thick and fast, Mary Martin remembers.

We were in Josh Logan's apartment in New York. Dick Rodgers had called and said, 'Come on over, I have a song, I have *the* song for you.' We went over, it was about midnight, and he was playing the piano and Oscar sang the song—'I'm in love with a wonderful guy'—in his darling, darling voice.

And I said, 'Could I have it, could I have the lyrics and sing it?' And I realised he expected me to sing twenty-six words on one breath. So I sat down beside Richard and he played it and I sang it. I sang it at the top of my voice, and when I finished I fell off the piano bench, because I was all in when I got to the end. And Richard Rodgers turned and looked at me on the floor and said 'That's exactly what I want. Never do it differently. We must feel you couldn't squeeze out another sound.'

'Happy talk' was done in about twenty minutes, so the story goes. Oscar sent the lyric to Rodgers while the latter was in bed with a cold. He rang Rodgers half an hour later to check that the messenger had arrived. 'I've not only got the lyric,' Rodgers said. 'I've got the music, too!' Even so, 'Happy talk' nearly got thrown out; Oscar was convinced there was no way the song could be successfully staged. Joshua Logan said if he could have the song, he could stage it; it took him perhaps ten or fifteen minutes to create and shape the scene in which Bloody Mary sings the song and her daughter Liat expresses the words in mime.

Logan was fiery, demanding and brilliantly inventive during the rehearsals. In the second scene, he got the men pacing like caged animals, back and forth, killing time, breaking into random, rather than

South Pacific: 'I'm gonna wash that man right out of my hair' promises Nurse Nellie Forbush (Mary Martin) and she did— eight times a week for three and a half years. TMC

choreographic patterns. In less than half an hour, singing all the time, tramping about the stage, doing every gesture, every grimace, he had the scene fixed, and the entire company gave him a standing ovation. The staging was never altered, and 'There is nothing like a dame' became, and remains, one of the high points of the show.

Dick and Oscar had given Pinza a song called 'Will you marry me?' but it didn't fit the spot they wanted. 'We'll get it, we'll get it,' they told the impatient actor, who was a laboriously slow learner and who knew he hadn't much time to memorize, rehearse and perfect a whole new number. Dick and Oscar came up with a song called 'Now is the time' but this one made the situation even more unbelievable. Emil de Becque and Joe Cable were going off on a mission from which they might never return. It wasn't likely that they would stand around singing 'Now is the time to act, no other time will do.' Everyone agreed that what was needed was a lament. Dick, Oscar and Josh went into a huddle, out of which the title 'This nearly was mine' emerged, together with the decision that it would be a big, bass waltz. Despite his legendary slowness, Oscar wrote the lyric in a couple of days; it became Pinza's favourite.

More problems: Cable had no song to sing to Liat after their first lovemaking experience in the little hut on Bali Ha'i. Oscar went back to his notes. He was hypnotized by the idea of the girl waiting for Cable's boat to come around the bend of the headland. A few days later he and Dick brought Logan a song called 'My friend' which appalled the director. 'When I think about it now, I just can't believe they did it,' he says. 'I was so astonished that I said, "My God, that's awful! That's the worst song I ever heard in my whole life!" ' Dick and Oscar looked at Logan in shock. No one had ever said anything so damning about one of their songs before, or even spoken to them that way. But they were pros. As Rodgers says, 'I'm not married to my tunes. There are plenty more where they came from.' Oscar was not married to his words, either, and so the deathless lines 'My friend, my friend, is coming round the bend' were consigned to the limbo that they sound as though they deserved.

A few days later they came back with a lilting melody called 'Suddenly lucky'. It was something Rodgers had run up for Mary Martin to rehearse the show-within-a-show until they wrote the actual song, and the words went 'Suddenly lucky, suddenly our arms are lucky, suddenly happy, suddenly our lips have kissed'. Logan vetoed this one, too. The boy and girl have just made love, he explained. The song was too 'up' and he wouldn't be able to do it with true emotion.

South Pacific: the final scene. De Becque is back from his mission, and Nellie is waiting for him, her previous reservations about him and his half-white children all gone. The little girl who played Ngana is Barbara Luna, now a regular television performer. TMC

Now it was Rodgers's turn to dig in his heels. He announced that he was damned if he was going to go on writing tunes until he came up with one that Josh Logan just happened to like.

'Give me one more,' Logan said. 'Something slower, deeper.'

Rodgers thought for a moment, and then played a melody that he had written originally for *Allegro* and dropped. The rough lyric that Oscar had put to it went 'You are so lovely, my wife, you are the light of my life' and when he heard the melody Logan knew it was third time lucky. Two days was all Oscar needed to come through with a great lyric: the song became 'Younger than Springtime'. 'Suddenly lucky' was to have a reincarnation, as well. Two years later, Gertrude Lawrence needed a song with the children in *The King and I*. Mary Martin, who had always hoped that one day they would put a lyric to it for her, reminded them of 'Suddenly lucky' and they gave it to Gertie with a new lyric. It was called 'Getting to know you'.

By the time *South Pacific* opened out of town—on 7 March 1949 at the Shubert Theatre in New Haven—the word was beginning to spread

Mitzi Gaynor in love with a wonderful guy in *South Pacific* (20th Century Fox, 1958; dir. Joshua Logan). Try to imagine Doris Day in the part: she very nearly got it. RICHARD RODGERS AND THE ESTATE OF OSCAR HAMMERSTEIN, COURTESY NFA

'I'll never forget Oscar's face when he brought "Honey bun" to me,' Mary Martin said. 'Those twinkling eyes in that granite face—he just loved having written something so deliberately corny.' Here's Mitzi Gaynor doing the song in *South Pacific*. RICHARD RODGERS AND THE ESTATE OF OSCAR HAMMERSTEIN, COURTESY NFA

that it was going to be the biggest show ever to hit Broadway. This was partially due to a rehearsal in New York held one day before the New Haven opening; an audience of show business people had been specially invited to see the show. The cast worked with makeshift props, old benches, anything; the lighting wasn't even set. The seasoned professionals watching them gave them a standing ovation. Many of those who saw it still say it was one of the best performances they ever saw in any theatre anywhere. In New Haven, Mary Martin recalls meeting Mike Todd with his then wife, Joan Blondell, the same Mike Todd who had once damned *Oklahoma!* with his wisecrack about girls and gags. He came backstage and faced Mary Martin gravely, telling her not to take the show to New York. The actress could not believe her ears, and asked him why. 'Because it's too damned good for them!' Todd said, 'It's too goddamned good for them!'

Despite the enormous enthusiasm the show was generating, it was still far too long, and there were still a number of staging problems. One was with the song that Mary Martin sang in scene seven. The idea for the song had come to her one evening while she was in the shower; she realized that she had never seen anyone wash their hair onstage. She called Joshua Logan and asked him whether he had. 'Wow!' said Logan and called Oscar Hammerstein. Before you could say 'shampoo' there was a new scene in the show where Mary washed her hair onstage to the tune of 'I'm going to wash that man right out of my hair'. The trouble was, audiences were so intrigued by her doing it that they were ignoring the song. Nobody could come up with another way of doing it. Then Josh Logan had the idea of Mary singing the song first and *then* washing her hair, flinging suds about as she did the dance which followed the song. Mary Martin washed her hair onstage eight times a week for three and a half years—and loved it every time.

Logan also had completely to restage 'I'm in love with a wonderful guy', as well as reluctantly to cut two of the songs: Cable's 'My girl back home' and one of de Becque's numbers, 'Loneliness of evening'. (He would reinstate them in the movie in 1958, the latter as incidental music.) Still the show was too long. Logan asked his friend Emlyn Williams, who was in Boston with a play of his own, to take a look at the script and see if he could suggest some cuts, as he had done with *Mister Roberts*. Williams's technique, according to Logan, is brilliant; he goes for the shortest form of every verb, cuts all dependent clauses, all unnecessary adjectives and all repeated phrases. Most importantly of all, he goes for those bits of which the author says, 'Oh, that's rather nice, I'm rather proud of that.'

With the 'Emlyn Williams Cutting' done, the format tightened, the songs restaged, *South Pacific* got ovations every night in Boston. The advance sale for the show in New York was more than one million dollars, and it was fast becoming a mark of the utmost social distinction to possess tickets to see it. The advance was the highest in theatrical history, and the furore so great that playwright George S. Kaufman, no great admirer of either Rodgers or Hammerstein, threw down his paper with its glowing reports of the show's success and complained bitterly to his friend Moss Hart that people in Boston were so excited about *South Pacific* that they were shoving money under the doors of the Shubert Theatre when it was closed on Sundays. 'They don't actually want anything,' he said, disgustedly. 'They just want to push money under the doors.'

South Pacific opened at the Majestic Theatre in New York on 7 April 1949 and proceeded to write another incredible chapter in the success story of Rodgers and Hammerstein. So confident were the partners in the enterprise that they joined in throwing a gala party on the St Regis Roof for the cast, collaborators and friends—before the reviews were in. It was a risk, perhaps, but a calculated one. The reviews were in fact better than even the most optimistic had expected, hurling adjectives like bouquets at everyone involved. The excitement continued to mount as the show ran. Tickets became such precious commodities that columnist Leonard Lyons printed an entire column of stories about what people had paid or done to obtain a couple. Although the show would not, in fact, run as long as *Oklahoma!* it was to prove infinitely more profitable. Its gross of $2,635,000 was bigger than that of *Show Boat*. Of the $50,600 weekly gross, Rodgers and Hammerstein each took $2,227, Logan $1,518, Michener $506. Of the approximately $10,000 weekly profits, half went to the backers (among whom, of course, were Rodgers, Hammerstein, Logan, Hayward, Reinheimer and their wives) and the other half to the producers. Rodgers and Hammerstein took $1,667 each of this half, Logan $1,111, Hayward $556. Weekly, remember; and the show was to run profitably for five years in New York, two and a half in London. Then there were to be the equally profitable touring companies. The national company began a several-year tour in 1950; after one year, its gross was over three million dollars, its profit $1,500,000. By August of 1949, the sheet music sales were in excess of one million copies; it had taken *Oklahoma!* six months to achieve in sheet music sales what *South Pacific* did in four. The backers who had put up the $225,000 budget (the show cost $163,000 to bring to Broadway) received their money back in four months. After a year

John Kerr, Mitzi Gaynor and Oscar Hammerstein II on the Fox sound stage during the filming of *South Pacific*. RICHARD RODGERS AND THE ESTATE OF OSCAR HAMMERSTEIN, COURTESY NFA

their return on investment was 1000 per cent and by the end of the run nearer five times that. By January 1957 the show's profit was nearly five *billion* dollars. (This figure, by the way, does not include revenue from the sale, in 1956, of the motion picture rights to 20th Century Fox.) The long-playing record album of the score with the original cast sold more than a million copies at $4.85—the income from this single venture alone being very probably more than that from any of the shows Dick Rodgers ever wrote with Larry Hart.

There were artistic as well as financial rewards. *South Pacific* swept the Antoinette Perry Awards—best musical, best male and female performers (Pinza and Martin) best supporting male and female performers (Myron McCormick and Juanita Hall) best director, best book, and best score. The Donaldson Awards went to the same starry roster: Pinza, Martin, McCormick, Hall, Logan, Hammerstein and Logan, and Richard Rodgers. The show walked away with the New York Critics Circle Award as best musical of the season 1948–9, and in 1950 came its greatest accolade: *South Pacific* won the Pulitzer Prize in drama. Not a consolation award, such as had been given to *Oklahoma!*, but

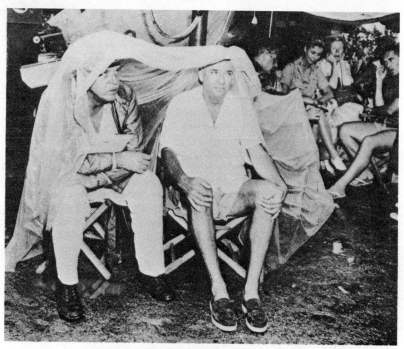

Joshua Logan (*l.*) and Oscar Hammerstein sheltering from a tropical downpour on the location set of *South Pacific*. In the background are Rossano Brazzi, who played de Becque, and Mitzi Gaynor, Ensign Nellie Forbush. Not an enchanted evening, by the look of it. RICHARD RODGERS AND THE ESTATE OF OSCAR HAMMERSTEIN, COURTESY NFA

the full prize, something which had not happened to any musical since 1933, when it went to the writers of the Gershwin show *Of Thee I Sing*, George S. Kaufman, Morris Ryskind and (as lyricist) Ira Gershwin. This time, the citation included Rodgers as composer, making him the first ever to receive the award. Unfortunately, the Pulitzer committee neglected to include the name of Joshua Logan. Like everyone else, they had accepted the show as Rodgers and Hammerstein's. Even though the omission was later remedied, and Logan got his Pulitzer, he was served with all the proof he needed that his part in the creation of *South Pacific* was being smothered by the legend of the other two. Such was his feeling about them that, although they offered him full co-authorship and direction of their next show, Logan turned them down. He has regretted the decision all his life; the show he refused was *The King and I*.

6. Broadway's Miracle Men

Too many people cling to the grief that comes from failure and too few people cling long enough to the thrill that comes from success.
Oscar Hammerstein II

South Pacific was a stunning success, a marvellous achievement with which to celebrate Rodgers's twenty-fifth anniversary on Broadway. The name of the show was licensed for cosmetics, clothing and fashion accessories. Every single member of the cast seems to have been interviewed about his or her rôle in the play: Myron McCormick, Juanita Hall, Joshua Logan, Jo Mielziner, Betta St John, James Michener, musical director Salvatore dell'Isola, Mary Martin, Ezio Pinza— especially Ezio Pinza, who had become a matinée idol and was living it up in a spectacular way—and most of all Rodgers and Hammerstein. Reporters described life at the Rodgers house in Connecticut, Hammerstein's work methods at Doylestown. *Ladies Home Journal* published a novella-length essay on Rodgers's life and work, written by Lincoln Barnett. Earl Wilson went up to Highlands Farm and filled a column in the *New York Post* with Oscar's remarks about his collaboration with Rodgers. *Variety* ran banner headlines hailing *South Pacific* as the 'one-year Broadway box-office champ'. *Life* magazine did a pictorial feature on them and their Pulitzer prize. The partners themselves appeared on the Groucho Marx TV show *You Bet Your Life*. Groucho pretended to be unimpressed with them (perhaps he was) and referred to them throughout as Roy Rogers and Trigger. When Oscar remonstrated that his name was Hammerstein, Groucho looked at him contemptuously.

'That's a funny name for a horse,' he snarled, and then, almost as an afterthought, 'It's a funny name for a man, come to think about it.' Dick and Oscar didn't even mind being told they looked like a 'couple of chiropractors'—they got in the plug for 'Some enchanted evening' and 'There is nothing like a dame'.

Rodgers himself was formally honoured in many other ways. The Theatre Guild commemorated his twenty-fifth anniversary on Broadway with a presentation and a party attended by some of the original members of the first *Garrick Gaieties* cast. He was presented by Dwight D. Eisenhower with the Hundred Years Association's award for his distinguished contributions to the American theatre. *Variety* reported in July that some fifteen Rodgers and Hammerstein concerts had been performed by symphony orchestras up and down the country, playing to standing room only audiences of 10,000 at a time. (These concerts led, the following year, to the establishment of a unit managed by Jim Davidson which toured the country for an entire season, playing a twenty-two-number Rodgers and Hammerstein concert). On 4 March, NBC Television devoted an hour to 'An Evening with Richard Rodgers' starring Mary Martin, Bing Crosby, Celeste Holm, Vivienne Segal and Alfred Drake. On 6 August the first Rodgers and Hammerstein concert (it was to become an annual event) was held at Lewisohn Stadium in New York. Despite a ten minute downpour which threatened to wash out the performance, 19,000 people turned up and waited the storm out. The very name of Rodgers and Hammerstein was box-office. Well, almost.

Surrey Enterprises, the Rodgers and Hammerstein producing arm, decided to present a new play by Samuel Taylor, based on Robert Fontaine's novel about a French-Canadian family, *The Happy Time*.[1] Taylor was an old friend of Rodgers; he had begun his theatrical apprenticeship when the Dramatist's Guild had asked the composer to let him watch the preparation and staging of *The Boys from Syracuse*, and had kept in touch with Rodgers ever since. The play, which starred Claude Dauphin and also featured Kurt Kaznar and Eva Gabor, was presented at the Plymouth Theatre in New York on 24 January 1950. The critics and the public liked it enough to keep it there for almost eighteen months, and a movie sale was clinched, making it another solid success for Rodgers and Hammerstein.

Then, in fairly rapid succession, they produced two thundering flops: *The Heart of the Matter* and *Burning Bright*. The first play was written by Graham Greene and an actor friend of his, Basil Dean, based on Greene's novel of a couple of years before. It just didn't work and there

The King and I: Yul Brynner as the strutting, swaggering King—and looking not a bit like the man who made the part of Chris, the gunfighter, in *The Magnificent Seven* his own. TMC

was no alternative but to close the play in Boston. This sharp reversal of their fortunes made the partners look very closely at their rôle as producers. They had several properties under their wing for posssible production: a new play by John O'Hara, another by John Steinbeck and the dramatic rights in a book by Sholom Aleichem called *Tevye's Daughters* which they though might make a musical. (It later did, with a score by Sheldon Harnick and Jerry Bock. It was called *Fiddler on the Roof*, and it became the longest-running musical in the history of the theatre.)[2]

They decided to go ahead with *Burning Bright*, the Steinbeck play, partly because it was already a well-advanced project, and partly out of loyalty to and friendship with the author. (His wife, Elaine, had been stage manager for *Oklahoma!*.) *Burning Bright* was another failure, folding after two weeks at the Broadhurst in October 1950.

By the time *Burning Bright* had died its death, however, the partners had withdrawn from the producing business, except where it concerned their own shows. They composed a long rationale called *The Pleasures of Producing* which appeared in *The New York Times* the day after they closed *The Heart of the Matter* in Boston. Their friends had been asking them for years, they said, why they functioned as a producing team when, with their own created hits and the others they had produced, they were working mostly for Uncle Sam. They pointed to the satisfactions in their producing rôle, not the least of which was the fact that they had been financially successful. That there was little profit in it all was outweighed by the sense of accomplishment, the knowledge that people were enjoying, and being emotionally engaged by, their plays. 'It would be difficult to imagine any greater fun'; they said,

than taking a little blonde girl with one line to speak out of the cast of *South Pacific* and putting her in the lead of the company of *Oklahoma!* which is now touring the country. On dreary March mornings with not enough sun the memory of Patricia Northrop's face when she learned she had the part of Laurey, and would eventually play it before her parents and school chums in California, is something to turn a dull day into a very happy one. What we are trying to explain is that in this sense alone producing can be creative, perhaps almost as much as writing itself, but there are other reasons. We are as aware as anyone that the theatre is having difficulty in maintaining itself, and it is our deep feeling that so long as we can help to keep some of the theatres lighted here and throughout the country and contribute towards the employment of actors, stagehands, musicians and hard workers in the theatre, we are in the position of having to do so, whether we like it or not.

These and many more hundreds of brave words on the subject

notwithstanding, Surrey Enterprises was effectively out of the producing business as of the failure of the two plays. Hence, perhaps, Joshua Logan's dry comment, 'I've always had a suspicion that Dick was more interested in money than art.'

Of course, there was another reason for their putting aside the burden of being producers, and that was the fact that—sooner or later—they had to find a property to follow *South Pacific*. Big as that show was, they had the need to do another. Neither man was the kind who can deliberately not work. So, by the summer of 1950, the word was already out that the next Rodgers and Hammerstein show would be a musical based on Margaret Landon's novel of 1944, *Anna and the King of Siam*.

Its genesis as a musical by Rodgers and Hammerstein is no less unusual than all the others. Both Dorothy Hammerstein and Dorothy Rodgers had read the book when it first appeared, and both had enthusiastically recommended it to their husbands as material for a musical. Both men had as strenuously resisted. *Anna and the King of Siam* was a novel based on fact, about the English governess Anna Leonowens who went to the court of the King of Siam in the 1860s to teach the King's many children English. The form of the book was to present, chapter by chapter, vignettes of life at the court of Siam and, through the character of the King, to heighten the exotic and sometimes savage aspects of daily life there.

The book was very successful, and was produced as a movie by 20th Century Fox, starring Rex Harrison as the King and Irene Dunne as Anna. The film was a big hit (even though Fox had wanted James Mason or Robert Montgomery as the King), and after seeing it, musical comedy star Gertrude Lawrence became convinced that she and only she should play Anna on the stage, and that she should do so in a show written for her by Rodgers and Hammerstein. She got her lawyer, Fanny Holtzmann, to try to talk Dick and Oscar into doing it, but they were still unconvinced. Gertrude Lawrence had been in a huge hit a couple of years back called *Lady in the Dark* but her vocal range was, to say the least of it, limited, and she had a distressing tendency to sing flat. They had never set out before to write a show with a specific star in mind. Still, they had to do something; and so they asked Fox to screen the movie for them. They emerged determined to do the show no matter what.

The obvious choice for the rôle of the King was Harrison, and they got in touch with him right away, but he was committed to doing a film called *The Long Dark Hall* and had an offer to do a play—T. S. Eliot's *The Cocktail Party*—in London.

Gertrude Lawrence as Anna and Yul Brynner as the King in *The King and I*. She got ten per cent of the gross even if she did sing off key. TMC

Celeste Holm made a charming Anna during the summer of 1952 while Gertrude Lawrence was on vacation from the cast of *The King and I*. TMC

I'd seen Alec Guinness playing it in New York and I wanted to try my hand at it, it was such a marvellous play. I also had to do the film because I'd found a plot of land in Portofino that I wanted to build a house on, and the film was really to pay for it. It turned out to be one of the worst pictures I've ever done. I don't think that more than twenty people ever saw it. Of course, if I had done *The King and I* for five years, and then the film afterwards, I probably never would have got *My Fair Lady*.

Oscar was already at work on the libretto. He found the key to the story in the account of the slave writing about Abraham Lincoln, an episode in the novel which would finally grow into the delightful story-ballet 'The small house of Uncle Thomas'. He altered the King's physical appearance (Mrs Landon described him as excessively thin and of medium height) and built up the romantic sub-plot about the slave-girl Tuptim from a small vignette which occurs about three-quarters of the way through the novel. (The man involved is a priest, and there is no amorous relationship with the girl whatsoever.) Hammerstein added the 'arranged' marriage and made the priest into a slave, Lun Tha. In fact, hardly any aspect of what was to become *The King and I* remains literally true to the original. Yet throughout, it is totally true to the spirit and intention of the book. Oscar's most radical alteration, and his most daring unorthodoxy yet in terms of the musical, was to have the King die at the end of the play.

Examined in isolation and without hindsight, the show should have been a failure. There was no conventional love interest between the two principal characters—they do not even kiss. There were no Americans in the story; all the characters were either British or Siamese. The setting was Bangkok (name any ten other musicals with a similar setting!) and the period Victorian. There was precious little humour—as Oscar pointed out, he had been especially wary of jokes about harems, and dancing girls with Oriental costumes who sang 'chingalingaling' with cymbals on their fingers. Instead he aimed his libretto towards the pageantry and dignity of the East, succeeding so admirably that Rodgers confessed himself 'crazy about Oscar's book' which was 'a wonderful job'. Anyone who knows Rodgers will know that this is almost rhapsodic praise; he usually says 'adequate' or 'very adequate' if a performer or a performance pleases him specially. By Christmas, Rodgers had written six or seven songs, and expected to write perhaps another dozen. Rehearsals were scheduled for January 1951, and casting was going apace.

Failing to get Rex Harrison for the King, Rodgers and Hammerstein now went after the biggest musical star on Broadway. He was, curiously enough, their own discovery, Alfred Drake, the original Curly of *Oklahoma!*. Drake had just left the cast of the smash-hit Cole Porter musical *Kiss Me, Kate!* and Dick and Oscar thought he would be ideal as the strutting King. Drake decided to play hard to get, however, making conditions and demands that Dick and Oscar decided were too high a price to pay. No doubt reflecting upon the irony that had made Drake too big a star for them to hire, they finished their lunch and went back to the Majestic, where John Fearnley was still auditioning. 'They told us the name of the first man and out he came with a bald head and sat cross-legged on the stage. He had a guitar and he hit this guitar one whack and gave out with this unearthly yell and sang some heathenish sort of thing, and Oscar and I looked at each other and said, "Well, that's it!" '[3]

The name of the actor was Yul Brynner, and he proceeded to make the part of the King—and indeed, much of the play—his own. The director of *The King and I* was John van Druten, but van Druten wasn't tough enough to handle Gertrude Lawrence, who was insecure and temperamental. Brynner had directed on Broadway and in television. He had made his movie debut in 1949 in *Port of New York* (which nobody anywhere seems ever to have seen) and he was as hard as nails. When he spoke, Lawrence listened. Rodgers confesses that they would have been in a lot of trouble had Brynner not been around, and just how important Gertrude Lawrence found his strength may be gauged from the fact that just before she died, still playing the lead, she asked for Brynner to be given star billing. 'He's earned it' she said, and she was not just talking about acting.

The King and I was a lavish and expensive show. The budget was a quarter of a million dollars, three times that of *Oklahoma!*, with an overcall of $50,000 and a further $40,000 underwritten by the producers. Six carloads of sets designed by Jo Mielziner were shipped up to New Haven for the tryouts. Irene Sharaff used genuine imported Thai silks and brocades for the costumes. The show was going to look, as well as sound, stunning.

The money for *The King and I* was raised in the usual Rodgers and Hammerstein manner. They were firm believers in bringing outside capital into the theatre, and in their own words, sternly averse to this 'procedure of peddling family jewels' to finance shows, which they deemed 'violently unhealthy'.

The backers of *The King and I* (their investment shown in brackets following their names) were: 20th Century Fox, represented by Joseph H. Moskewitch ($40,000); Theatrical attorney Howard Reinheimer

Yul Brynner as the King in *The King and I* (20th Century Fox, 1956; dir. Walter Lang). Compare with his appearance in the stage version to see how much Hollywood 'enhances' appearances.
NFA

The King and I (20th Century Fox). What Hollywood can do that Broadway cannot, and why the movie won Oscars for best art direction (Lyle R. Wheeler and John De Cuir) and best set decoration (Walter M. Scott and Paul S. Fox).
NFA

Yul Brynner and Deborah Kerr in *The King and I* (20th Century Fox). Her voice was ghosted by Marni Nixon, who got her own showing as a singing nun in the film *The Sound of Music*. NFA.

($37,500); Billy Rose ($15,000); Dorothy Rodgers ($10,000); Dorothy Hammerstein ($5,000); Leland Hayward ($12,500); Joshua Logan ($1,000) and his wife Nedda Harrigan ($1,000); theatre owner Howard Cullman ($15,000); Producer and theatre owner Anthony Brady Farrell ($12,000); Mrs William Hammerstein ($5,000); Reginald Hammerstein ($5,000); Oscar Hammerstein's stepdaughter, Mrs Susan B. Fonda ($2,500); her husband Henry Martin Fonda ($2,500); Richard M. Blow ($10,000); Bandleader Meyer Davis ($2,500); Producer Sherman Ewing ($2,500); Souvenir programme agent Hal Greenstone ($5,000); Mary Martin ($2,500); and her husband Richard Halliday ($2,500); Nancy Hawks (Mrs Leland Hayward) ($2,500); Theresa Helburn ($5,000); Lawrence Langner ($2,500); and his wife Armina Marshall ($2,500); designer Jo Mielziner ($5,000); general manager Morris Jacobs ($2,500); lighting technician Edward F. Cook ($2,500); former silent movie star Carmel (*Ben Hur*) Myers ($2,500); Mrs Howard Reinheimer ($7,500); The Author's League of America ($5,000); stage manager Jerome Whyte ($2,500); ad executive Lawrence Weiner ($2,500).

Once again the financial arrangements reveal how closely Rodgers and Hammerstein were involved with both the financing and the rewards of their work. As authors, they took eight per cent of the gross, giving one per cent to the original author, Margaret Landon. As usual, they took a further two per cent as managers. John van Druten got three per cent as director, and Gertrude Lawrence ten per cent of the gross and five per cent of the profits until her untimely death in 1952. Brynner got no percentage (neither did any of the actresses who followed Lawrence) but choreographer Jerome Robbins got $350 a week, with Mielziner again drawing $100. Irene Sharaff took $50 a week. The theatre shared a flat twenty-five per cent.

The profits of the show—at 30 June 1953, they were over $700,000—were to be shared 60–40 between backers and management. In taking the extra ten per cent up front, the backers waived all rights to any share in the movie rights or any foreign incomes from the show. Even so, they would eventually draw 117 per cent profit on their total investment of $360,000. Thus attorney Reinheimer's profits, for instance, would be $43,875 at the end of the show's run on Broadway. All that, however, was some way in the future.

Tryouts began at the Shubert Theatre in New Haven on 26 February 1951. There was still a lot of work to do, especially in trying to cure Gertie Lawrence of her insistent propensity to sing off key, so noticeably as to make audiences uncomfortable. Rodgers had taken as few chances with her songs as possible, keeping them all within a relatively limited range. His score was not yet complete, but he already had some delightful melodies for the huge cast to work on, among them 'I whistle a happy tune', 'Shall we dance?' and 'Hello, young lovers'.

The last song had given Oscar Hammerstein some of the most agonizing weeks of his career entire. In trying to create a lyric by means of which Anna can describe her dead husband, Tom, to the ladies of the court, he wrote—and threw out—seven different songs. He kept coming back to the line 'When I think about Tom', and finally, after weeks of work, got his lyric together and sent if off to Rodgers. He was especially proud of 'Hello, young lovers', which he considered one of the best things he had ever written, and couldn't wait to hear from Rodgers. Dick didn't call. He didn't call that day or the next day or the next. By this time, Oscar could no longer work. Yet there was something that made him wait, something that kept him from calling Rodgers to ask him whether he had liked the song. Finally, on the morning of the fourth day, Dick called him about something else entirely. They talked for ten minutes about various things in the show—everything except 'Hello, young lovers'. Then finally, Rodgers remarked that he'd received the lyric, and told Oscar it was 'okay'. 'It works just fine' he said and hung up, leaving Hammerstein completely wrecked.

Oscar called Joshua Logan and told him what had happened. Logan tried to reassure Oscar, but Oscar was so embittered that he poured out all the hurts, all the slights, all the frustrations he had undergone in all these years of working with Dick. He had made a very conscious effort—both of them had—to avoid jeopardizing their working relationship. In doing so, although he was the older and in many ways more experienced half of the partnership, Oscar had accepted second place in his relationship with Rodgers. When the limousines came to the door, it was Dick who drove away first. If there was only one suite at the Ritz, Dick was the one who got it. Rodgers was a brilliant man, a near genius, but, as Logan tellingly remarks, he was not a generous one. So Oscar had made all the adjustments, without complaint until now, when something he considered as good if not better than anything he had ever done was dismissed with a casual 'okay'.

'Dick would never have any idea of how hard it was for Oscar to write that lyric,' says Logan. 'He just figured that was what Oscar could do. He had no idea of the agonies Oscar went through because Oscar would never show Dick that side of him at all. I don't think he showed it to anyone. He never talked about his work at all, with anybody, except to me that one time.'

Work went apace at New Haven. Leland Hayward came up and saw the show, at the conclusion of which he astonished Rodgers by advising him to close it before it went any further. They moved on to Boston with at least forty-five minutes too much play, and maybe three or four songs that either had to be cut or replaced, somehow, somewhere. 'Waiting', 'Who would refuse?' and 'Now you leave' went back into the trunk, never to re-emerge. Even with the substantial cuts they had made to the text, however, Dick and Oscar felt that the show still lacked a vital lightness of touch. The King was well served with a number aptly expressing his bewilderment at the number of options he had to consider in his diplomatic dealings with the West, all of which he declared 'A puzzlement'. Lady Thiang, his head wife (played by Dorothy Sarnoff) had a beautiful song, 'Something wonderful', which explained to 'Mrs Anna' her love for and devotion to the King. The slave Tuptim's bitterness towards the King was shown in 'My Lord and Master', as was Anna's vexation in 'Shall I tell you what I think of you?' The march which accompanies the entrance of the King's children, with its dynamics increasing in proportion to their size (and with its curious echoes of the verse of a 1927 Rodgers and Hart song called 'On a desert island with thee'), was stunningly staged. So, too, was Jerome Robbins's balletic divertissement, in which the slave Tuptim strives to explain the concept of freedom to the King by means of a free Siamese interpretation of Harriet Beecher Stowe's *Uncle Tom's*

Cabin. With all this, the first act still lacked that 'lift' they were all looking for.

Then Gertrude Lawrence came up with an idea. Couldn't they give her a song to sing with the children? Something to explain that she was becoming attached to them, getting to know and like them? That was all Dick and Oscar needed. Mary Martin reminded them of the lilting schottische that had been used to rehearse *South Pacific*'s show-within-a-show (until it was replaced by 'Honey bun'), the song which had lived but briefly as 'Suddenly lucky'. Oscar put the lyric of 'Getting to know you' to the melody, and the first act had all the lift it could use. It is one of the few Rodgers and Hammerstein songs which bears a family resemblance to a Rodgers and Hart melody: no one who hears 'Getting to know you' could doubt that it springs from the same melodic source as 'Manhattan'.

There were a few further changes to be made, another couple of songs to write, and then they were ready to take the show to New York. They closed in Boston on 24 March and that day, critic Elliott Norton dashed off the following report to his paper:

THE KING AND I LEFT HERE WITH THREE NEW SONGS ALREADY INSERTED. GER-
TRUDE LAWRENCE HAS 'GETTING TO KNOW YOU' IN ACT ONE, DOROTHY SARNOFF
HAS 'WESTERN PEOPLE FUNNY' OPENING ACT TWO, DORETTA MORROW HAS 'I
HAVE DREAMED' ALSO IN ACT TWO. 'WESTERN PEOPLE' NOT MUCH BUT OTHER
TWO LOOK LIKE BIG HITS. UNDERSTOOD BING CROSBY AND OTHERS ALREADY
RECORDING SCORE ALSO SINATRA.[4]

Good auguries indeed, and when *The King and I* opened on Broadway on 29 March 1951—in the same theatre and almost eight years to the day that *Oklahoma!* had burst upon the world—the critics tossed their hats into the air and hailed another triumph from the miracle men of Broadway. Yul Brynner became a star overnight, his swaggering, likeable King a perfect foil for the fey charm of Gertrude Lawrence's Anna. The Robbins ballet was hailed as a tour-de-force, which it was (he would go on to create the sensational dances in *West Side Story*), and the words used to describe the score were 'exuberant' and 'radiant' and 'glorious'. *The King and I* was another solid gold hit.

One sad event marked the three year Broadway run of *The King and I*. Gertrude Lawrence, although no one knew it, had leukaemia. She left the cast after a year for an extended vacation (her replacement was the original Ado Annie of *Oklahoma!*, Celeste Holm) and returned in mid March 1952, looking rested and well. She continued to play the part of Anna until three weeks before she died on 6 September 1952. Her understudy, Constance Carpenter, took over the rôle.

Rodgers and Hammerstein had yet another clean sweep. They were making the astonishing look normal. Three years on Broadway (1,246 performances) and another eighteen months on tour. Two and a half years at London's Drury Lane Theatre, where Valerie Hobson played Anna to Herbert Lom's King. Antoinette Perry Awards for best musical, to Gertrude Lawrence, for Rodger's score. Donaldsons for Brynner, Morrow, Robbins, Mielziner and Sharaff. A stunning movie in the works, it was the old story all over again. Was there anything that these men couldn't do? And more important, what would they do next?

The answer was totally unexpected: they split up.

It was not a parting, a sundering such as had occurred between Rodgers and Larry Hart but, nevertheless, for the best part of a year Rodgers and Hammerstein worked apart. That is not to say that they did not pursue their mutual endeavours, nor is it to say that they were not actively considering another joint project—Oscar already had an idea for a new show by the end of 1951. All the same, either by accident or design, they were more apart in the final months of 1951 than at any time in the preceding decade.

If there was a rift between Dick and Oscar, it has never been mentioned or acknowledged. It would be presumptuous to suggest that there was one at all, were it not for the story Joshua Logan told about 'Hello, young lovers' and Oscar's deeply wounded feelings about Dick's reception of it. What is certain is that Rodgers accepted a commission from NBC Television to write a background score for a proposed documentary series about the exploits of the United States Navy during World War II. He also involved himself enthusiastically in a revival of the 1940 Rodgers and Hart show, *Pal Joey*, which his friend Anthony Brady Farrell (one of the backers of *The King and I*) was producing in collaboration with song-writer Jule Styne and Leonard Key. There were also plans for a spectacular television salute on two consecutive Sunday evenings telling the Richard Rodgers story.

So, in that autumn of 1951, Dick and Oscar worked apart. It was, of course, unthinkable that they separate, and they knew it. Perhaps it was just a breathing space, Rodgers working on music unsupported by libretto or lyric (the first time he had done anything of the kind for more than ten years) and taking a nostalgic but far from unhappy look back at his finest collaboration with Larry Hart. Ahead of him was an eventful Silver Jubilee year.

Oscar Hammerstein does not seem to have been giving any interviews around this time.

7. Only human

'The audience are the only smart people in show business'
Richard Rodgers

There are one or two people in show business who have had harsh things to say about Richard Rodgers, but there does not seem to be anybody around who has a bad word to say about Oscar Hammerstein. 'He was a very sensitive, very poetic, very dreamy man,' Joshua Logan says, 'who had many dreams of beautiful things he wanted to do. He had a doggedness, too. He was a delight. He had the most marvellous judgement.' 'To meet Oscar was to love him,' says Jan Clayton. 'He wasn't obvious, not a man for small talk. And he had a great sense of humour.' 'He was so warm and so enthusiastic,' Lucinda Ballard said. 'He was a big, tall man, with a big head and wide shoulders, he had a look that my mother always used to call philoprogenitive. Some people say his songs were too sweet. They're not if you knew Oscar. Oscar was like that. His warmth and kindness were genuine. He'd never put on airs like some people do.' William Hammerstein, his son, agreed that Oscar has been given a Pollyanna aura that he may not have entirely merited. Was he really such a nice guy? 'Well, I think he tried to be. He didn't always succeed, of course, but it was something he tried as much as he possibly could to be.' 'Oscar was able to write about dreams and grass and stars because he *believed* in them,' says Stephen Sondheim. Richard Rodgers agreed. 'He always wrote about the things which affected him deeply. What was truly remarkable about him was his never-failing ability to find new ways to reveal how he felt about nature and music and love.'

Oscar was always willing to do battle for any cause in which he believed, and was among the first of the Hollywood community in the Thirties to take a positive stand against Nazism. He reacted equally promptly against McCarthyism when it reared its head in the Fifties. He was on innumerable theatrical and charitable committees, from the Dramatists' Guild to the World Federalists.

Oscar Hammerstein liked to leave parties early. His edgy shuffle towards the door was known as 'the Hammerstein glide'. LFG

In the upside-down world of show business, where everyone stays up until three and sleeps until midday, Oscar Hammerstein was an anomaly.

> I'm not a nighthawk. Unlike so many of my friends, I hardly ever stay up until midnight. Usually I'm in bed by around eleven, although I always take some books with me. I'm asleep in a few minutes. This allows me to get up around eight in the morning, feeling quite rested—an hour which would seem like the middle of the night to most people in show business. I have a hot bath, followed by a massage and a cold bath, then a leisurely breakfast during which I usually read through the New York morning papers. Around 9.30 I go off to my work room. I plug away at my writing until lunch, occasionally going for a walk around the farm whenever I've struck a snag and need a change of scenery. By two o'clock or thereabouts I'm back at the job, but my wife, who is an Australian, has taught me the British custom of breaking off at about 4.30 p.m. for tea. Frankly, I look forward to it every day with a lot of pleasure.
>
> I like to walk a lot when I'm working. If it's a bad day I stay on the porch. I like the country because you can sing to yourself and not feel silly. I make up dummy tunes, usually something corny. I started going to vaudeville at three, and all those songs are still in my head. It angers me that I can't write music. I've got no creative ability with melody.[1]

Oscar was, as he had often remarked, foolishly in love with the theatre. His unformulated idea now was to write a play about something in which he felt well qualified: what happens to a theatrical company during a long running hit show. There would be real people in it, not just the usual stereotyped Star, Ingénue, Bitch and so on. It would be a many-layered story charting how a rag tag of performers grows into a family, a community unto itself—a show within a show in the truest sense of the words. He warmed to the idea, striding around the snowy pastures of Highlands Farm, a tall, lumbering, crew-cut, pock-marked man with gentle blue eyes, surrounded by the people of his imagination: chorus boys, musical conductors, stage managers, understudies, electricians and grips, their interrelated loves and hates, the things that, as Oscar knew only too well, could happen to them. After the première of *Pal Joey* he told Rodgers his idea. Dick was enthusiastic about it, and they agreed to get together to work on it as soon as Rodgers was free of his committment to NBC on *Victory at Sea*.

When *Pal Joey* opened in New York on Christmas Day, 1940, it met as we have seen, with a very mixed critical and public reception. It was seamy; its people were not the nice, normal, wholesome sort one usually expected in a musical. They were hard and hip and heartless. Perhaps, in 1940, Broadway wasn't ready for it. Certainly critic Brooks

Atkinson wasn't, when he waspishly commented that if it was possible to make a musical comedy out of an odious story, *Pal Joey* was it. We have seen how Atkinson's reaction affected Larry Hart, who always thought *Joey* the best thing he had done.

The revival of *Pal Joey* brought Vivienne Segal back in her original rôle as Mrs Vera Simpson (John O'Hara had given the character the same initials as the star when he wrote the original libretto) and paired her with a Joey played by Harold Lang, who had just scored in *Kiss Me, Kate!*. Elaine Stritch had the part of Melba Snyder, the girl reporter who does the hilarious skit striptease 'Zip', originally performed by Jean Casto. This time around Brooks Atkinson and the rest of the critics saw *Pal Joey* clear, and hailed it as the landmark of musical theatre it had always been. Alas, their well-eaten words came a little late for Larry Hart, but they were highly rewarding for Richard Rodgers.

Pal Joey settled down for a comfortable fifteen-month run which would make it the longest-running of all the Rodgers and Hart shows, and turned Shubert Alley into Rodgers's personal domain. *South Pacific* was still at the Majestic, *The King and I* at the St James. Now *Pal Joey* completed a very satisfying hat-trick, and nobody enjoyed it more than Rodgers himself. He would often visit one or two or all three of the theatres in the course of an evening, checking the performances, listening to the songs and—some say—counting the receipts.

He is not uncharming, Richard Rodgers, but he does not try to be lovable. Brilliant, intelligent, witty and incredibly gifted, he seems to have chosen a *persona* to be, rather than to be the person he is. He has a strong sense of purpose, he loves his work and is perfectly happy as long as everyone around him meets his extraordinarily high standards. When they do, no matter at what cost to themselves, he accepts them as his due, no less than what was expected. He is sparing with praise, although always supportive with advice and help. Despite his stated aversion to it, he actually enjoys the hurly-burly of business, and even today, when he is far from strong and it is far from necessary, he commutes regularly to his office on Madison Avenue and 57th Street, located not inappropriately above the Chase Manhattan Bank. 'He's a fantastic workman,' says Jan Clayton. 'Stern, you bet, but fair, courteous and confident. Everyone who worked with him knew he expected, demanded, the very best we could give.' Mary Martin agrees. 'He's very exact and demanding of an artiste,' she says. 'But he gets it back because he gives so much. He is also terribly reserved and terribly emotional, but you'd never know it to see him or be with him.' She

Richard Rodgers's face is described as 'incandescent' when he conducts his own music, so he must have been conducting someone else's here. LFG

adds the story that Dorothy Rodgers told her. Often, after playing a new song for an audience for the first time, Rodgers has gone into the bathroom and been physically ill, so tense and strung-up is he about reactions to his work. 'He's very paternalistic,' George Abbott says. 'Maybe because he's a doctor's son, he has this bedside manner. He talks to actors and actresses at auditions in a very personal way, encouraging them even when he's turning them down.' 'The only way I can define it,' Robert Russell Bennett said, 'is that deep down somewhere in that soul of his there must be a warm beautiful thing that produces all these melodies.' Dorothy Fields referred to him as a 'gentle' man, but Helen Ford recalled that beneath the gentleness was 'the steel fist in the velvet glove', the temper that would 'burn, but deep down'.

A man, then, of many contradictions. A theatrical song-writer who prefers to be called a composer and dresses like a banker. A hugely successful creator of melodies who, according to John Green, does not care for poetry when it is not married to music. A man who, says writer George Oppenheimer, hates homosexuality, cliques and in-groups, yet worked for a quarter of a century with a homosexual, and all his life in that most cliquey and in-group-ish of all professions, the theatre. A man of infinite talent and limited soul, according to Stephen Sondheim. A blessed man who has led a blessed life, according to Mary Martin.

Kurt Singer, author and literary agent, tells an anecdote which illustrates a little more clearly than most how Rodgers sees himself and his profession. Singer came to America in 1943 and was invited by a friend to dinner at the Players' Club in Gramercy Park. He knew no one there—they were all theatre people—and found himself sitting next to an unspectacular-looking man who looked like a shoe clerk. Singer asked the man what he did for a living. 'I'm a musician,' the man said. 'That must be a difficult profession at the moment,' Singer remarked, referring to wartime conditions. 'Oh,' said the musician, 'I'm managing.' Later, Singer was told that his 'shoe clerk' was Richard Rodgers, who was then riding the crest of the biggest wave in the history of the musical theatre, his new show *Oklahoma!* Perhaps, then, as Joshua Logan hypothesizes, Rodgers is somehow embarrassed by the ease with which he writes his songs, and added the hard-bitten, ruthless businessman exterior only to find that he enjoyed the rôle.

For all that, Rodgers is unfailingly courteous, endlessly patient, infinitely available to the hundreds and hundreds of people who still feel they have to talk with him, offer him ideas, seek his support. In several hours of interviews with me, at a time when he was suffering very badly from a diseased larynx, he never once expressed impatience or referred to his own discomfort. In our last interview, at a time when he was learning to 'talk' all over again after the removal of his larynx, he was as urbane and helpful as before.

Rodgers is not a demonstrative man, and yet he delights in the company of beautiful women—a fondness, by the way, which it has been

Dick and Oscar at work in the Ritz at Boston: some of the best songs in theatrical history were written in hotels or ladies' rest rooms. CP

taboo to discuss in writing about him for as many years as he has been working in the theatre. He is a loyal man to his close friends, but he never forgets his mistakes and rarely makes the same one twice. He does not seem to know, or chooses not to explore, the wellsprings of his own talent. In preparing this book I asked him the following question: 'Perhaps at this point I could ask you to describe your own working method by putting it thus: you have worked out where the song will appear, its mood, its motivation. The lyric arrives from Oscar. It is called 'Will you marry me?' and Pinza will sing it. What happens now?'

'I write the music,' was Rodgers's answer.

In the spring of 1952, Dick and Oscar got together in Palm Beach where Rodgers and his wife were vacationing while Dick put the finishing touches to his melodic sketches for *Victory at Sea*. They discussed Oscar's tentative ideas for a new show, agreeing that if they did it, the action would have to be confined to the various parts of one theatre: the wings, stage, dressing-rooms and even the lobby. Rodgers put up the suggestion that they dispense with an overture, saving it for the 'overture' of the show within the show.

By summer, Rodgers had completed the main musical themes for the television series, and he handed them over the brilliant orchestrator and arranger Robert Russell Bennett, whose job it would be to extend, expand and score them in line with Rodgers's basic intention. The final score for *Victory at Sea*, if played in one piece, would run for some thirteen hours but, of course, Rodgers did not compose anything like thirteen hours of music. The nine-movement symphonic suite contained such evocative sub-titles as 'Song of the High Seas', 'Guadalcanal March', 'Theme of the Fast Carriers' and 'Under the Southern Cross'. The last, in the unusual tempo of the tango, became very popular when the programmes were premièred in October, 1952. Rodgers was to receive two of the highest awards television could confer upon his work for *Victory at Sea*: the 'Emmy' of the Television Academy and the George Foster Peabody citation. The composer was also given the Distinguished Public Service Award of the United States Navy, but before all this could happen he had already plunged back into preparing another show with Oscar Hammerstein. Dick's fiftieth birthday celebrations included two Sunday evening hours on CBS Television's 'Toast of the Town' programme, in which host Ed Sullivan introduced, among others Yul Brynner, Vivienne Segal, Lisa Kirk, Jane Froman, William Gaxton, John Raitt and Rodgers himself. One evening was devoted to Rodgers and Hart songs, the second to those of Rodgers and Hammerstein. Cementing their relationship publicly, Oscar Hammerstein filled a page in the June 1952 issue of *Town & Country* magazine with an affectionate salute to his collaborator entitled 'Happy Birthday, Dear Dick'.[2] On 28 June, Rodgers's birthday, the Hammersteins hired a boat, brought aboard an orchestra and sailed a huge party of theatre people, including members of the casts of the three Rodgers shows now playing on Broadway, up the Hudson River and back again, serenading Rodgers all night with his own music. If there had been any difference between Dick and Oscar, any sort of rift, it had been resolved.

Through the summer, Dick and Oscar worked in their usual fashion, blocking out the story, talking over every aspect of the production. Not one word or one note would be written until they were finished with these preliminaries. There were one or two mechanical problems, so they called in Jo Mielziner. He reassured them: they could play scenes on the light bridge or partly-onstage and partly off. It would be expensive, but it could be done (In fact the enormously complicated sets for what was to become *Me and Juliet* added a crippling $300,000 to the budget, more than the entire cost of *South Pacific*). By August Oscar had begun working on the script.

His original idea of a show within a show had now been expanded. There was a sub-plot interwoven into the main story which, by autumn, was taking definite shape. In October Oscar told a newspaper reporter that he had done some dialogue for the first act, but no lyrics at all. 'We have no title in mind yet. All I can tell you about the theme is that it's about the theatre. We are going to do our utmost to avoid the usual clichés of show business musicals.'

With a rough script from which to work, Mielziner and his three assistants began to draw up designs for the twelve sets. At the Rodgers and Hammerstein offices wheels started turning. Robert Alton was engaged as choreographer, Salvatore dell'Isola to conduct the orchestra (although as yet there was no music for him to conduct), and Don Walker to do orchestrations and vocal arrangements. The Majestic Theatre was booked for 28 May 1953, which in turn necessitated the relocation of *South Pacific*, which showed no signs of running out of steam. Frantic revisions of theatrical schedules were made; *South Pacific* could move into the Broadway Theatre, but not until 29 June, and so it was scheduled into the Opera House, Boston, for a five-week engagement from 18 May to 27 June of the following year. Cleveland and Boston theatres were also booked for the tryouts of the new show, and production manager Jerome Whyte began to interview stage managers, master carpenters, chief electricians, property masters and wardrobe mistresses. First rehearsals were pencilled in for 19 March, auditions beginning nine days earlier.

Dick and Oscar had decided by now that *Me and Juliet* (the title was announced on 18 December) would be a 'musical comedy' and not, as formerly, a 'musical play'. Oscar had the book pretty well in working order, and Dick began work on the songs. By the end of the year they had three of the thirteen songs finished; one of them had been lifted from Rodgers's score for *Victory at Sea*, the tango 'Under the Southern Cross'. It became 'No other love' and, incidentally, the only hit song in the show.

In an interview in December 1952 Rodgers's happiness at being involved in a new show with his partner is evident. 'It's wonderful to be writing again,' he said, 'to sit quietly in a room and work. It's what I was meant to do, but somehow I became a producer along the way.

Me and Juliet: Joan McCracken doing a little vamping during
'rehearsals' of the show within the show. CP

Me and Juliet: Isabel Bigley (*l.*) and Joan McCracken (*extreme r.*)
with Bill Hayes (*centre*) and Ray Walston on the floor (in sports
jacket). Walston played the part of Billis in the movie of *South
Pacific* some years later. CP

I like having a say in the way our shows are staged, but composing is really my business.'

With the book and some of the songs ready, Dick and Oscar now went to a man both of them regarded as one of the very best directors in the musical comedy business, George Abbott. They asked him to do *Me and Juliet* and he accepted, a decision he began to regret almost as soon as he started reading Oscar's libretto. It was melodramatic and sentimental, and Abbott didn't like it. He convinced himself that he must be wrong, however; Rodgers and Hammerstein were two smart men with a string of big hits behind them. Just the same, he told Dick and Oscar about his reservations concerning the book, and Oscar told him to take it home, cut it, make notes, do what he liked. 'Treat it as ruthlessly as if it were your own,' he said. Abbott did just that, but it was still a clumsy book.

Chorus auditions began on 10 March 1953 at the Majestic. There were parts for seventeen male singers and dancers, and twenty-five female. They were being offered $90 a week in town, $100 a week on the road. More than 1,000 turned up; Dick, Oscar and George Abbott saw and heard every one of them.

On 19 March the first rehearsal was held. Rodgers and Hammerstein had a technique for presenting the story to the cast. Oscar would read from the libretto, playing different parts, then sing the songs while Dick Rodgers played them. *Me and Juliet* was no exception, and the cast gave composer and lyricist a warm round of applause before splitting up to get to work. Singers and dancers rehearsed at the Alvin Theatre; the principals at the Majestic. Isabel Bigley had been chosen to play Jeanie, the chorus singer with whom Larry, the assistant stage manager (Bill Hayes) is in love. His boss, Mac (Ray Walston) is having an affair with the principal dancer, Betty (Joan McCracken). Stage electrician Bob (Mark Dawson) has had an affair with Jeanie. Mac is taken off the show. Larry and Jeanie get married secretly. Bob finds out and gets drunk, then tries to kill them during the performance of *Me and Juliet*, the 'show' within the show. Most of the cast were alumni of other Rodgers and Hammerstein hits: Isabel Bigley, fresh from her triumph in *Guys and Dolls*, had played in the English production of *Carousel*, and in the chorus of *Oklahoma!*, as had Joan McCracken. Ray Walston had played Billis in the English company of *South Pacific*, and so on.

After about a week of rehearsal, the actors begin to work without scripts. The director maps out their movements, instructs them in how to play the rôles as he sees them from the auditorium. The players in *Me and Juliet* were 'on their feet' on the second day, blocking out their exits and entrances with chairs and makeshift props.

By mid April Dick and Oscar were furiously rewriting. As Rodgers remarked once, 'Anybody can fix things with money. It's when things need brains that you have a little trouble.' *Me and Juliet* needed all the brains they could muster. They took out two entire production numbers, 'Wake up, little theatre', and 'Dance' in order to speed up the action. The actress playing 'Juliet' in the interior play was replaced by Helena Scott. Visitors drifted in and out making comments, some useful, some not. Oscar later recalled that he made eight pages of notes at the first full dress rehearsal. Between the afternoon and evening rehearsals he and Dick cut out two minutes of 'Juliet's' solo and the verse of the song 'No other love'.

Another rehearsal before moving to the Hanna Theatre in Cleveland. Do it again, do it again, and again and again. They ended at 2.45 a.m. in a complete shambles. Bigley was in tears. The lighting cues were out of synch, the curtain was coming down at the wrong moment, the vital sandbag (by means of which Bigley and Hayes are supposed to be killed) had not fallen properly.

There was one afternoon rehearsal prior to the opening in Cleveland, as dispiriting as the one which had preceded it. Seamstresses were still sewing and pressing Irene Sharaff's three hundred costumes beneath the stage as the curtain went up on opening night. Rodgers sat in his accustomed place in the last row of the orchestra, Hammerstein in the eighth row, note pad ready.

Both men changed abruptly as soon as one of their shows was staged for the first time. Rodgers was a dynamo at rehearsal, his eye on every aspect of the production, checking, advising, gesturing, talking. Hammerstein would be much more aloof, sitting in the auditorium and making copious notes. 'He had very definite and fixed opinions,' Abbott said, 'but he took his time about asserting them.'

On opening nights, they changed rôles. Rodgers became imperturbable while Hammerstein fumed and swore audibly beneath his breath when things went wrong onstage. Dorothy Hammerstein said he sometimes came out with the most awful remarks. On the opening night of *Me and Juliet*, the wayward curtain failed once more to come down on cue and Oscar was heard to mutter 'Damn and damn and damn! This is a new way: they saved it for the performance!'

The audience, however, failed to notice the fluffs and errors, and gave the show a rousing welcome. The critics, while reserving judgement on the weak story, liked it too. They called it 'big' and 'beautiful' and 'ingenious'.

The show moved to Boston's Shubert Theatre on 6 May, rewriting every inch of the way. The show-within-a-show was changed yet again. Another song, 'Meat and potatoes' was dropped, lest it might be considered suggestive, and was replaced by one called 'We deserve each other'. They finally brought *Me and Juliet* into the Majestic in New York on 28 May 1953, anything but optimistic. As Dick Rodgers said, 'When you hear people leaving the theatre raving about the sets, without a word about the rest of your show, it doesn't make you feel too confident.' He was right; despite an advance sale of $500,000, despite a ten-month run (which, for anyone except Rodgers and Hammerstein, would have represented a success) and despite an eventual profit in excess of $100,000, *Me and Juliet* has to be classed as a failure.

The show's director, George Abbott, always felt that there were two major factors in the failure of *Me and Juliet.* One was Oscar's nebulous play-within-a-play. No one had thought it out, and since Oscar remained 'positively Sphinxlike' on the subject, Bob Alton was at a loss to come up with the kind of divertissement which Jerome Robbins had done in *The King and I.* So the song and dance routines were just that, routine. The second factor, Abbott felt, was Rodgers and Hammerstein themselves. They were the golden boys. They hadn't had a flop since *Oklahoma!*—with the honourable exception of *Allegro.* They were too sure of themselves, and perhaps therefore did not try as hard as they should have done. They also craved personal publicity far too much for Abbott's liking. He noted one other thing about their relationship: how each made a conscious, and visible effort not to jeopardize it, which would seem to indicate that both were aware of its fragility. At one point, Rodgers told Abbott, 'I never want to have another collaborator as long as I live.'

Even if *Me and Juliet* did not succeed in its intention to toss a bouquet to the theatre they both loved, even if it had no tour and no London showing, even if at times it was downright embarrassing (showbiz insiders still get dinner party laughs with 'The Big Black Giant', a song which tried to describe how an audience appears to the performers onstage)³ it did one very important thing. It re-established the strong working relationship of Richard Rodgers and Oscar Hammerstein. It remained thus until the very end.

In 1953, Mayor Impellitteri proclaimed that the week of 31 August would be 'Rodgers and Hammerstein Week' in New York. A revival of *Oklahoma!* at New York City Centre had brought the total of Rodgers and Hammerstein shows in town to four, *South Pacific, The King and I* and *Me and Juliet* completing the quartet. There were presentations

Rodgers and Hammerstein receiving yet another award, this time the Alexander Hamilton Award, April 1956. LFG

of scrolls, and later in the year more honours: doctorates, elections to the boards of trustees, directorships, awards, dinners. Dick and Oscar appeared in an MGM documentary about the Broadway stage called *Main Street to Broadway*, for which they wrote a song 'There's music in you' which was sung by Mary Martin. There was a 'Person to Person' TV appearance by Dick and Dorothy Rodgers, Ed Murrow interviewing. Both men, but especially Rodgers, were honoured as no song-writing team in the history of the theatre had ever been honoured before. They became an institution, and as such, they in turn became benefactors. The Rodgers and Hammerstein Foundation (launched the preceding year on the proceeds of the sale to *Life* magazine of a Christmas song published on 29 December) was one such venture, established to provide help for talented youngsters wishing to make a career on the musical stage. (The song, by the way, was called 'Happy Christmas, little friend'. It has become—deservedly—forgotten.)

Rodgers now set up in his own name a permanent scholarship to be given annually to a talented musician. Rodgers and Hammerstein financed a scholarship in the name of their publisher, Max Dreyfus, to be given annually to a talented singer. And more, and more. Broadway regarded these benefactions with its customary cynicism, a cynicism best expressed by Irving Berlin when Dick and Oscar established yet another annual scholarship in Berlin's name at the Juilliard School on the occasion of Berlin's sixtieth birthday.

'They didn't do it for me,' Berlin is reported to have said. 'They did it for *them*.'

A St Louis lawyer named David Merrick had acquired theatrical rights to Marcel Pagnol's film trilogy about life on the Marseilles waterfront, *Marius*, *Fanny* and *Cesar*. Merrick aspired to be a theatrical producer (he would eventually create that resounding hit *Hello, Dolly!*) and asked Joshua Logan to see the movies in the hope he might be interested. Logan liked *Fanny* and he and Merrick agreed to offer it to Rodgers and Hammerstein who, to quote Logan, 'were put on earth to do the score'. To Logan's joy and delight, Dick and Oscar were as impressed with *Fanny* as he was. His joy and delight were quickly dissipated when they insisted that the credits begin 'Rodgers and Hammerstein present ...' with no other producer mentioned. *Fanny* was to be Merrick's chance to establish his name. He had put up the thirty thousand dollars for the rights and spent years persuading Pagnol to allow the adaptation, as well as lining up backers for the production. Joshua Logan knew that Oscar wanted to do *Fanny*—'He said he had never wanted to do any show more than this one'—and he put Merrick's case as forcefully as he could to the lyricist. It was no use, Hammerstein said; Rodgers was adamant. Rodgers and Hammerstein would never share credit with an unknown.

Merrick, who went on to become one of America's leading producers, decided to go ahead alone. He asked Sam Behrman to work with Logan on the book, and he and the director jointly produced the show, which had a score by Harold Rome and a cast led by Ezio Pinza. It was a big hit, an ambitious and moving work that Oscar regretted to the end of his days that he had not written.

Rodgers and Hammerstein's next project came to them from Cy Feuer and Ernie Martin. Feuer had been head of the so-called Music Department at Republic Pictures, the renowned low-budget studio which gave the world the movies of Vera Hruba Ralston, and Martin was a former television executive. After the war they teamed up and decided to get into producing musicals. They approached Howard Reinheimer and persuaded him to option them the rights of Brandon Thomas's classic farce *Charley's Aunt*, with the intention of turning it into a musical with a score by Frank Loesser. Since Loesser had a big name as a lyricist (for such songs as 'Two sleepy people', 'Slow boat to China', 'Praise the Lord and pass the ammunition' and 'I wish I didn't love you so') but had none at all as a composer, Feuer and Martin were getting nowhere fast until they enlisted the aid of Rodgers and Hammerstein through lawyer Reinheimer. The new producing team had no track record, but Dick and Oscar had enough faith in them— and more especially in Loesser—to take two investment units in the projected show. Once they had the names of Rodgers and Hammerstein on their list of backers, Feuer and Martin were in business. With Ray Bolger in the lead and George Abbott directing, *Where's Charley?* was an unqualified hit, and Feuer and Martin went on to further triumphs which included *Guys and Dolls*, *The Boy Friend* and Cole Porter's *Can Can*.

All producers have ideas for shows. Some of them jell, and some do not. Rodgers and Hammerstein, as we have seen, considered and rejected *Tevye's Daughters*, concluding that there wasn't a musical in it. They also considered and rejected George Bernard Shaw's *Pygmalion*, which Lerner and Loewe transformed into *My Fair Lady*, and James Michener's second book, *Sayonara*, which Joshua Logan made into a movie. Feuer and Martin, too, had their near misses. They worked for a long time on a show with a young composer named Meredith Willson, whom Loesser had brought to them. No dice. Willson went elsewhere with what was to become *The Music Man*.

Feuer and Martin had another idea: a musical based on John Steinbeck's 1945 novel *Cannery Row*, with music and lyrics by Frank Loesser and the author producing the libretto. Steinbeck liked the idea and went to work, but Loesser baulked. He had a dream about a show which would be closer to an opera than a musical, based on Sydney Howard's play *They Knew What They Wanted*. It would eventually take him more than three years to write and produce it, under the title *The Most Happy Fella*, but he was so preoccupied with it at the time when Feuer and Martin came to him with the Steinbeck project that he had no difficulty in turning down *The Bear Flag Café*, as the property was then known.

Steinbeck, meanwhile, had realized that he was on the threshhold of something interesting, and decided to complete the project as a novel rather than a play. 'I was trying to write a musical,' he said. 'When I realized I couldn't do it, I went back to writing a book.'

Convinced that there was still a show in it, Feuer and Martin asked Dick and Oscar if they would be interested. Rodgers and Hammerstein were great friends of the Steinbecks, and anxious to work with the novelist again. The idea appealed to them enormously, and, since Feuer and Martin knew that Rodgers and Hammerstein shows were just that and nothing else, they sensibly offered to step out of the picture, leaving the question of whatever rewards might come to them from the idea to Dick and Oscar. (As it turned out, the question was academic: the show was destined never to make a cent.)

By the autumn of 1954, Dick and Oscar were in London producing the English company of *The King and I*. Throughout the rehearsals they were sent batches of the Steinbeck manuscript hot off the typewriter. Well before Steinbeck had finished his novel (and before *The King and I* opened in London on 8 October 1953), Dick and Oscar were already at work adapting it for the stage.

By the beginning of 1954, Oscar was writing dialogue and lyrics. Steinbeck's novel, which he called *Sweet Thursday*, was published in the spring to mixed reviews which touched off the novelist's short fuse. 'I was just having fun,' he growled, 'but according to some critics this is a serious crime. Some of the critics are so concerned for my literary position that they can't read a book of mine without worrying where it will fit in my place in history. Who gives a damn?'

Well, Rodgers and Hammerstein, for two, Oscar was off to Hollywood and later Arizona to work on the screen version of *Oklahoma!* for which he and Dick were executive producers. Before he left, he and Dick signed Harold Clurman (who had been a performer in and the stage manager of the original *Garrick Gaieties*) to direct the show. By this time Oscar had completed about five scenes of the first act, and about as many lyrics. While at MGM, he again met Helen Traubel, whom Oscar's brother Reginald had seen on a television show and recommended for a part in the forthcoming musical, some of which he had read. The Metropolitan Opera star was in Hollywood to work on a film about the life of Sigmund Romberg called *Deep in my Heart* which must have provided Oscar with a few chuckles, knowing what he knew about 'Rommie'.[4] To make the coincidence even more pleasant, the film was being directed by Stanley Donen, who had been in the chorus of *Pal Joey* along with Van Johnson. Oscar had seen Helen Traubel perform at the Copacabana night club in New York, and he and Rodgers were of a mind: she would be ideal in the part of Fauna, the warm-hearted madame of *Sweet Thursday*, which was now going by the Rodgers and Hammerstein title of *Pipe Dream*. The opera singer grabbed the chance they offered her.

Throughout the summer, Oscar remained with the *Oklahoma!* crew which, true to Hollywood logic, filmed the picture in Arizona. During this time, Oscar continued work on one song, 'The man I used to be': 'During the day and between shots, I would walk out over the prairies keeping my eyes peeled for snakes and my brain alert for rhymes. I found no snakes at all and very few rhymes. By the end of August, however, I had managed to complete one verse and one refrain of this song.'[5]

The casting of principals was not completed until August. Depending on whichever newspaper you check—and only one in six gets it right anyway, according to Rodgers—their original idea was to co-star Henry Fonda and Julie Andrews. They discovered, however, that Fonda couldn't sing, and that Julie Andrews, fresh from her big success in *The Boy Friend*, had just signed a two year contract with Fritz Loewe and Alan Jay Lerner for a new musical they were writing called *My Lady Liza*. It was announced in October, and opened the following March as *My Fair Lady*, setting records that even Rodgers and Hammerstein were going to have to wait awhile to match. So they settled for Bill Johnson, who had made a hit with Ethel Merman a couple of years earlier in *Something for the Boys*. The female lead was given to Judy Tyler, a singer Rodgers had spotted on television.

The partners were facing a much grimmer crisis than any which could arise out of the show, however. Rodgers had been suffering throughout the summer from intense pain in his lower jaw. Cancer was diagnosed and immediate surgery recommended.

With remarkable *sang-froid* Rodgers spent the weekend prior to his hospitalization finishing up the score for *Pipe Dream*. He had several songs composed which needed committing to paper, and he wrote one new song. Then he went in for his operation, determined to survive. He did. After an operation to remove his left jawbone and some glands in his neck, Rodgers was told that the prognosis was favourable. Eight days later, he was out in the park for a ride with his wife. Ten days after the operation, still sleeping at the hospital, he was back at rehearsals.

He supervised them with a handkerchief in his hands to stem the uncontrollable flow of saliva. He could not even speak properly, and his discomfort throughout the New Haven and Boston tryouts was constant. Such dedication is rare, and hard to comprehend, but the truth of the matter was that Rodgers was unhappy anywhere else than

Pipe Dream: Judy Tyler as Suzy and Helen Traubel as Fauna, the unlikeliest brothelkeeper in history, in the 'Suzy is a Good Thing' sequence. LFG in the theatre, working on a new show. Especially when that show was in trouble, and *Pipe Dream* certainly was that. The composer wryly comments today that if someone in Hollywood had been writing a movie about his life at that time, they would have had him battling gamely through his illness to bring the show triumphantly into New York to a thunderous ovation and instant success. What happened was the opposite.

Perhaps Oscar's gently tolerant and optimistic attitudes did not sit comfortably on the shoulders of the raffish denizens of Cannery Row. His story, and Steinbeck's, was about the attempts of the residents of a flophouse in Monterey, California, to marry off their hero, the marine biologist Doc, to an itinerant hitchhiker called Suzy. Neither Steinbeck nor Oscar had been able to do much with it, and *Pipe Dream* suffered from the additional handicap of having opera star Traubel, a buxom lady, trying to convince the audience that she was a brothel-keeper, albeit one with a heart of gold. It might have seemed like inspired casting at the time, but in Boston it no longer looked so cute. There were rewrites and then more; a song called 'Sitting on the back porch' was cut; but still *Pipe Dream* remained weak and unconvincing. They brought it, reluctantly one feels, into the Shubert Theatre on 30 November 1955, where it proceeded to lay the biggest egg in Rodgers and Hammerstein's career.

The songs over which Oscar had laboured so arduously in the Arizona sun (he said that his notes for 'All at once you love her' made a folder thicker than the actual libretto of the show) were, well, adequate. The book was too high-minded for such low-life people and, as the critics were quick to point out, it was minor-key Rodgers and Hammerstein throughout. So, in spite of the largest advance sale of any show they had written thus far ($1,200,000) *Pipe Dream* had the shortest run (seven months) and incurred the greatest financial loss. Once again there was no touring company, no British production, no movie sale. Even the première of the movie *Oklahoma!* starring Gordon MacRae[6] and Shirley Jones that October to generally good reviews did little to lessen their disappointment. They took their beating like the pros they were, but Oscar made no bones about his feelings. 'If anybody else had produced it,' he said, 'we'd say that these are producers we wouldn't like to work with again.'

Rodgers's reaction to the failure of *Pipe Dream* was predictable: he began immediately looking for another project. He was, as he had always been, the driving force of his partnerships. He had wheedled, nagged, flattered, begged or bullied Larry Hart into putting some words on paper. Even with Oscar, who was as disciplined in his work habits as any man, Dick remained the pusher. Perhaps he could not stop; perhaps, as he has said, he wouldn't know what to do with himself if he wasn't writing for the stage. Paradoxically, it might very well have been his insistence upon their doing shows at this time which contributed to their lack of success. We have seen how Rodgers vetoed a number of projects, some of which Oscar was crazy about; they had also taken on themes which they were far from ideally suited to. Additionally, Oscar had been confiding to friends that now he was past sixty, he would like to spend more time with his large and noisy family— three children by both his marriages, two stepchildren and their further nine children—and less time writing. He was no longer dependent on his pen for a livelihood. There was the farm, and plenty of theatrical committees, if he wanted something to do. Rodgers, anxious to work, had stirred him into action twice following *The King and I* and on shows which had been considerably less than successful. Maybe they both needed a rest?

No, said Rodgers. Mary Martin had starred in a theatrical version of J. M. Barrie's *Peter Pan* which had been so successful that it was televised nationally early in 1955 and again in 1956. CBS Television was now looking for another children's show, and had suggested *Cinderella*. Coincidentally, Jerome Whyte, Rodgers and Hammerstein's business manager (he later headed their London operation) had bumped into Lou Wilson, Julie Andrews's American representative. Wilson's client was the hottest star on Broadway, the Eliza of *My Fair Lady*, the biggest musical sensation since *Oklahoma!* (which it would eventually outrun, as it did everything else until *Fiddler on the Roof* came along). Julie was interested in doing a television spectacular, Wilson said. Did Jerry Whyte think Rodgers and Hammerstein might be interested in writing one for her? 'There's only one way to find out,' Whyte said. 'Ask them'.

The combination of Julie Andrews, Rodgers and Hammerstein, and *Cinderella* was a natural, and CBS snapped it up, scheduling for it a television hookup of proportions hitherto undreamed-of in the medium. They paid Rodgers and Hammerstein's $300,000 fee without blinking, and the partners went to work on the project. Oscar decided early on that he wasn't going to 'trick up' the traditional fairy story, changing Cinders to a Macy's shopgirl and such. It would be—except for presenting the Ugly Sisters as comic, rather than cruel characters—the story with which everyone was familiar. Music would marry the characters to the dialogue in a way that had not been done before.

Dick and Oscar were later to remark that writing the television show took them longer (six months in the writing, and ten more weeks of rehearsals and tryouts) and required more music (fourteen songs and various other transitional music) than a full-scale Broadway show. Prior to the transmission, Dick and Oscar staged two full productions of the show which were recorded by kinescope (they were a year too soon for videotape). After these equivalents of New Haven and Boston try-outs (they performed without an audience, however) they did such re-writing as they felt necessary. One song 'If I weren't king' was cut, and they were ready. The show was telecast on the fourteenth anniversary of the première of *Oklahoma!*, 31 March 1957.

With Howard Lindsay (that same Howard Lindsay who had co-authored and starred in *Life with Father* and who would soon collaborate with Dick and Oscar on their last show together) in the rôle of the King, Dorothy Stickney (Lindsay's wife) as the Queen, Ilka Chase as Cin-derella's stepmother, Kaye Ballard and Alice Ghostley as the stepsisters, *Cinderella* was in good hands. Julie Andrews was a delightful Cinders; Edith Adams her Fairy Godmother; and a newcomer aptly named Jon Cypher was her Prince Charming. The songs Rodgers and Hammer-stein had given them included 'A lovely night' and 'Do I love you because you're beautiful?' and among Rodgers's instrumental pieces were a march, a gavotte and a sweeping waltz to be played at the Ball.

Between 8.00 p.m. and 9.00 p.m. that March night *Cinderella* was transmitted, via a chain of 245 stations, to what was probably the lar-gest TV audience ever assembled up to that time. According to CBS the programme was seen by 107,000,000 viewers, which was more people than had seen every one of the preceding Rodgers and Hammer-stein shows combined. The following year Harold Fielding adapted the show and presented it at the London Coliseum for the Christmas season, with Tommy Steele as 'Buttons' and three songs from *Me and Juliet* interpolated into the score, one of which was 'No other love'. Seven years later, CBS filmed the show again, with a new cast that included Walter Pidgeon and Ginger Rogers as the King and Queen, Celeste Holm as the Fairy Godmother, and Lesley Ann Warren as Cinderella. All of the original score, plus 'Loneliness of evening' which had been written for *South Pacific* and cut, was used. *Cinderella* has become an annual event on American television ever since.

In 1958 another of the theatrical Fields family came into the life of Rodgers and Hammerstein. They had worked with Herb Fields and his sister Dorothy, but never with Joe Fields, who had become a theatri-

Various forms of strain, pain and disdain during auditions for *The Flower Drum Song*. LFG

Rodgers's face looks like a sour apple when he is making a decision, says Joshua Logan. He appears to be making one here at rehearsals of *The Flower Drum Song* with producer Joseph Fields. LFG

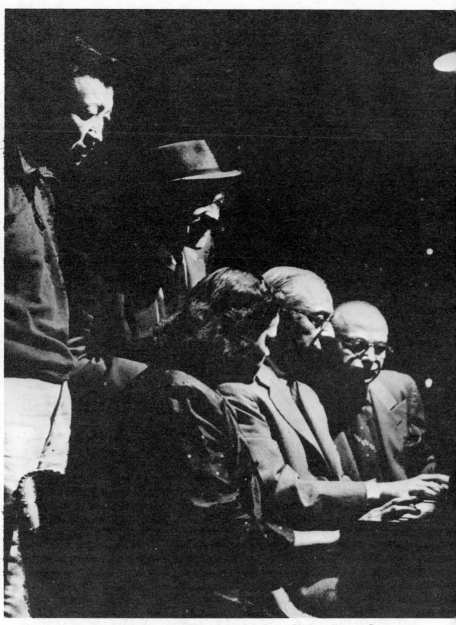

Rehearsing *The Flower Drum Song* Larry Blyden, director Gene
Kelly, pianist Trude Rittman, Rodgers and Fields. LFG

cal producer like his father before him. Joe was responsible for such shows as *My Sister Eileen*, *Wonderful Town* and the wartime comedy *The Doughgirls* and early in 1958 he was in Hollywood trying to produce a movie based on the Peter de Vries novel *The Tunnel of Love*. Fields was having the usual trouble: both stars wanted 100 per cent of the gross, and the producer was contemplating introducing a new system, the 300 per cent gross. That way, he reasoned, the stars could have 100 per cent each and Uncle Sam could take the rest. (The movie was eventually released starring Doris Day, Richard Widmark and Gig Young, although it is doubtful if anyone now cares. Precious few did at the time.)

Simultaneously, Fields was negotiating the purchase of dramatic rights in a novel published the preceding autumn to much acclaim, C. Y. Lee's *The Flower Drum Song*. Chin Lee's agent, Ann Elmo, agreed to a deal, and Fields mentioned the book to Oscar Hammerstein, who was in town supervising the filming of *South Pacific*. Oscar liked the sound of the title, and asked Fields to send a copy over to his hotel.

South Pacific was giving him his share of troubles. Mitzi Gaynor had won the Nellie Forbush rôle coveted by Doris Day, and Rossano Brazzi was set for the Emil de Becque part. Unfortunately for all concerned, Brazzi believed he was God's gift to musical films, and it was a long time before he could be persuaded to let Giorgio Tozzi do his singing for him. In addition, Oscar had a couple of clashes with director Joshua Logan. 'He made me reshoot a scene that had cost an awful lot of money—the one where Mitzi sang "I'm gonna wash that man right out of my hair"—because he thought it wasn't as effective on the screen as it had been on the stage,' Logan said. 'And he was right.' Oscar also rewrote the lyric for the song 'My girl back home' which had been dropped from the original show and which Logan wanted to reinstate in the movie 'because I loved it'. Logan had experimented with a technique of flooding the entire screen with a single colour during some of the solos—notably 'Younger than springtime' and 'Bali Ha'i'—with the intention of introducing a mood matching that of the song. Oscar disliked it intensely and Logan agreed to take the experiment out. 20th Century Fox had assured him that this could be done, but it was not. The film was released in March 1958 and, despite its treacly pace and disastrously self-indulgent direction, was well-received. It was not, however, a patch on the movie of *The King and I* which followed in June, starring Yul Brynner and Deborah Kerr, whose singing had been skilfully and believably dubbed by Marni Nixon. Director Walter Lang had taken no chances, sticking to an almost carbon copy of the

Rodgers and Gene Kelly at a run through of *The Flower Drum Song*. Chin on hand, Miyoshi Umeki doesn't look half as thrilled as Pat Suzuki. but then, Rodgers isn't patting her on the back. LFG

Opening night of *The Flower Drum Song*, 1 December 1958: *l* to *r*. Joseph Fields, Rodgers, Hammerstein and Gene Kelly, whose hat seems to have been a permanent fixture throughout. LFG

stage production, but giving designers Walter Scott and Paul Fox, and Irene Sharaff in charge of costumes, a blank cheque. The result was a stunning, a sumptuous-looking film.

Meanwhile, Oscar had agreed with Dick Rodgers that *The Flower Drum Song* might be much better as a musical than a straight play, and they got together with Joe Fields on a co-production deal. Oscar and Joe would write the book, and Rodgers and Hammerstein would produce the show in collaboration with Fields. Oscar began work, but in July he was hospitalized for a month with a stomach ailment which required surgery. Rehearsals, which had been planned for the beginning of September, were postponed for a fortnight. Oscar was released from hospital with a clean bill of health, and returned to the show with a 'deficit' of three songs due to his absence. He professed himself unworried by this. 'Both "Happy talk" and "Younger than springtime" were written in rehearsal,' he told an interviewer, 'and "Getting to know you" was written on the road. I don't prefer to do them that way, but I'm not unused to it.'

The Flower Drum Song was a lightweight story which pointed up generation gaps in the Chinese families of San Francisco, the conflict between traditional ways and the new American lifestyles. A 'picture bride' Mei Li, comes from the old country to marry Sammy Fong, a man she has never seen, at the behest of Sammy's parents. Sammy, however, is a with-it character who is crazy about Linda, a stripper at his club. He tries to get his friend married off to Mei Li, but Wang Ta isn't interested—he, too, is in love with Linda (or so he thinks). He is blind to the love of Helen Chao, thinking of her as a friend, and his intention of marrying Linda appals his very traditionally-minded father. It all comes out right in the end, of course.

Joshua Logan had discovered a delightful Oriental actress to play opposite Marlon Brando and Red Buttons in the movie *Sayonara* and suggested her to Rodgers for the part of Mei Li. Her name was Miyoshi Umeki and she joined Keye Luke (Charlie Chan's Number One Son in those far-off days of 'Ah, so!' movies) as Wang Chi Yang, Wang Ta's father, Ed Kenney as Wang Ta, Pat Suzuki as Linda, and Juanita Hall as Madam Liang. An actor named Larry Storch was given the part of Sammy Fong, but he was replaced by Larry Blyden during the Boston tryouts, which were extended to four weeks so that the young newcomer could get into the part in time.

Altering the staging of one song 'She is beautiful' consumed a good deal of time. Only when Oscar hit upon the idea of rewriting the song as 'You are beautiful' could director Gene Kelly make it jell. He re-

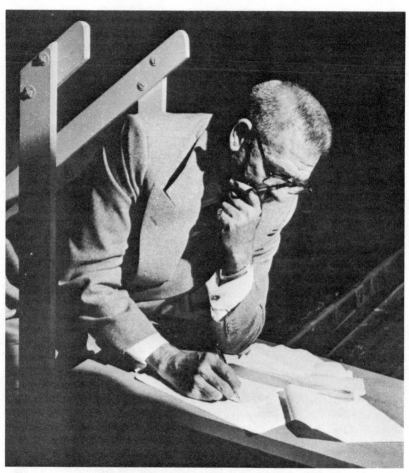

Oscar working on a lyric during rehearsals of *The Flower Drum Song*. LFG

members Dick Rodgers rehearsing Pat Suzuki in singing 'I enjoy being a girl'. She kept on hitting the beat a little late, and Rodgers went over and over it with her until she got it the way he wanted it. 'Exactly,' he said, when she did. 'Don't ever do it better.' Don't ever change it,

he meant. Another song, 'My best love' was cut. Keye Luke was supposed to have sung it, but it didn't work. They gave it to Hall, but
that did not work either, so they discarded it and set to work on another.
Then they decided to have Sammy explain to Mei Li that he was a
poor matrimonial risk, as Gene Kelly remembered.

> In one afternoon, Dick wrote this song 'Don't marry me' and Oscar wrote
> the lyrics in one afternoon. So you see, slow as Oscar was reputed to be,
> he was the complete pro. Dick was always fast, but so was Oscar that day.
> And Dick took me out to the ladies' room, and said, 'Listen to this,' and
> I said, 'It's fine, I'll stage it, I'll have it in the show tomorrow.' 'I'm glad
> you like it,' he said, 'because we think it's terrific.'

The Flower Drum Song was a hit, if not a smash hit, when it opened
at the St James on 1 December 1958. Its songs were good, if not top-
drawer Rodgers and Hammerstein: 'Grant Avenue', 'Chop suey' being
okay 'Chinese' songs, 'Don't marry me', 'I enjoy being a girl' and the
deliberately-awful 'Gliding through my memoree' the Occidental ones.
There were some quite beautiful numbers which are today sadly
neglected, including 'Love look away', a soaringly eloquent Rodgers
melody, and a song particularly dear to Oscar's heart, 'A hundred million miracles'. At least *The Flower Drum Song* put Rodgers and Hammerstein back upon the pinnacle to which they had become accustomed.
The show ran a year and a half on Broadway, had a fifteen month
tour, a year at London's Palace Theatre, and was filmed three years
later with Nancy Kwan as Linda, James Shigeta as Wang Ta, and with
Myoshi Umeki and Juanita Hall repeating their stage rôles.

Even before *The Flower Drum Song* opened on Broadway, however,
Dick and Oscar had already agreed to do another show, on which they
planned to begin work the following spring. It would star Mary Martin,
Rodgers announced, and would be based on the real-life story of the
Trapp Family Singers. Dick was feeling good again, free of the depression which had brought him to commit himself briefly to an institution
during the preceding year. He was looking forward immensely to working again with Mary Martin. He was back on Broadway with a solid
hit. He saw nothing in the future which could stop him.

8. *So long, farewell*

Who are we going to offend—people who like Nazis?
Richard Rodgers

Vincent J. Donehue was a stage and television director who had gone to work at Paramount late in 1956. One day he was asked to look at a German film which had been a big success in Europe and South America, with a view to making a movie in English based upon it and starring Audrey Hepburn. The German film was based on the life story of Maria, Baroness von Trapp, and told of her beginnings as a postulant nun in Austria who was sent to be governess to the seven children of the widowed Georg von Trapp. They were later married and escaped from Austria just before the *Anschluss*, finding their way across the Alps into Switzerland.

'It was in many ways amateurish,' Donehue said of the film, 'but I was terribly moved by the whole idea of it, almost sobbing.' He saw it immediately as a perfect vehicle for Mary Martin, whose husband, Richard, was one of his closest friends. When Paramount lost its enthusiasm for the project and let its option lapse, Donehue sent the German film to Richard Halliday. Both he and Mary Martin loved the film. 'The idea was just irresistible,' Mary said, 'a semi-Cinderella story, but true.'

Halliday began to try to locate Maria von Trapp and her children, all of whose permissions would be required if they were to be portrayed live on stage or in a movie. There was not the slightest doubt in his or Mary's minds that it would make a great musical, and both agreed from the outset that they wanted Dick and Oscar to produce the show.

Baroness von Trapp, however, was hard to find. She was on a world tour, establishing missions in the South Seas. Letters addressed to her in Australia, New Zealand, Samoa and other locations failed to reach her. In addition, the seven von Trapp children were scattered in various places around the world and were proving just as difficult to locate.

At this point Halliday's lawyer Bill Fitelson (who also represented Joshua Logan) brought in producer Leland Hayward, and Hayward became as enthusiastic as everyone else about the possibilities of the story. Together Hayward and Fitelson chased all over Europe picking up hints and clues as to the whereabouts of the Trapp children. By the autumn of 1957, they had all the necessary permissions sewn together. The seven von Trapp children had been traced and had signed on the dotted line. The contract with Baroness von Trapp was finalized in a hospital ward in Innsbruck, where she was recuperating from malaria contracted in New Guinea. Leland Hayward, who spoke no German, concluded his negotiations with the representative of the German film company, who spoke no English, in Yiddish!

At this point, Howard Lindsay and Russel Crouse, the successful team who created *Life with Father, Arsenic and Old Lace,* and the libretto for the Irving Berlin show *Call Me Madam,* were contacted by Leland Hayward about writing the book for the musical. They agreed to write a sixty page outline; if Mary Martin didn't like it, they would bow out quietly. Hayward accepted with alacrity, and Lindsay and Crouse turned their synopsis in soon afterwards. Mary liked it, but wanted to show it to Rodgers and Hammerstein. 'Ever since I first worked for them,' she says, 'I've always asked their opinions about scripts I was thinking of doing.' Although she and her husband were inclined towards Rodgers and Hammerstein as composers, Lindsay and Crouse were still thinking in terms of using the original German songs sung by the Trapp Family Singers, with perhaps just one or two new songs by Dick and Oscar.

When they read the outline, Rodgers and Hammerstein both agreed that it was a good story, but they felt that the idea of using the Trapp songs would be a mistake.

'Either you do it authentically,' Rodgers said, 'all actual Trapp music, or you get a new score.'

'It would be great if you wrote it,' Lindsay said.

'Well,' said Rodgers, 'you haven't asked us.'

Everyone was excited at the idea of Dick and Oscar doing the score, but that was the good news. The bad news was that they were so deeply involved in *The Flower Drum Song* that they couldn't even think about

Oscar in his workroom at Highland Farm: the book-keeper's desk was a gift from Jerome Kern, the sampler on the wall sewn by his wife Dorothy. The last thing he wrote was an apology. LFG

a new show for at least a year. Mary Martin recalled that she went out on the balcony of her apartment with Dick Rodgers one evening after they had yet again discussed the show, and he said 'You know, Mary, it's up to you. If you want us, you're just going to have to wait.' Lindsay, Crouse, Hayward, Halliday and Mary Martin had no choice but to bow to the inevitable: they waited.

Thus Rodgers and Hammerstein became co-producers with Hayward and Halliday, and while they completed the job of putting *The Flower Drum Song* together, Lindsay and Crouse set to work on the book for the new show. They realized that they were going to have to fight operetta every inch of the way. 'The minute you say "Vienna" everybody thinks of chorus boys in short pants, and the minute you have a waltz, you're sunk,' Lindsay said. 'We had to work to keep the story believable and convincing and not letting it get into the never-never land operetta lives in.'

The Sound of Music had a 'family' atmosphere almost right from the start: everyone working on it knew everyone else and the 'family' conference became the accepted method for planning and discussing every aspect of the show. Dick and Oscar would play and sing the songs as they were completed for choral arranger Trude Rittman, music director Fred Dvonch, Theodore Bikel (cast as Captain Georg von Trapp) Mary Martin, Richard Halliday, Leland Hayward, Lindsay, Crouse, or anyone else who happened to be around. Everyone attended Mary's costume fittings; she showed off Lucinda Ballard's charming gowns and the special wedding dress created for her by Mainbocher with the delight of a kid going to a party. The seven children: Lauri Peters (Liesl), William Snowden (Friedrich), Kathy Dunn (Louisa), Joseph Stewart (Kurt), Marilyn Rogers (Brigitta), Mary Susan Locke (Marta) and Evanna Lien (Gretl) made a habit of rushing Rodgers from all sides and hugging him until he said he felt like 'a Rodgers sandwich'.

The composer was at first apprehensive about writing liturgical music. He had had no problems painting musical impressions of Siam or Oklahoma or the South Pacific, but the prospect of composing a Catholic prayer was something else again, for badly done, it could easily give more offence than pleasure. For the first time in his life, he did musical research. Mother Morgan of the Manhattanville College in Purchase, New York, staged a special concert for Dick and Dorothy Rodgers at which the nuns and seminarians sang a selection of works which ranged from Gregorian chants to more modern works by Fauré and others. With this experience to guide him, Rodgers had little difficulty in composing the *Preludium* which opens the show. Indeed, the score seems by and large to have come very easily. There was one verse that he cut because it sounded 'like a damned five finger exercise' but apparently few other problems, unless one counts the problem of trying to write music which gives a church flavour and at the same time creates the feeling of the national background and period in which *The Sound of Music* is set.

Mary Martin, too, got into shape in her own idiosyncratic way. Her voice teacher, William Herman, had her work out every day with boxing gloves, whacking away at a punchbag and singing while she did it. The idea was to strengthen the diaphragm and produce big tones,

The Sound of Music: Theodore Bikel as Captain von Trapp and Mary Martin as Maria. You may remember him better as Zoltan Karpathy in *My Fair Lady* (the movie, not the show). LFG

and anyone who has ever heard Mary Martin singing 'The lonely goatherd' can attest to its efficacy. The star also visited Maria von Trapp. No longer a Baroness (she had taken out American citzenship in 1948) Maria von Trapp now ran an Alpine-style family lodge in Stowe, Vermont. The two women became fast friends, and Maria taught Mary how to cross herself, to kneel properly and to play the guitar.

Rehearsals were set for the late summer, tryouts scheduled; the Schubert Theatres in New Haven and Boston were booked for the month of October, the New York opening fixed for November. The show was virtually complete within six months of the opening of *The Flower Drum Song*, astonishingly fast by Rodgers and Hammerstein's painstaking standards.

'Usually, we take a couple of years,' Rodgers said. 'Of course, Oscar didn't have to work on the libretto in this case, so we didn't have quite so much to do.'

Just how much Howard Lindsay and Russel Crouse had done is indicated by their notes on the scenic production, which were stored for some inexplicable reason among the yellowed press cuttings for the show in the archives of Lincoln Centre, neither credited nor identified. It is rare indeed to be able to get an insight into the mechanics behind the creation of a show, and since they are a remarkably prescient forecast of how the show finally looked (only two minor scenes were added) they are worth examining in detail.

THE SOUND OF MUSIC
NOTES ON SCENIC PRODUCTION

Since this musical does not have a dancing chorus or, in fact, a chorus as such (with the exception of the nuns who will sing) this comes closer to being a 'play with music' than a musical play. We feel this demands that some of the scenes will have to have a somewhat realistic treatment, especially in the distribution of furniture, etc.

In the scene on the terrace we hope that the Captain and Elsa will dance, also the Captain and Maria. This scene also includes a 'step-out' number for the children. At the same time, both the terrace and the living room, which are the two largest sets, must permit the playing of two-scenes and still hold the audience. If they are too spacious in appearance the characters will have difficulty in playing intimate scenes.

In the living room in Scene 8 of Act I, there is a party of neighbours and it will probably open with an informal dance, but the furniture could probably be deliberately moved to make room for this. We liked very much the staircase which was seen in the picture starting on one side of the stage and running across the top of the back as a balcony but the problems of the Lunt-Fontanne Theatre may not permit this.

We are not entirely clear where all of the entrances and exits are in the various scenes. This can only be decided after the stage director and the scenic artist have all met in conference.

Act I, Scene I: THE CORRIDORS OF NONNBERG ABBEY

We hear the nuns chanting, and we see groups of them appear and disappear through vaulted arches as different areas of the stage are lighted. Toward the end of this montage we hear the abbey bells and the movement takes on purpose and direction. A nun with a large ring of keys crosses, speaking to other nuns as she passes. Gradually we hear the question they are all asking each other: 'Where's Maria?', 'Where's

Maria?', 'Where's Maria?' This builds to something of a climax as we fade out.

Act I, Scene 2:

We fade in a spot in the forest on the mountainside towards sundown, and Maria, in her nun's habit, perhaps slightly torn, is sitting on the branch of a tree, listening. She sings 'The Sound of Music'. Whatever staging of this number there is will be devised later. Perhaps at the end of the number we hear the abbey bells and see her hurry off.

Act I, Scene 3: THE ABBESS'S OFFICE

This calls for a desk, two chairs, a footstool and possibly a prie-dieu. The scene suggests the use of a window and a door. (These may be made impossible by the problems of the theatre.)

Act I, Scene 4: THE LIVING ROOM OF THE VON TRAPP VILLA

We have imagined the French windows being upstage looking out on the terrace and the Alps. They would be under the balcony, if there is one. There will be, also, entrances left and right, perhaps more than one on one or the other sides.

Act I, Scene 5: OUTSIDE THE BACK DOOR OF THE VON TRAPP VILLA

We have imagined a two-step leading up to the door which has to look practical enough for Liesl to pretend to try to open it. It is, however, never opened.

Act I, Scene 6: MARIA'S BEDROOM

Here a practical window—at least one through which Liesl can crawl—is necessary. There also needs to be a bed and perhaps a wardrobe. At one side of the stage we envisioned a curtained alcove. This scene also calls for a practical door in the upstage wall.

Act I, Scene 7: THE TERRACE OF THE VON TRAPP VILLA

We have imagined the house stage right. The entrance from the house being perhaps the French window we have seen in the living room. At the back is a drop of the Alps, and perhaps this drop is continued around and downstage left for masking purposes. There can also be box hedges stage left . . . to create an entrance. There can be a marble bench to the left by the hedges, and somewhere on the stage, well down front, should be a terrace table where coffee can be served. It may be this set should have a garden wall to make for some intimacy. There will be some remarks about this drop when we discuss Act II, Scene I.

Act I, Scene 8: THE VON TRAPP LIVING ROOM

It is the occasion of a small party given in honour of Elsa, to which some of the neighbours have been invited. This may open with a dance.

Act I, Scene 9: WE ARE BACK IN THE ABBESS'S OFFICE, THE SAME AS ACT I, SCENE 3.

Act II, Scene 1: THE TERRACE OF THE VON TRAPP VILLA

(THE SAME AS ACT I, SCENE 7)

In this scene we go into twilight, and on the mountains on the backdrop we want the effect of one or more bonfires in the shape of swastikas. This can be on St John's Eve, June 23, or perhaps the bonfires may be a personal warning to Captain von Trapp.

The Sound of Music: Captain von Trapp (Theodore Bikel) and Maria (Mary Martin) dance the 'Laendler' at a party given to honour his fiancée, and the Captain realizes he may be making a mistake because he is falling in love with Maria. Well, it was that kind of show. LFG.

Act II, Scene 2: A SCENE IN THE ABBEY
>It could be the Abbess's office. It is in this scene that Maria is being dressed for her wedding.

Act II, Scene 3: A SCENE IN THE ABBEY
>There is a drop of latticework behind which the nuns are looking into the church watching the wedding. The wedding is, of course, taking place where the audience is sitting.

Act II, Scene 4: THE LIVING ROOM OF THE VON TRAPP VILLA
>It is in this scene that the Trapp family including both Maria and the Captain, start to sing the song they would sing in the festival. We dim out during the song, they continue to sing and when we dim up they are singing in front of a rich velour drop which should suggest to the audience that they are now singing in the contest in the festival hall.

Act II, Scene 5: THE ABBESS'S OFFICE
>We would like to see over the walls of the office again the backdrop of the Alps. It may be that we should have the same effect in Act I, Scenes 3 and 9. In this particular scene, however, we have hoped that we might see the headlights of automobiles up and down and along roads through the mountains perhaps even suggesting that one car is being pursued and headed off by others.

Act II, Scene 6: THE FINALE
>It may well be we will want to suggest that this is high in the Alps on the Swiss border.

With so detailed a blueprint to guide them, Dick and Oscar had no difficulty in finding melodies for most of the spots they needed. The first scene opened, as Lindsay and Crouse had indicated, with the 'Preludium' Rodgers had written after his sessions at Manhattanville and segued beautifully into the first major song, 'The sound of music'. In the original film, Maria had made her entrance sliding down a banister, to the dismay of the assembled nuns. For the show, the fade in on the forested mountainside, with Mary Martin in her tree, regretting that her day in the hills has come to an end, was infinitely more effective. In the third scene, the Mother Abbess and Sisters Margaretta, Berthe and Sophia wonder 'What are we going to do about Maria?' 'How do you catch a moonbeam in your hand?' they sigh, knowing the task is hopeless. So it is decided that perhaps Maria should go to live outside the Abbey for a while, as governess to the motherless von Trapp children. The Mother Abbess cheers Maria up by reminding her of some of the lovely things they both like in the song 'My favourite things'. (In the movie, and perhaps more effectively, Maria sings this song to the children.) An additional transition scene set in the corridor of the Abbey was added later between the original scenes three and four, but everyone will remember the overburdened Maria, guitar around her neck, arriving at the von Trapp villa and teaching the children the

Mary Martin and the children in *The Sound of Music*. On the night
Oscar died they had to perform just as if he hadn't. CP

Maria (Julie Andrews) sings 'My Favourite Things' to the
children in *The Sound of Music* (20th Century Fox, 1965, prod. and
dir. Robert Wise). They are from *l.* to *r.* Duane Chase (Kurt)
Charmian Carr (Liesl) Nicholas Nammond (Friedrich) Heather
Menzies (Louisa) Kym Karath (Gretl) Angela Cartwright
(Brigitta) and Debbie Turner (Marta). 20TH CENTURY FOX.

rudiments of the musical scale in 'Do-re-mi'. Scene five (six in the final version) had the oldest von Trapp girl, Liesl (played by Lauri Peters) secretly meeting her boyfriend behind the villa. Rolf (played originally by Brian Davies, and two years later by a newcomer named Jon Voight who would go on to fame and fortune as the drifting *Midnight Cowboy*) and Liesl sing 'Sixteen going on seventeen' in this scene. The next sequence is set in Maria's bedroom. A thunderstorm brings the frightened children to her, and Dick and Oscar managed to demonstrate the growing affection between her and the children with the whimsical story of 'The lonely goatherd'. The scene on the terrace provided an opportunity for Captain von Trapp, his fiancée Elsa, and their old friend Max (Elsa was played by Marion Marlowe, Max by Kurt Kaznar) to comment on the creeping horror of Nazism threatening their homeland ('How can love survive?') and for a reprise of the title song by the Captain, Maria and the children.

The party in the living-room contains the charming sequence where Maria and the Captain dance the *Laendler* and realize the growing affection between them. The children perform their party piece 'So long, farewell', each disappearing in order of size during its singing. In the final scene of the first act (again, Lindsay and Crouse inserted a transitional scene set in the abbey corridors) Maria has returned to the abbey, and confesses her love for the Captain. The Mother Abbess reassures her, singing the moving 'Climb ev'ry mountain'.

Rodgers and Hammerstein dispensed with tradition again, in their now-usual no-nonsense fashion, by adding only two new numbers—and both of them completely minor ones—in the second act. Every other musical piece was a reprise of something already heard. The first scene of Act II opened with the Captain, Max and Elsa singing 'No way to stop it', a song really inserted to supplement the dialogue in a musical way. During the rehearsals, they realized that although the Captain and Maria were by now obviously in love, they had no duet. 'We didn't have anything until they wrote "An ordinary couple",' Mary Martin said. 'I never was happy singing it. It went downhill. I liked the lyrics but I never did like the music.'

As rehearsals got under way, Oscar Hammerstein went once again into hospital, ostensibly to be operated on for an ulcer. He had been complaining throughout the writing of the score of a recurrence of the stomach pains for which he had been operated on the preceding July. After exploratory surgery, his wife and Dick and Dorothy Rodgers were told the grim news: Oscar had a malignant cancer from which the chances of recovery were nil. It proved impossible to keep the truth from him; and once he knew it, Oscar accepted it with equanimity and told his wife and his partner that he intended to go on working as long as he could.

'It was typical of Oscar that he didn't tell anyone,' Lucinda Ballard says. 'I don't think he wanted anyone to know, I remember him singing "My favourite things" in that darling croaky voice of his. Everyone knew he wasn't well, of course, but nobody knew that he'd been told he had six months to live. We all worked harder on *The Sound of Music* than we ever had before, because we all loved Oscar and we missed him so dreadfully.'

It fell to Richard Rodgers to break the news to the cast. Mary Martin remembers how she learned of Oscar's illness:

> They had put in the song 'Sixteen going on seventeen' for Lauri Peters to sing and it was darling. Then, after I (as Maria) married the Captain, they wanted a moment for Lauri and I to be together. This was while we were still in rehearsal, getting ready to go on the road, and we still didn't have the scene between Lauri and myself. One day I was getting out of the car and going into the theatre when I saw Oscar coming out of the stage door. He didn't see me. He was walking sort of bent over—for him— and he didn't look at all well. Then he saw me and he straightened up. He had a little piece of paper in his hand, and he said, 'Here are the words for the scene between you and Lauri. Dick already has the music. We're adding a verse to "Sixteen going on seventeen". I would have loved to enlarge it and make it a complete song, but we'll have to use it this way now. Don't open it yet. Just look at it when you have time.'
>
> Then later on Dick Rodgers came to my dressing room and he said, 'Did you see Oscar?' I said yes, and he said, 'Well, Mary, you're a big girl now, and you're old enough to take things. I have to tell you that Oscar has cancer and it's really bad. He didn't want to tell you himself, so he asked me to tell you. But he's given you the lyrics?'
>
> I said he had, and Dick said, 'Now, we're not going to be sad about this, Mary. We don't know how long he will be with us, but he will work to the very end. If you feel badly, stay in here for a while, and then come out and rehearse and forget it. We're all going to forget it and that's it.'
>
> I opened the piece of paper Oscar had given me. This is what it said: 'A bell is no bell till you ring it. A song is no song till you sing it. And love in your heart wasn't put there to stay. Love isn't love till you give it away.'[1]

It was awful, of course: everyone pretending that nothing was wrong, everyone knowing and pretending not to. 'It was devastating, but we all went out and carried on,' says Mary Martin. 'New Haven, Boston, as if nothing had happened at all.' The tryouts were very encouraging; the audiences responded well to the score and the story. A few minor changes were made in New Haven; the fade-out at the end of the scene envisaged by Russel Crouse and Howard Lindsay in their original book which takes the Trapp family from their home to the festival was altered to allow for a reprise of 'Do-re-mi', and in Boston, the authors took further note of a critic who complained that the ending was melo-dramatic. The writers went back to work adding an extra explanatory scene and rewriting the ending. The original version had the Nazis pur-suing the Trapp family—among them the treacherous boyfriend Rolf—actually coming onstage all jackbooted and swastika'd. They were made into an offstage presence, all the more menacing because unseen.

Lucinda Ballard remembered one amusing incident during the Boston tryouts. It was very hot, and during a break in rehearsals, some of the chorus, still wearing their nuns' habits, went out to get a drink. For a long time they sat in the nearby bar, totally unaware of the fact that outside, a large crowd of very proper Bostonians were gawping in appalled horror at the sight of a dozen nuns with their shoes kicked off, their habits hiked up around their knees, their feet on tables as they smoked cigarettes, drank beer and swapped decidedly un-nun-like anecdotes containing very un-nun-like adjectives! The 'nuns' were hastily shepherded back to the safety of the theatre before a riot began.

On another occasion, a party of genuine nuns was invited backstage between the matinée and evening performance to meet the star, Mary Martin. Before they could reach her dressing-room, however, musical staging director Joe Layton came bustling through, saw the nuns stand-ing about looking understandably uncertain, and tore into them. 'God-dammit!' he yelled, 'You girls know you're not supposed to stand out here in the hall in your goddamned costumes! Now get back to your dressing rooms right this minute and get them off!'

'But—but—but—' the nuns tried to protest. Layton would have none of it, and heckled them for about ten minutes until the real actresses emerged from their dressing-rooms in their street clothes, and his face fell about four yards. Exit one chorus of nuns, giggling.

Advance word on the musical was all good, and in New York the advance sale, encouraged by the reunion of the *South Pacific* team of Rodgers, Hammerstein and Mary Martin, soared over three and a quarter million dollars, a record for the partnership and for the Broad-way musical. There seemed little they could do to improve, and yet Rodgers was still unhappy with the festival sequence. He felt that Theo-dore Bikel needed a solo in the scene preceding the finale, in which the children slip offstage one by one in a reprise of their party piece 'So long, farewell' and begin their flight to Switzerland. Unusually for him, Rodgers came up with the melody before Oscar had given any

The Sound of Music (20th Century Fox). Christopher Plummer (Captain von Trapp) sings 'Edelweiss'. He said acting with Julie Andrews was 'like being hit over the head with a Valentine's Day card'. (His voice was dubbed by Bill Lee, who ghosted for John Kerr in *South Pacific*.) 20TH CENTURY FOX.

Julie Andrews as Maria Rainer in the movie version of *The Sound of Music*. 20TH CENTURY FOX.

thought to a lyric for the spot. Bikel learned to play it on the guitar while they waited for words to fit to it. Rodgers remembered how it happened: 'Oscar was sick and couldn't come to the tryouts in Boston, and I felt that Bikel needed another song. In the plot there was a concert and I wrote a tune that Bikel could play on his guitar and sing. Then Oscar finally got up to Boston and I played the tune for him. He agreed Bikel should have it and he wrote the lyric.'

The name of the song was 'Edelweiss'. It was the last one that Oscar Hammerstein wrote.

The Sound of Music opened at the Lunt-Fontanne Theatre in New York on 16 November 1959. It would run for almost four years, sweep the Antoinette Perry Awards, tour for almost three years and establish new records in London with an astonishing five and a half years at the Palace Theatre. The critics were in the main kind, although some expressed dismay at the saccharine sweetness of the story. Rodgers and Hammerstein had not written it but they stepped forward, as always, to defend it as if they had.

'Sentiment', Oscar riposted, 'has never been unpopular except with a few sick persons who are made sicker by the sight of a child, a glimpse of a wedding or the thought of a happy home. *The Sound of Music* was based on the autobiography of Maria von Trapp. No incidents were dragged in or invented to play on the sentimental susceptibilities of the audience as some critics seem to feel.' 'Most of us,' added Rodgers, 'feel that Nature can have attractive manifestations, that children aren't necessarily monsters and that deep affection between two people is nothing to be ashamed of. I feel that rather strongly, or obviously it would not be possible for me to write the music that goes with Oscar's words.'

At the time of the show's opening, in the usual fashion, Rodgers and Hammerstein made themselves available to the Press for the standard interviews about the show. One of them—among Oscar's last—had him recalling for the *New York Journal-American* the days of his first collaboration with Rodgers.

> I was very conscious that Dick had worked for years with Larry Hart. I admired Larry's lyrics greatly. They were wittier and brighter than mine. In writing *Oklahoma!* his image was dangling in front of my face. I *had* to be witty, and as a result I never had or have since done funnier lyrics.

And today? asked the reporter, never realizing the poignancy of the answer he was eliciting. Do you think you're getting slower as you get older?

I don't think it's that I'm getting old. I'm getting more critical all the time. I was fast in my youth—and not very good. I used to dash off lyrics on a commuter train with no trouble at all, but now I dig, dig, dig. I sometimes think that if I had a bad case of amnesia and forgot that I had been a writer of songs, I would never again do a lyric. I might start one, realizing that I had a bent for poetry, but I wouldn't think that I could ever finish it.[2]

It was Oscar's valedictory statement, made in full awareness of the sentence of death. As he had vowed, he intended to go on working as long as he was able, and that was just what he did. During the following winter he and Dick auditioned for cast replacements, talked of future things they might write together, oversaw the activities of their publishing and producing empire, even flew to London to supervise the London première of *The Flower Drum Song* on 24 March 1960. The end, however, was very near, and Oscar was soon too sick to do any more. Rodgers immersed himself in writing the background score for another television series, this time about Winston Churchill, called *The Valiant Years*.

They met for a final lunch one summer day in 1960. Oscar told Dick that he had given due consideration to the possibility that he might go into hospital yet again for a battery of last-ditch attempts to arrest his cancer, and had decided against it. He said that he was going up to Highland Farm and die there, as matter of factly, Rodgers says, 'as if he had been discussing a set of rhyming alternatives'. Oscar told his partner that he hoped, after he was gone, that Dick would try working with a younger man. He was sure that would be good for him.

Halfway through their luncheon, a man seated a few tables away came over and introduced himself. After asking them to sign his menu, he ventured to wonder how it could be that here were Rodgers and Hammerstein, two of the most famous men in the history of the musical theatre. They were both brilliantly talented and successful men. They had the biggest hit on Broadway playing in a theatre around the corner. They couldn't possibly have a worry in the world, he said, so what on earth could be making both of them look so sad?

Oscar Hammerstein died at Highland Farm, Doylestown, on 23 August 1960. 'When he died it was a matinée day,' Mary Martin remembered. 'The phone rang and it was Dorothy Hammerstein. "Do the two shows, Mary," she said, "and do them well, because that's what Oscar would want." It was just ghastly, but we all did it. I think I broke down on every second line, they were all so much Oscar, and he was gone and none of us wanted to believe it.'

Years before Oscar died, his son Billy Hammerstein had asked

Julie Andrews as Maria and Christopher Plummer as Captain von Trapp in the movie *The Sound of Music*: Rodgers wrote words and music for this song 'Something Good' and another 'I have confidence in me'.
20TH CENTURY FOX.

Roger Dann and Jean Bayliss as von Trapp and Maria in the London production of *The Sound of Music*—the longest running musical in British theatrical history. LFG him to start working on an autobiography. Oscar pooh-poohed the idea, but Billy insisted, saying that if Oscar wouldn't settle down to a formal book, what he ought to do was to write it all down in a series of letters and send them out to Billy, who was going to California to work at Paramount. Oscar agreed, and for about three months, Billy received a daily letter from his father. Some of the stories in them were hilarious, he says, especially those about Oscar's early days in show business and vaudeville. Then work intervened; there were rehearsals for *The King and I*, then another show, and another. Oscar never did get around to resuming the letter-writing, although his son thinks he always intended to. On the night that Oscar died, his family were sitting in his study at the farm. Billy Hammerstein wandered over to the old writing desk that had been a present to Oscar from Jerome Kern, many years before. On it was a sheet of yellow work paper, a note to his son written by Oscar just a few days earlier. The last thing he had written was an apology for never having finished the letters.

There was a simple funeral, attended only by Oscar's family and closest friends. The words of 'Climb ev'ry mountain' were read, and Howard Lindsay delivered the eulogy. 'We shall not grieve for him. That would be to mourn him and he would not want that. On the occasion of Gertrude Lawrence's services he said, in so many words, "Mourning does not become the theatre. Mourning is a surrender to the illusion that death is final."'

That night, in an unprecedented salute to a great theatrical talent, the lights of every theatre on Broadway and in London were dimmed for three minutes while the world he had lived in all his life paid silent homage to Oscar Hammerstein. There had never been such a tribute before; there has not been one since.

The most successful collaboration in the history of the musical theatre was ended. The statistics it had generated were (and still are) formidable. For fifteen years—from 1 July 1946 to 11 July 1961—*Oklahoma!* held the record as the longest-running musical in Broadway history. A record number of four Rodgers and Hammerstein musicals passing the one thousand-performance mark: *Oklahoma!*, *South Pacific*, *The King and I* and *The Sound of Music*. The latter is the longest-running American musical in London theatre history. Rodgers and Hammerstein's shows occupied the Theatre Royal, Drury Lane, continuously from 29 April 1947 to 14 January 1956 inclusive, *Oklahoma!*, *Carousel*, *The King and I* and *South Pacific* racking up a total of 3,842 performances.

Oklahoma!, *Carousel*, *South Pacific*, *The King and I*, *The Flower Drum Song* and *The Sound of Music* were all awarded Gold Records by the Recording Industry Association of America, signifying that the soundtrack or original cast album of the shows had sold more than one million dollars' worth of records. On 24 February 1950, *Variety* noted that $65,000,000 worth of Rodgers and Hammerstein albums had been sold since 1943.

There was to be one further, total triumph ahead, one which Oscar would sadly never see—sadly because it confirmed that his approach to the musical was what the public wanted to see and hear, confirmed Dick's oft-quoted statement to the effect that the only smart people in show business were the audiences. It was, of course, the 1965 movie of *The Sound of Music*.

Within two years of its release, *The Sound of Music*, starring Julie Andrews as Maria and Christopher Plummer as Captain von Trapp, would gross $66,000,000. It went on to outdistance such box office champions as *Gone With The Wind*, *The Ten Commandments*, *Ben Hur* and *Doctor Zhivago*, and remains one of the most successful audience-pullers in the history of the movies.[3] The soundtrack album, released on 2 March 1965, the same day as the film, has become the world's all time best-selling long-playing record album. Up to 1972 alone it had sold over fourteen million copies, which is more records than Frank Sinatra has sold in his entire career. And the strange thing is that the film very nearly never got made at all.

After its forty-million-dollar debacle with the Elizabeth Taylor–Richard Burton turkey *Cleopatra*, and further losses incurred through the cancellation of Marilyn Monroe's last, uncompleted movie *Something's Got To Give*, 20th Century Fox was over sixty million dollars in the red. Irate stockholders demanded new management, and Darryl F. Zanuck was called in to put the company back on its feet. The first thing Zanuck did was to fire two thousand people, and then he instituted a set of economies so swingeing that they reduced the staff on the lot to around one hundred people. He put his son Richard (later to co-produce the ultimate blockbuster *Jaws*) in charge of stopping every project in sight.

One day, Richard Zanuck ran into Irving Lazar, the agent who had sold the movie rights in *The Sound of Music* to Fox for $1,125,000. Lazar was sure that in the present climate, Fox would never make the movie. He told Richard Zanuck that he had someone else anxious to make it, and offered him two million dollars on the spot for the return of the rights. The offer was more than tempting, but pride kept Zanuck from admitting how tight things were strapped. His father decided to go ahead on the movie, and it was a major factor in restoring Fox to profitability. Darryl Zanuck always referred to it as 'the miracle movie' and from where he was sitting, one can see why.

Richard Rodgers wrote two new songs for the film version, putting his own lyrics to them: 'I have confidence in me' and 'Something good'. He is unashamedly delighted by the success of the movie.

> It's the most successful picture that's ever been made and that's very pleasurable. It isn't just a question of money. What I enjoy particularly is what it has done for the un-selfconscious people of the world—the selfconscious ones sneer a little at it. It *is* sentimental, but I don't see anything particularly wrong with that. I think people have been given a great deal of hope by that picture.[4]

A fitting enough epitaph for the Rodgers and Hammerstein partnership, surely. Oscar Hammerstein would have been more than pleased: he would have been satisfied.

9. Finale

'I want to do something good or not do anything.'
Richard Rodgers

For a year, Rodgers nursed his loss. 'I am permanently grieved' was all that he would say, but even grief as deep as he felt at the loss of Oscar could not keep him away from the theatre for ever. As he himself has said, 'I was only fifty-eight at the time of Oscar's death, and while my career had been long and fulfilling, I could not imagine spending the rest of my days reliving past glories and withdrawing from the vital, exciting world that I loved.' Yet with Oscar gone, what could he do? It was too much to make again the kind of adjustment that he had done after the death of Larry Hart, even if there had been another lyricist of the calibre of Hammerstein to do it with. Rodgers certainly did not expect to be able to do it, and set out to be his own lyricist. As a sort of practice run, he used the opportunity presented by Twentieth Century Fox, who had decided to remake *State Fair* yet again. The film this time starred Pamela Tiffin (whose voice, like Jeanne Crain's, was ghosted—this time by Anita Gordon) and Pat Boone, with Ann-Margret and the late Bobby Darin supporting, and Tom Ewell taking the old Charles Winninger rôle. Alice Faye unwisely came out of retirement to play the part of Ewell's wife, and went right back in again afterwards. 'More than just a friend', 'Willing and eager', 'Never say no to a man', 'This Isn't Heaven' and 'It's the little things in Texas' were the new Rodgers songs. Alas, they were not a patch on the five retained from the original score.

Nevertheless, the experience must have started Rodger's creative juices flowing again, for he was soon deeply involved in a couple of new projects. The first was an idea to write a musical for a lovely black singer named Diahann Carroll, whom he had seen in a television show. He remembered her from the 1954 Harold Arlen musical *House of Flowers* (the book and some of the lyrics of which were written by Truman Capote) which, despite a superb score, had lasted only 165 performances on Broadway. Rodgers got the idea of putting Carroll into a show as a chic, sophisticated woman of the world rather than as a representative of her race, or as some kind of symbol. He thought that in doing so he might possibly help in breaking down the racial stereotyping then, and still, all too prevalent along Broadway. It was a daring idea made even more daring by adding an interracial love affair.

Now he turned to his old friend Samuel Taylor, whose play *The Happy Time* Rodgers and Hammerstein had produced. Taylor had since written two more successful plays, both later filmed: *Sabrina Fair* and *The Pleasure of His Company*. Although he had never written the libretto for a musical, Rodgers persuaded Taylor that he could, and they set to work on the story. Barbara Woodruff (Carroll) is an American model who meets and falls in love with David Jordan, a Pulitzer Prize-winning novelist turned expatriate sponger, in Paris. Barbara tries to make him return to his profession, but David prefers the easy life. Finally, she makes him see that he must do it, and he reluctantly decides to return home—alone. They part, as they agreed, with no strings.

Even as Rodgers set to work on the score, he was following the advice that Oscar had given him at their final lunch. It was an open secret on Broadway that Frederick Loewe and Alan Jay Lerner, creators of the fabulous score for *My Fair Lady*, were no longer able to work together. So reverberating had been their last explosion of temperament that Loewe had vowed he would retire and never write another note again. He moved to Palm Springs and, as far as is known, has done precisely that. Broadway matchmakers saw the pairing of the witty, elegant lyrics of Lerner and the lush, melodious music of Rodgers as guaranteed Box Office. So the two men met and discussed a couple of ideas the lyricist was mulling over. One was a musical based on the life of 'Coco' Chanel, and the other was about extra-sensory perception and reincarnation. They agreed that as soon as *No Strings*—the title given to the Diahann Carroll show—was out of the way, they would set to work on one or other of Lerner's ideas.

With Joe Layton (who had worked on *The Sound of Music*) as director, Rodgers worked out a way of taking the orchestra out of the pit and putting it on the stage. 'I wanted them there in order to blend the orchestral sounds with the other elements so completely that they would seem to be an integral part of the proceedings, just as much as the dialogue, the lyrics or the action. I also wanted to eliminate the chasm between the audience and the stage that has always existed because of the orchestra pit,' he said.

He went even further, indulging the whimsy of actually having no strings in the orchestra except for a harp and a bass violin. With Richard Kiley (who later played Don Quixote in *Man of La Mancha*) as David Jordan, the show went into rehearsals. The score contained a number of light and felicitious songs which showed that, even if he was no Lorenz Hart or Oscar Hammerstein, Rodgers could write a professional and even admirable lyric when he had to.

> There's a vast difference in writing lyrics as opposed to writing music. Lyric writing is mosaic work. You have to pick up little bits, little syllables and put them all together painstakingly and, naturally, slowly, which accounts for the fact that lyric writing takes up so much more time. Melody writing, on the other hand, to go into another medium, is done in broad strokes and can come quickly. I found that if it didn't come quickly for me I either went away from it entirely or just put it off and tried again, and then I'd get the whole thing very rapidly.

'The sweetest sounds', with its almost autobiographical lyric, is probably the show's best-known song, but 'Look no further' deserves more recognition than it has had. 'Loads of love' and an ironic waltz called 'Love makes the world go' were the other big numbers. It was a vivacious and romantic score, and when *No Strings* opened at the 54th Street Theatre (later the George Abbott) on 15 March 1962, it was enthusiastically greeted by the critics. Although it was never a smash hit, it had a very respectable seventeen-month run (580 performances) on Broadway, and a little over four months at Her Majesty's in London, where Beverly Todd and Art Lund took the leads. Encouraged by the show's reception, reassured by the critical reaction to his lyrics, Richard Rodgers returned now to the ideas he had discussed with Alan Jay Lerner. They decided to do the story about extra-sensory perception, and gave it the tentative title *I Picked A Daisy*. However, there was a clash of temperaments. Rodgers was autocratic. Lerner's working habits were often as erratic as Larry Hart's had been—although inspired by different reasons. He would miss appointments with the crushingly punctual Rodgers or worse, fail to deliver material he had promised. Unpunctuality Rodgers might have swallowed, but to him unprofessionalism was beyond the pale. When one holiday weekend (which Lerner had told him he was going to use to work in the country),

Rodgers telephoned to find that Lerner had gone to Capri, it was the end. In the summer of 1963 they called it a day, and the partnership was dissolved, but not without any hard feelings. Publicly, Rodgers may have been philosophical about the whole thing, but privately he was incensed. 'How dare this young man cause me to waste a year of my life?' he said to one friend. 'I don't have·that much time any more.'

As if conscious of its passage Rodgers plunged again, and again unwisely. This time it was into the idea of a musical based upon Arthur Laurents's play *The Time of the Cuckoo*. It had originally starred Shirley Booth in its 1952 Broadway production, and was later filmed (as *Summertime*) in 1955 with Katharine Hepburn in the starring rôle. Laurents had always felt it would make a good musical and had at one time even interested Oscar Hammerstein in the project. Oscar had suggested leaving it a few years until people had had time to forget the Hepburn movie, which was somewhat less than a box office smash, but he had died before the project could be revived again. Rodgers knew of Oscar's former interest in the property, and was very favourably inclined towards it. When Laurents suggested that he team up with Stephen Sondheim, Dick again agreed. Sondheim had been a protégé of Oscar's. He had already made a substantial reputation for himself, notably with the lyrics for *West Side Story* and *Gypsy*. It seemed like a marvellous idea. It turned out to be a nightmare.

Sondheim had doubts from the start: 'He [Rodgers] had previously asked me to write songs with him,' Sondheim said, 'and although I didn't want just to write lyrics again, I told Dick I'd be honoured to write with him if a project came up that excited me.' Hoping against hope that such a project never would come up, Sondheim found himself with his back against the wall when he was pressed to do the Laurents-Rodgers show by Arthur Laurents and by Dick's daughter, Mary. He agreed to do it, and that was the first mistake.

They called the project *Do I Hear A Waltz?* The idea behind it was straightforward: to do something that would make a lot of money. That was the second mistake. There were to be plenty more. Elizabeth Allen was selected for the rôle of Leona (the lady who goes to Venice in search of love) after Anne Bancroft had been considered, and Mary Martin rejected. The male lead was played by Sergio Franchi, and John Dexter, assistant director of London's National Theatre, was brought in to direct. All these choices were nails in the show's coffin, as was the decision early on not to have any dancing in the show. It was all supposed to be a musical feast, but it never even approached that ideal.

Insecurities lurking just beneath the skin erupted; cracks which had been papered over reappeared. The show was a mess because it had no real *raison d'être*. By the time they opened in New Haven for the tryout on 1 February 1965, they knew they had to do something drastic. Herbert Ross was brought in to assist in the enormous job of putting some dances into a danceless show, but he found he could make little headway. The factions had polarized. Rodgers was insisting that the rôles be played sentimentally; Laurents and Sondheim wanted a tough, dry interpretation. Liz Allen was in shreds, Franchi sterile: they had nothing to work with. When Rodgers would come into the theatre, everyone would say 'Here comes Godzilla'.

Rodgers himself hated the whole in-crowd atmosphere, and was scathing about many of Sondheim's offerings. One day, out of town, Sondheim came in with a new lyric. In front of the entire company Rodgers said 'This is shit!' Since he was producer as well as composer, what he said was law, so many of the faults of *Do I Hear A Waltz?* must be laid at his door. The blame for Broadway disasters usually falls on poor direction, or poor choreography, a poor score, a poor book, poor acting. Invariably, however, it is the producer who is at the root of the trouble. A producer's job is infinitely more complex than raising capital. He has to see that the right people are in the right jobs, and that they get along with each other. He has to see that every fragment of the show, from the props to the lights to the costumes to the songs to the script to the actors to the electricians to the theatre are absolutely correct. It is his job to ensure that when the show opens, it is ready to open. Rodgers and Hammerstein were sensational producers. Rodgers alone appears to have been less sensational.

It seems astonishing that the mixture of such talents should have resulted in so lachrymose a musical, but that is what happened. 'It was a workmanlike, professional show', Sondheim says. 'Period. And it deserved to fail.' Even so, there were moments when the score made one wish that Rodgers and Sondheim had persisted: a song called 'What do we do? We fly!' that has zest and gaiety and sufficient intricacy of rhyming to have aroused envy in a Larry Hart, and the waltz which takes the show's title is both charming and unusual. They were, however, a long way from being enough.

Do I Hear A Waltz? opened on 18 March 1965 at the 46th Street Theatre, and ran for two hundred and twenty performances, which was far short of what was needed to pay off its $450,000 investment. Rodgers is still reluctant to talk about the experience. As late as 1973, he was asked to comment on a *Newsweek* cover story on Sondheim, in which Sondheim referred to Oscar Hammerstein as a man of limited

Richard Rodgers: his most recent formal portrait. AC

talent but infinite soul and Rodgers as a man of infinite talent and limited soul. 'The less said, the better,' Rodgers said, and said no more.

In 1967, Rodgers was approached by NBC to write a score for a television adaptation of George Bernard Shaw's *Androcles and the Lion*. Apparently undismayed by the bizarre casting—Norman Wisdom was Androcles, Noël Coward Caesar—Rodgers produced lyrics and music for the show, which premièred on the NBC network on 15 November of that year. The songs were apposite but unremarkable.

Rodgers had by now ruefully concluded that he would never again have the kind of long-term working relationship he had once had with Larry Hart and again with Oscar Hammerstein. He saw his rôle now as overseer of the publishing empire he and Oscar had created. If a good idea for a musical came along, he was always open to ideas. So he sat and waited.

Musicals had changed vastly, drastically. The revolution that Rodgers himself had helped to bring about was now paradoxically responsible for his being unable to find another show. One of the major reasons for this was the astonishing escalation in the costs of producing a new musical. Whereas in 1943, something as lavish as *Oklahoma!* then was could be produced for $83,000, *Me and Juliet*, which came ten years later, cost four times as much to stage. *West Side Story* ate up $300,000 four years after that, in 1957. That kind of money up front is a lot of risk to take, and backers were understandably nervous about taking it. Nevertheless, when Rodgers announced that he would write the score for a new show based on Clifford Odets's play *The Flowering Peach*, the auguries were again good. The libretto was to be by Peter Stone, who had just had a big hit with the musical about the American Revolution, *1776*, and the lyrics by Martin Charnin, who had done a couple of successful off-Broadway shows with Dick's daughter Mary, a promising composer and author (*Once Upon a Mattress*, *The Mad Show*, *Freaky Friday*). The musical, *Two by Two*, which would deal with Noah, the flood, and such then-topical themes as ecology, the generation gap and atomic extermination, was announced in June, 1969. In the following month, Rodgers was felled by a heart attack.

He had survived cancer; now he survived cardiac arrest. Indomitable, Rodgers simply will not be stopped. He is a survivor, and at this time he had something to survive for: a new show. He was back at work as soon as they would sign him out of the hospital, supervising auditions, staging, casting. One of his first steps had been to sign Danny Kaye for the rôle of Noah. Kaye's film career, which had begun so brightly with *Wonder Man* and *Up in Arms* at Sam Goldwyn's glossy studios in the late Forties, was floundering. Audiences had seen everything that he could do, and no longer wished to see it again. Kaye was anxious to try something meatier than the rôles he had been getting in Hollywood, and the part of Noah was certainly that: he was required to age from a 'sprightly' ninety to a doddering six hundred and something.

Two by Two eventually ran for more than a year, but not necessarily because it was a great show. In February, 1971, soon after the opening, Kaye tore a ligament in his leg during a performance. He returned to the show with his leg in a cast, and proceeded to adapt the whole thing around his infirmity, riding around the stage in a wheelchair trying to run down the other actors, goosing the girls with his crutch, improvising lines, and altering lyrics and tempos. At the end of his performances—and 'performances' was what they were—he would tell the audience that he was glad that they had come and even gladder the authors hadn't. People went to see the show for the same reasons they had many years earlier gone to see *Hellzapoppin'*: word had got around that you never knew what was going to happen next, except that it would be anything but what you expected. Nothing Rodgers or anyone else could do or say succeeded in making Kaye stick to the original script. In the end, they washed their hands of the whole thing, and left it alone. It is not, however, inapposite to note that Kaye has been conspicuously absent from the Broadway stage since.

Rodgers had plenty to do, although he was not a well man. His throat gave him constant trouble, and his voice was petering out. He persisted, appearing before the cameras for a salute to his old partner Larry Hart when the University of Southern California devoted an evening to the memory of the lyricist,[1] and again for Tony Palmer, who filmed Rodgers for his television series *All You Need Is Love*. In August, 1974, he could avoid the inevitable no longer, and underwent a laryngectomy. Although the operation was a success, it required Rodgers to devote a great deal of time to mastering what is known as esophageal speech, but even that was not enough to keep him away from assisting in the production of a revue conceived by his old casting director John Fearnley and Richard Lewine called *Rodgers and Hart*. Produced by Lester Osterman, Jr, the show opened on 13 May 1975, a bright *Babes-in-Arms*-ish presentation of some of the best-known (and also some of the least-performed) songs in the Rodgers and Hart song book. The show was not a great success, although it was a treat to hear audiences chuckling at the felicity of some of Larry Hart's lyrics.

Despite the limitations placed upon him by his inability to talk—

all he will say about it is that 'sometimes it's a bloody nuisance'—Rodgers was already involved in a major new show by the time *Rodgers and Hart* premièred at the Helen Hayes Theatre. Producer Richard Adler had come to him with the idea of doing a musical based on the life of Henry VIII. Lyrics, he proposed, would be written by Sheldon Harnick, who had done *Fiddler on the Roof*. The libretto would be by Sherman Yellen, who had written *The Rothschilds*. Nicol Williamson would play Henry, and Penny Fuller (who had been a big hit in the Lauren Bacall musical based on *All About Eve, Applause*) would play Anne Boleyn. Why any one of them or all of them collectively should have thought that there was anything left to say on the subject of Henry VIII after—for it was after—Keith Michell's definitive renderings on television (followed by a further series about Elizabeth I of England starring Glenda Jackson, and a veritable tide of books on every aspect of Tudor England 'tied in' with them) is open to conjecture. Putting on a show of such scope would require an enormous investment: millions. They went ahead.

Rex, it was called. It was the story of Henry VIII's quest for a male heir, his succession of wives, his ruthless machinations to satisfy his personal desires and ambitions. 'He is much less of a monster than he used to be,' Rodgers said, during rehearsals. 'It's just our vision of him.' Old pro that he was, he made sure that when Tony Palmer filmed him for *All You Need is Love*, he filmed him playing one of the songs from the score; but *Rex* was dead long before the film ever saw the light of day. The show tried out in Wilmington, Delaware; in Washington, D.C.; and in Boston, before opening on Sunday night, 25 April 1976, at the Lunt-Fontanne Theatre, the same theatre that had played *The Sound of Music* seven years earlier.

The critics descended upon *Rex* and rent it with tooth and nail. *Time* magazine was typical. Henry, it said, was a 'male chauvinist executioner' and they noted that 'although Rodgers is incapable of writing an uningratiating [sic] tune . . . several of the numbers seem more suitable for rocking a cradle than stirring a realm'. Harnick's lyrics confused spareness with childishness, they went on, and Dania Krupska's dances were derivative and few.

The show was a massive and catastrophically expensive failure which no effort of Rodgers's or anyone else was able to prevent. Rodgers felt that his score was a good one, and indeed, several of the songs, including 'So much you loved me' and 'From afar', are as good as any he has written since the halcyon days of his partnership with Oscar Hammerstein. Nevertheless, he should have known, they all should have known, that it just wouldn't work. The trouble was that *Rex* had got to that point where it was so big that nobody could call it off. As for failing, Rodgers shrugs. 'I never take success for granted,' he says. 'If you get up to bat often enough, it's very easy to fail. I've always known that.'

There was a small consolation prize that summer when the Circle in the Square revived *Pal Joey* as part of the 1975–6 season of plays marking its 25th Anniversary, but in that show, too, artistic temperaments clashed, and it was not the success it could have been. It did not altogether lend itself to being played 'in the round', but there was a tellingly pantherish performance by Joan Copeland in the part originally played by Vivienne Segal.

In 1977, Rodgers's seventy-fifth year, he was back on Broadway with a revival of one of his biggest successes: *The King and I*, starring the original King, Yul Brynner, with Constance Towers as Anna, celebrating that show's silver jubilee. Audiences are still as smart as they always were, and a good show is still a good show. The Rodgers and Hammerstein era lives on for one very simple reason: they don't write shows like that any more.

Notes & Sources

The material for this book came from three principal sources: the reminiscences given in interviews with the author between 1970 and the present; from contemporary newspapers and magazines; and from the biographies or autobiographies listed in the bibliography. Where no other indication is given, the quotation comes from the taped interviews.

Newspapers and magazines consulted: *The New York Times, The New York Post, The New York Herald Tribune, The New York World-Telegram and Sun, The New York Journal-American, The New York News, The New York Mirror, The Boston Post, The Boston Herald, The Boston Globe, The Los Angeles Times, The Akron* [Ohio] *Beacon-Journal, The Brooklyn Daily Eagle, The New York Morning Telegraph, Dance Magazine, Cinema Magazine, The Hollywood Reporter, Variety, Time Magazine, Newsweek, Current Biography* and *Town and Country Magazine.* In one or two cases I have taken the liberty of joining together two separate newspaper interviews and making one quotation, since the subject matter is common.

Notes on the text

Chapter 1: Away We Go!

1 Richard Rodgers, interview with Arnold Michaelis, 18 December 1957.
2 ibid.
3 Lincoln Barnett, 'With Songs in His Heart', *Ladies Home Journal*, Nov. 1950.
4 David Ewen, *Richard Rodgers*, Holt, New York, 1957.
5 *New York Journal-American*, 13 November 1959, and Ewen, op. cit.
6 *Green Grow the Lilacs.* Copyright, 1930, 1931, by Lynn Riggs. Copyright, 1957 (In Renewal), by Howard E. Reinheimer, Executor. Copyright, 1958 (In Renewal), by Howard E. Reinheimer, Executor. Reprinted by permission of Samuel French, Inc.
7 Oscar Hammerstein, interview with Arnold Michaelis 9 November 1957.
8 Just for the record, *Dancing in the Streets* folded in Boston.
9 In the roster of Broadway's longest-running shows, *Oklahoma!* today stands eighth (fifth if you count only musicals).

Chapter 2: Oscar

1 From the Introduction to *The Rodgers and Hart Song Book*, Simon & Schuster, New York, 1951.

2 The lyric of 'Always Room for One More' is used by permission of the Estate of Oscar Hammerstein II.

3 *Miss 1917* was produced at the Century Theatre by Florenz Ziegfeld, who had a lot of other things on his mind at the time. He was getting over losing his mistress and principal *Follies* showgirl, Olive Thomas (who had just married Mary Pickford's brother Jack), by consoling Lillian Russell (Diamond Jim Brady died that April), overseeing the building of an ornate swimming pool at Burkley Crest, his palatial home, and pouring gifts (including a diamond tiara and a baby elephant) on his new-born daughter Florenz Patricia. One other item: the rehearsal pianist for the show was a young man named George Gershwin.

4 Marilyn Miller (originally Marilynn) was a former member of the famous family vaudeville act, The Five Columbians. She had a well-known passion for chorus boys and became Ziegfeld's mistress. She had a tinny voice and could not act her way out of a paper bag, but when she opened in *Sally* the audience would not let her leave the stage. Finally she ran down through the auditorium and out of the theatre, followed by the entire audience. They went around the block and then came back into the theatre, where the show was resumed. Those were the days!

5 According to William Hammerstein, it was Oscar who gave Kern the idea for the melody of 'Ol' Man River'. Kern had already written the opening 'Cotton Blossom' sequence, and when he was casting around for a theme to express the unchanging river Oscar suggested he take a musical phrase played on a banjo in the overture, slow it down and use that: it became the first bars of the refrain.

6 Quoted in *Ziegfeld* by Charles Higham, W. H. Allen & Co. Ltd, London, 1973.

7 Myers was the author of *The Blond Beast*, which Milton Wynn and Edward Justus Mayer had acquired the right to stage on Broadway. Larry Hart was its director, and the idea was to stage one performance and invite all the producers to see it—a revolutionary kind of way to submit a play. Unfortunately, the night it was staged word reached the theatre that there was going to be an actor's strike and every producer in the theatre left to attend an emergency meeting at the Belasco offices.

8 Oscar Hammerstein worked on the following films (an asterisk denotes a song of the same title) between 1930 and 1942: *Viennese Nights** (Warner Bros, 1930); *Children of Dreams* (Warner Bros, 1931); *The Night is Young** (MGM, 1935); *Reckless** (MGM, 1935); *Give Us This Night** (Paramount, 1936); *Show Boat* (Universal, 1936); *High, Wide and Handsome* (Paramount, 1937); *Swing High, Swing Low* (screenplay only) (Paramount, 1937); *I'll Take Romance** (Columbia, 1937); *The Lady Objects** (Columbia, 1938) and *The Great Waltz* (MGM, 1938). Other pictures which he either adapted or contributed to include *The Story of Vernon and Irene Castle* (RKO, 1939); *New Moon* (MGM, 1940); *One Night in the Tropics* (Universal, 1940);

Sunny (RKO, 1941); *The Desert Song* (Warner Bros, 1942) and *Broadway Rhythm* (MGM, 1943).

Chapter 3: Dick and Larry

1 According to Philip Leavitt, Larry was also enamoured of the songs of Wodehouse and Kern, his shrine a phonograph upon which he listened to the music of the Princess Theatre shows for hours. He felt sure that he could in some ways do better than Wodehouse and was working on a lyric called 'Venus' (There's no diff'rence between us).

2 The first song Arthur Schwartz was ever paid money for was written with Larry Hart and another fellow named Eddie Ugast. They wrote it over-night for a vaudeville act and got $75 for it (twenty-five dollars each). It was called 'I know My Girl By Her Perfume'.

3 'The Midnight Supper', 'Lady Raffles—Behave', 'The Gown is Mightier Than The Sword', 'Let Me Drink In Your Eyes', 'Will You Forgive Me?', 'The Lord Only Knows' and 'I Surrender' were the Rodgers and Hart songs Fields discarded. The Romberg–Gerber replacements were possibly even more forgettable.

4 Max Dreyfus was of German origin, and his first job was playing the cornet on a Mississippi riverboat. He was a frustrated composer who gradually worked his way up in the music business, from errand boy to arranger, then salesman and finally as publisher—the most powerful one in the business. Originally his company was called T. B. Harms, Inc., but when he bought the English firm Chappells in the late 1920s he changed the name, selling off part of the Harms catalogue to Warner Bros. for more than eight million dollars. His hobby was reading orchestra scores for operas or symphonies. He was in his ninetieth year when he died in 1964.

5 'I think Larry and I got fifty dollars a week,' Rodgers recalls, 'and for the month that I conducted the orchestra, I also got $83 a week, the union minimum.'

6 Sam Marx asked Howard Dietz if Milton Bender was still alive. 'Doc Bender was *never* alive!' snapped Dietz.

7 From the Introduction to *The Rodgers and Hart Song Book*, op. cit.

8 Richard Rodgers, interview in *Cinema* magazine, 1930.

9 'Running Up A Score', *The New York Times*, 29 October 1939.

10 Cohan met producer Sam Harris, librettists Kaufman and Hart, Dick and Larry to listen to a run-through of their score. He sat through it without so much as moving a facial muscle, and when they had finished, got to his feet, tipped his hat over his eyes and, bidding them not to take any wooden nickels, sauntered out without another word. And this was the man to whom Oscar Hammerstein erected the statue on Times Square.

11 Kaufman had one of the most biting tongues on Broadway. With two wives, an unknown number of mistresses, sixteen known collaborators, two Pulitzer prizes, forty-five plays, twenty-six hits, he was credited by *Variety* with one of the greatest track records in the history of the American theatre. His last Broadway show was also Cole Porter's: *Silk Stockings* in 1955. He was visiting Oscar and Dorothy Hammerstein the day the Nazis invaded Russia, and Dorothy asked him what he thought about it. 'From now on,'

Kaufman said, darkly, 'they're shooting without a script.' And when Moss Hart invited Kaufman up to his new and sumptuously-landscaped country home, Kaufman sourly observed: 'This is what God could have done if only He'd had money.'

12 Cecil B. de Mille cast Lucille Ball in *The Greatest Show on Earth* for Paramount when she assured him she could get out of her Columbia contract. Harry Cohn of Columbia had other ideas and handed her a turkey called *The Magic Carpet*, hoping she would turn it down and let him off the $85,000 fee he would have to pay her. Lucy did the movie anyway, but by the time she reported to de Mille her pregnancy was getting to the point where, as the old joke has it, she couldn't do the part for reasons that were obvious. She and Desi broke the bad news to de Mille, who told Arnaz, 'Congratulations! You're the only man in history who screwed Lucille Ball, Columbia Pictures, Paramount Pictures, Harry Cohn and Cecil B. de Mille, all at the same time'.

13 One of the reasons for *Pal Joey*'s 'failure' legend is that it opened just before the outbreak of war between ASCAP and the radio networks, which resulted in the banning from the air of all music by ASCAP members. The score of *Pal Joey* lost its most potent promotional medium, and in that era of 'Ooooo-oo-oo' vocal accompaniments few of its songs became well known. 'Bewitched' turned up a year or so later as a French *chanson* called 'Perdu dans un rêve immense d'amour' and in 1950 became a world-wide hit as a piano solo by Bill McGuffie.

14 Lorenz Hart's net estate was $196,971. His will left $26,828 to charity, $5000 and the life interest in a trust composed of seventy per cent of the residue to his brother Teddy Hart of 333 West 57th Street, $2500 in cash and the succeeding interest to Mrs Teddy (Dorothy) Hart. A life interest in thirty per cent of the residue was bequeathed to Larry's business manager, William Kron of 865 West End Avenue. His brother attempted to prevent probate shortly after Larry's death, charging that Kron had exerted 'undue influence' on his alcoholic brother. It was an unsavoury squabble and a sad end to Larry's career.

Chapter 4: About As Far As They Can Go!

1 Benjamin Glazer (Barney, to his fellow Broadway *bon-viveurs*) reportedly paid Larry $200 to translate *Liliom* because he was too lazy to do it himself. Then he reworked the translation for the Theatre Guild. It's a good story, anyway.

2 Bothered by lyricist Leo Robin's lack of progress, Kern got 'Yip' Harburg, Johnny Mercer and Oscar Hammerstein to each do a song for the movie. Go to the top of the class if you can name any of them.

3 Coincidence: Molnar was also the author of *The Guardsman* which, you'll remember, Rodgers and Hart asked the Theatre Guild to take off to make room for *The Garrick Gaieties*. He died in 1952.

4 Rodgers did not know until I told him that 'You'll never walk alone' was the nasal anthem of Liverpool Football Club and that it was sung by up to 50,000 Liverpool supporters every week. 'It makes me go cold to think about it,' he said, and I still don't know if he was pleased or appalled.

5 The beautiful Miss Fields's career began in the Twenties with such oldies-but-goodies as 'I can't give you anything but love, baby' and 'On the sunny side of the street' and 'Exactly like you'. With 'Don't blame me', 'I'm in the mood for love', 'The way you look tonight', 'A fine romance' and many others, she would have been a star in the song-writing pantheon even had she had nothing to do with the other aspects of musical theatre. She also wrote the lyrics for *Sweet Charity* (including 'Big spender' and 'If they could see me now'). I called her in December 1973, at which time she was abed with a bad back. 'Come back and see me in the Spring,' she said, 'and I'll chase you round Central Park.' Alas, she died the following April, before she could do it.

Chapter 5: The South Pacific Years

1 Hayward's marriage broke up disastrously, and he remarried, this time to Nancy 'Slim' Hawks.
2 Michener told this story at the benefit show staged by the Friends of the Theatre and Music Collection of the Museum of the City of New York to celebrate Rodgers's fiftieth birthday, in 1952.

Chapter 6: Broadway's Miracle Men

1 *The Happy Time* went on to become a musical, with songs by John Kander and Fred Ebb, which opened in 1968. It was produced by David Merrick and directed by Gower Champion, but its score was not a patch on Kander and Ebb's earlier one for *Cabaret*.
2 Second longest running musical is *Hello, Dolly!* (Merrick again); third, *My Fair Lady*; fourth, *Man of La Mancha*; and fifth, as earlier observed, *Oklahoma!* The respective run figures are, 3,242, 2,844, 2,727 and 2,212.
3 Richard Rodgers, interview with Arnold Michaelis 18 December 1957.
4 Sinatra recorded 'Hello, young lovers' and 'We kiss in a shadow' on 2 March 1951. On 27 March, he added 'I whistle a happy tune'.

Chapter 7: Only Human

1 Oscar Hammerstein, interview with Earl Wilson, *New York Post*, 5 March 1950, and another in *The New York Times*, October 1952.
2 Rodgers reciprocated with a 'Happy Birthday, Dear Oscar' page on Hammerstein's 58th birthday, in August of the following year.
3 Larry Adler says that 'The Big Black Giant' was one of the most squeamish-making numbers he had ever seen performed in the theatre, and that at the after-première party, he kept away from the people who were telling Dick and Oscar that it was all superb, marvellous, best thing they had ever done. A little while later he felt a tap on his shoulder and turned to see Dick Rodgers grinning at him. 'Well, Larry,' Rodgers said, 'are you one of those people who say "They don't write them the way they used to"?'
4 'Rommie' was famous for, among other things, his massacre of the English language. He once told Jerome Kern, who was wearing a brightly checked coat and cap, 'Jerry, you look like a racecourse trout!', and on another occasion lost his temper with a rehearsal pianist at whom he shouted, 'The

trouble with you, Miss, is you haven't got enough shows behind your belt!'
5 Oscar Hammerstein, interview in *The Boston Post* 30 October 1955.
6 Jan Clayton tells a lovely story of how MacRae got the part of Curly. Oscar was watching off camera when Macrae performed in General Food's one and a half hour television salute to Rodgers and Hammerstein on 28 March 1954. Jan asked Oscar if Gordie had the part and Oscar said he had. 'Then why in heaven don't you tell him and put him out of his misery?' she asked. 'Well,' Oscar said, 'we'd just like to sweat a few more pounds off him first.'

Chapter 8: So Long, Farewell

1 'Sixteen going on seventeen' from *The Sound of Music*. Music by Richard Rodgers, words by Oscar Hammerstein. Copyright 1959 by Rodgers and Hammerstein. Reproduced by kind permission of Williamson Music Ltd. in all territories of the world excluding the Western Hemisphere and Japan for which the owner of publication and allied rights is Williamson Music Inc. All rights reserved.
2 Oscar's attitude to his work is best summed up in his reply to TV host Mike Wallace's question asking whether he had written 'Ol' Man River' as a protest song. 'No,' replied Oscar, 'I wrote it because we needed it for a spot in the first act.' Incidentally, his widow Dorothy Blanchard Hammerstein has been known to intervene when someone introduces the song as 'Jerome Kern's "Ol' Man River"'. 'Jerome Kern wrote da-da-dada,' she says. 'It was my husband who wrote "Ol' Man River".' And she is right.
3 According to *Weekly Variety* in 1976, *The Sound of Music* lies fourth in the list of the top twenty-five box office champion films, behind *Jaws*, *The Godfather* and *The Exorcist*. Its earnings at that time stood at $78,400,000.
4 Richard Rodgers, interview with Geoffrey Millais, November 1968.

Chapter 9: Finale

1 *The Hart of the Matter:* A Celebration of Lorenz Hart had been staged by the Friends of the USC on 30 September 1973. Among those performing were Geraldine Brooks, Jack Cassidy, Saul Chaplin, Betty Comden, Nanette Fabray, Henry Fonda, Helen Ford, Adolph Green, John Green, Shirley Jones, Gene Kelly, Lisa Kirk, Donald O'Connor, Harve Presnell and Benay Venuta.

The Rodgers & Hammerstein Years: A Chronology

1895	2 May	Lorenz Milton Hart born, New York City.
	12 July	Oscar Greeley Clendenning Hammerstein born, New York City.
1902	28 June	Richard Charles Rodgers born, Long Island, New York.
1913		Hammerstein and Hart at Columbia University (until 1917).
1916		Rodgers's first songs written at Camp Wigwam, Maine ('Dear Old Wigwam' and 'Campfire Days').
1917		Rodgers's first copyrighted song written ('Auto Show Girl', lyric by David Dyrenforth).
	29 Dec.	Rodgers's first amateur show, *One Minute, Please* (book and lyrics by Ralph G. Engelsman).
1919	spring	Philip Leavitt introduces Rodgers to Hart.
	8 Mar.	Rodgers's first published songs from amateur show *Up Stage & Down* include two with lyrics by Oscar Hammerstein: 'Weaknesses' and 'Can It'.
	24 May	Oscar Hammerstein's play *The Light* fails in New Haven after four performances.
	26 Aug.	Rodgers and Hart's first published song 'Any Old Place With You' in the show *A Lonely Romeo*. It was copyrighted on 19 December.
1920	5 Jan.	*Always You* at the Central Theatre. Book and lyrics by Hammerstein, music by Herbert Stothart (66 perf.).
	6 Mar.	Rodgers's first (amateur) score with Hart for Akron Club's *You'd Be Surprised*. 'Don't Love Me Like Othello', 'Mary Queen of Scots' (lyric, Herbert Fields) and 'That Boy of Mine' (lyric, Hammerstein).
	24 Mar.	Rodgers and Hart score for Columbia Varsity show *Fly With Me*. 'Always Room For One More' (lyric, Hammerstein).
	27 July	First professional Rodgers and Hart score, *A Lonely Romeo*, at the Central Theatre (119 perf.). 'You Can't Fool Your Dreams' and 'Love's Intense in Tents'.

17 Aug.   *Tickle Me* (book by Hammerstein, Harbach and Mandel, lyrics by Harbach and Hammerstein, music by Stothart) at the Selwyn Theatre (207 perf.).

17 Nov.   *Jimmie* (book by Hammerstein, Harbach and Mandel, lyrics by Hammerstein and Harbach and music by Stothart) at the Apollo Theatre (71 perf.).

The most successful musical of 1920 (570 perf. at the New Amsterdam Theatre) was produced by Florenz Ziegfeld: *Sally*, starring Marilynn (as she then was) Miller, and including Jerome Kern's 'Look For The Silver Lining' (lyric, B. G. de Sylva).

1921   10 Feb.   Rodgers and Hart's score for The Akron Club's amateur show *Say Mama*. Their first collaboration with Herbert Fields, with whom they also write an unproduced show called *Winkle Town*. 'Manhattan'.

20 April   Rodgers and Hart's final Columbia Varsity Show, *You'll Never Know*. Rodgers quits Columbia for Institute of Musical Art (later the Juilliard School of Music).

1 June   *Say It With Jazz*, amateur musical produced by the IMA, has a Rodgers and Hart score consisting mostly of old songs already written.

'Rommie' Romberg had a huge hit with *Blossom Time* (book and lyrics by Dorothy Donnelly) purporting to be the story of Schubert's life and loves. Buddy de Sylva, Lew Brown and Ray Henderson had given Al Jolson two enormous successes with 'Avalon' and 'April Showers' for his show *Bombo*. Kern's *Good Morning Dearie* (book and lyrics by Anne Caldwell) was playing to capacity houses where they emerged humming 'Ka-lu-a' and 'Blue Danube Blues', while Irving Berlin's *Music Box Revue* was making 'Everybody Step' or at least 'Say It With Music'.

1922   22 Mar.   *Daffy Dill* (book by Guy Bolton, lyrics by Hammerstein and music by Herbert Stothart) at the Apollo Theatre (71 perf.).

2 June   Rodgers and Hart, still amateurs, score *Jazz à la Carte* for the IMA.

Rodgers tours (as musical conductor) with Lew Fields's show *Snapshots of 1922*. Also writes three songs for a show put on by the Benjamin School for Girls (which Dorothy Fields attends).

10 Oct.   *Queen O'Hearts* (book by Frank Mandel, lyrics by Hammerstein and Sidney Mitchell, music by Lewis Gensler and Dudley Wilkinson) at the George M. Cohan Theatre (39 perf.).

Hits of the year included Victor Herbert's 'A Kiss in the Dark' and 'I'll Build a Stairway to Paradise' from *George White's Scandals*, scored by the Gershwins.

1923   7 Feb.   Oscar Hammerstein's first big hit with *Wildflower* (music by Vincent Youmans, book and lyrics by Hammerstein and Otto Harbach, music also by Herbert Stothart) at the Casino Theatre (477 perf.). Its big hit is 'La Bambalina'.

25 Mar.   Rodgers and Hart play *If I Were King* for the Benjamin School.

31 May   Another amateur show by Rodgers and Hart at the IMA:
          A Danish Yankee in King Tut's Court.

25 Dec.   *Mary Jane McKane* (music by Vincent Youmans, book and
          lyrics by Hammerstein and William Cary Duncan, music
          also by Herbert Stothart) at the Imperial Theatre (151
          perf.).

1924 23 Mar. *The Prisoner of Zenda* by Anthony Hope adapted as a musical
          by Rodgers, Hart and Fields, presented at the Selwyn
          Theatre by the Benjamin School's Dramatic Art Depart-
          ment, with Dorothy Fields playing Rudolf Rassendyll.

13 May   *The Melody Man*, a comedy by 'Herbert Richard Lorenz',
          at the Ritz Theatre (56 perf.). Two songs by the boys in-
          cluded: 'Moonlight Mama' and 'I'd Love to Poison Ivy'.

2 Sept.   Oscar has another smash hit: *Rose Marie* (music by Rudolf
          Friml and Herbert Stothart, book and lyrics by Hammer-
          stein and Otto Harbach) at the Imperial Theatre (557 perf.).
          'Indian Love Call', 'Rose Marie', 'Totem Tom-Tom', 'The
          Mounties' Song'.

For the second year in succession Oscar was associated with one of
Broadway's biggest hits, but there were plenty of others. George Gersh-
win not only produced the 'Rhapsody in Blue' but also three show
scores with 'Somebody Loves Me' (lyric by B. G. de Sylva and Ballard
MacDonald), 'Fascinating Rhythm', 'So Am I' and 'Oh, Lady Be
Good!' Sigmund Romberg had another hit with writer and lyricist
Dorothy Donnelly: *The Student Prince in Heidelberg*. 'Deep in My Heart,
Dear' and the 'Drinking Song'.

1925 17 May *The Garrick Gaieties* (score by Rodgers and Hart), at the Gar-
          rick Theatre (211 perf.). 'Manhattan', 'Sentimental Me'.

6 Aug.   A Rodgers and Hart song, 'Anytime, Anywhere, Anyhow'
          in a Shubert musical, *June Days* (music mostly by J. Fred
          Coots, whose best known songs include 'Love Letters in the
          Sand' and 'You Go To My Head') which ran for 84 perf.

18 Sept. Rodgers and Hart's *Dearest Enemy* (book by Herbert Fields)
          at the Knickerbocker Theatre (286 perf.). 'Here in My
          Arms', 'Bye and Bye'.

22 Sept. *Sunny* (book and lyrics by Hammerstein and Otto Harbach,
          music by Jerome Kern) at the New Amsterdam Theatre (517
          perf.). 'Who?', 'D'ya Love Me?', 'Two Little Bluebirds' and
          the title song. Some of the dances were choreographed by
          a young man named Fred Astaire.

30 Dec.   *Song of the Flame* (music by George Gershwin and Herbert
          Stothart, lyrics and book by Hammerstein and Otto Har-
          bach) at the 44th Street Theatre (219 perf.).

A vintage year for musicals: The Gershwins had *Tell Me More!*, 'Why
Do I Love You?', which would become famous only when written by
someone else, and *Tip-Toes*, 'That Certain Feeling', 'Looking for a
Boy'. Rudolf Friml was packing them in to see *The Vagabond King*
('Only a Rose', 'Some Day') based on the same idea Dick and Larry

had used for *If I Were King*. (They got their own back some years later by using the title of one of Friml's songs—the lyrics were written by Brian Hooker and W. H. Post—for their 1932 film, *Love Me Tonight*.) Romberg's *Louie the 14th* was a hit without producing anything melodically memorable, bigger in fact than the show which became the archetypal 1920s musical: *No, No, Nanette!* (book by Otto Harbach and Frank Mandel, and lyrics by Irving Caesar ('Swanee'). 'Tea For Two', 'I Want To Be Happy' and 'Too Many Rings Around Rosie' are still as well known as anything written in the entire decade.

1926 Jan.   Rodgers and Hart write songs for Billy Rose's revue *Fifth Avenue Follies*.

17 Mar.   *The Girl Friend* (book by Herbert Fields, music by Rodgers and lyrics by Hart) at the Vanderbilt Theatre (301 perf.). Songs include the title number and 'The Blue Room'.

10 May   The second *Garrick Gaieties* scored by Rodgers and Hart at the Garrick Theatre (174 perf.). 'Mountain Greenery' and 'What's The Use of Talking'.

20 Oct.   *The Wild Rose* (music by Rudolf Friml and book and lyrics by Hammerstein and Otto Harbach) at the Martin Beck Theatre (61 perf.).

30 Nov.   *The Desert Song* (music by Sigmund Romberg, book by Harbach, Hammerstein and Mandel, and lyrics by Harbach and Hammerstein) at the Casino Theatre (465 perf.). 'The Riff Song, 'One Alone', 'The Desert Song', 'Romance'.

1 Dec.   *Lido Lady* (book by Ronald Jeans based on another by Guy Bolton, Bert Kalmar and Harry Ruby, and a score by Rodgers and Hart) at the Gaiety Theatre, London (259 perf.). 'Here in My Arms' (from *Dearest Enemy*), 'Try Again Tomorrow', 'Atlantic Blues'.

27 Dec.   *Peggy-Ann* (book by Herbert Fields based on 'Tillie's Nightmare' by Edgar Smith and A. Baldwin Sloane, and score by Rodgers and Hart) at the Vanderbilt Theatre (333 perf.). 'A Tree in the Park', 'Where's That Rainbow?' and 'A Little Birdie Told Me So'.

28 Dec.   *Betsy* (book by Irving Caesar and David Freedman, score by Rodgers and Hart) at the New Amsterdam Theatre (39 perf.). 'This Funny World' was the only song worth noting; seven were cut prior to the New York opening, no doubt because they were too fancy for Mr Ziegfeld's taste.

Rodgers and Hart were really into their stride: four hit shows in one year. Kern's only show that year was *Criss-Cross* which had in it a song called 'In Araby With You', whose lyric was by Oscar and Otto Harbach, but nothing else of note. The Gershwins had a big hit with Gertie Lawrence in *Oh Kay!* 'Someone To Watch Over Me' (the title suggested to Ira by Howard Dietz and used without formal acknowledgment ever since), 'Do Do Do', 'Clap Yo' Hands'. De Sylva Brown and Henderson gave the world 'The Birth of the Blues' and 'Black Bottom' in the 8th *George White's Scandals*, but Youmans, Cole Porter and Irving

Berlin produced no show songs of note, apart from Berlin's 'Blue Skies' in Rodgers and Hart's final show of 1926, *Betsy*, which was a flop.

1927   19 May   *One Dam' Thing After Another*, a revue by Ronald Jeans with music by Rodgers and lyrics by Hart at the London Pavilion (237 perf.). 'My Heart Stood Still' and 'Play Us A Tune' (by Cole Porter). Among the cast: Jessie Matthews, Max Wall, Sheilah Grahame.

3 Nov.   *A Connecticut Yankee* (book by Herbert Fields based on Mark Twain's novel, score by Rodgers and Hart), at the Vanderbilt Theatre (418 perf.). 'My Heart Stood Still', 'On a Desert Island With Thee', 'Thou Swell'.

30 Nov.   *Golden Dawn* (book and lyrics by Hammerstein and Otto Harbach, music by Emmerich Kalman and Herbert Stothart) at the Hammerstein Theatre (184 perf.). The songs were and are forgettable; among the cast was a newcomer, Archie Leach, who went on to fame and fortune as Cary Grant.

27 Dec.   *Show Boat* (book and lyrics by Hammerstein, music by Jerome Kern) at the Ziegfeld Theatre (575 perf.). 'Why Do I Love You?', 'Ol' Man River', 'Make Believe', 'You Are Love', 'Bill', 'Can't Help Lovin' Dat Man' and more.

Solid hits yet again for Kern and Hammerstein, for Rodgers and Hart. So, too, for Vincent Youmans, with *Hit The Deck* (book by Herbert Fields, lyrics by Leo Robin and Clifford Grey: 'Hallelujah' and 'Sometimes I'm Happy' (for which Irving Caesar did the words). George and Ira Gershwin had *Funny Face* starring Fred and Adele Astaire. ''S Wonderful', 'My One and Only', 'The Babbitt and the Bromide', 'He Loves and She Loves'; while De Sylva, Brown and Henderson had a hit of *Show Boat* proportions in *Good News*, which, as well as the title song, had 'Varsity Drag' and 'The Best Things in Life Are Free'. There was also *Rio Rita* (score by Tierney and McCarthy, composers of 'Alice Blue Gown') and another *Ziegfeld Follies* (the 21st) with an Irving Berlin score that included 'Shakin' the Blues Away'.

1928   3 Jan.   *She's My Baby* (book by Bolton, Kalmar and Ruby, score by Rodgers and Hart) at the Globe Theatre (71 perf.). 'You're What I Need' was probably its best song.

26 April   *Present Arms* (book by Fields, score by Rodgers and Hart) at the Mansfield Theatre (155 perf.). 'You Took Advantage of Me', which was sung by choreographer/actor Busby Berkeley.

19 Sept.   *The New Moon* (music by Sigmund Romberg, book by Hammerstein, Frank Mandel and Laurence Schwab, lyrics by Hammerstein) at the Imperial Theatre (518 perf.). 'Softly, as in a Morning Sunrise', 'Stouthearted Men', 'One Kiss', 'Wanting You' and 'Lover, Come Back To Me' proved that operetta was not dead, merely sleeping.

25 Sept.   *Chee-Chee* (book by Herbert Fields adapted from a novel by Charles Petit, score by Rodgers and Hart) at the Mansfield Theatre (31 perf.). This, Rodgers and Hart's worst flop, had

a lovely score which included 'Moon of My Delight', 'Singing a Love Song' and 'Dear, Oh, Dear'.

25 Sept. On the same day, *Good Boy* (book by Otto Harbach and Henry Myers, lyrics by Bert Kalmar and Hammerstein, music by Harry Ruby and Herbert Stothart) at the Hammerstein Theatre (253 perf.).

21 Nov. *Rainbow* gave Oscar a part in a bigger flop than *Chee-Chee* (book by Lawrence Stallings and Hammerstein, lyrics by Hammerstein, and music by Vincent Youmans) at the Gallo Theatre (29 perf.).

Operetta had made a comeback: (Rudolf Friml's *The Three Muske-teers*). Messrs Kern and Berlin had no show in 1928, but the Gershwins had two: *Rosalie* (a hit) and *Treasure Girl* (a flop). In the first, 'How Long Has This Been Going On?' and the second, 'I've Got a Crush On You' but they were nothing like the hits that De Sylva, Brown and Henderson had in *Hold Everything!* ('You're The Cream in my Coffee') or Cole Porter in *Paris* ('Let's Do It') or the new team of Jimmy McHugh and Dorothy Fields in *Blackbirds of 1928* ('I Can't Give You Anything But Love, Baby').

1929 21 Jan. 'Sing' and 'I love You More Than Yesterday', two songs by Rodgers and Hart, in the show *Lady Fingers* (129 perf.).

11 Mar. *Spring is Here* (book by Owen Davis, score by Rodgers and Hart) at the Alvin Theatre (104 perf.). 'Yours Sincerely', 'With a Song In My Heart', 'Baby's Awake Now'.

31 May Short movie *Masters of Melody* released.

3 Sept. *Sweet Adeline* (book and lyrics by Hammerstein, music by Jerome Kern) at the Hammerstein Theatre (234 perf.). It gave Helen Morgan a huge hit with 'Why Was I Born?' Also in the score: 'Don't Ever Leave Me'.

11 Nov. *Heads Up!* (book by John McGowan and Paul Gerard Smith, score by Rodgers and Hart) at the Alvin Theatre (144 perf.). 'A Ship Without A Sail', 'Why Do You Suppose?'

George and Ira Gershwin had another success with *Show Girl*, starring Al Jolson's new wife Ruby Keeler, which had 'Liza' among its songs and the ballet 'An American in Paris' among its set-pieces. Vincent Youmans had a catastrophic flop with *Great Day* despite such songs as 'More Than You Know', 'Great Day' and 'Without a Song'. De Sylva, Brown and Henderson did it again: *Follow Thru* (402 perf.) and everybody was singing 'Button Up Your Overcoat' and 'You Are My Lucky Star'—that is, when they weren't singing 'What Is This Thing Called Love' or 'You Do Something to Me', the hit songs from the two Cole Porter shows of that year, *Fifty Million Frenchmen* (book by Herbert Fields) and the revue *Wake Up and Dream*, which starred Jack Buchanan and Jessie Matthews. Among its dancers was Marjorie Robertson, later to metamorphose into Anna Neagle. New talent on the scene: the team of Arthur Schwartz and Howard Dietz, with their first big success, *The Little Show*. 'I Guess I'll Have To Change My Plan', 'Moanin' Low'. There was, of course, one other major flop in 1929:

the Stock Market, which crashed on 24 October and set off the greatest economic depression in American history.

1930   16 Feb.   *The Melody Man*, Columbia's film of the Rodgers and Hart show, released. The songs have been cut out.

18 Feb.   *Simple Simon* (book by Guy Bolton and Ed Wynn, who also starred, music by Rodgers, lyrics by Hart) at the Ziegfeld Theatre (135 perf.). 'Ten Cents a Dance', 'Send For Me'.

20 July   *Spring is Here*, First National-Vitaphone's movie of the Rodgers and Hart Show, is released. 'Yours Sincerely' and 'With a Song in My Heart' are retained. Two others by Harry Warren, Sam Lewis and Joe Young are interpolated.

12 Sept.   *Leathernecking*, movie of *Present Arms* is released by RKO. Two songs by Rodgers and Hart retained: 'You Took Advantage of Me' and 'A Kiss for Cinderella'. Five others, by Harry Akst and Benny Davis added.

24 Sept.   'I'm Hard To Please', 'Softer Than Kitten' and 'It Never Happened Before' by Rodgers and Hart in Paramount's movie of De Sylva, Brown and Henderson show, *Follow Thru*.

12 Oct.   Paramount releases movie version of *Heads Up* starring Victor Moore, Charles 'Buddy' Rogers and Helen Kane. Two songs from the original show retained: 'A Ship Without a Sail' and 'My Man is On The Make'.

3 Dec.   *Ever Green* (book by Benn W. Levy, score by Rodgers and Hart) at the Adelphi Theatre, London (254 perf.). 'Dancing On The Ceiling', 'Dear Dear' and 'If I Give In To You'.

22 Dec.   *Ballyhoo* (book and lyrics by Harry Ruskin and Leighton Brill, and additional lyrics by Hammerstein) opens at the Hammerstein Theatre (68 perf.).

Of the 32 shows which opened in the year (5 less than the preceding year), 18 were thundering flops, among them a show called the *9.15 Revue* which had songs by Gershwin, Friml, Ralph Rainger, Vincent Youmans and Victor Herbert. All of them were eclipsed by a neophyte named Harold Arlen, whose 'Get Happy' was the show's sole bright spot. George and Ira Gershwin had two solid hits, *Strike Up The Band* and *Girl Crazy*, which catapulted a new discovery named Ethel Merman to fame singing 'I Got Rhythm'. The score also included 'Bidin' My Time', 'Embraceable You' and 'But Not For Me' (the last two sung by another newcomer, Ginger Rogers). De Sylva, Brown and Henderson had the year's biggest (357 perf.) hit in *Flying High*, but the songs were unmemorable. Schwartz and Dietz unveiled 'Something To Remember You By' in *Three's A Crowd* (which also contained Johnny Green's torchy 'Body and Soul'), and Cole Porter's hymn to the oldest profession, 'Love For Sale' made its bow in *The New Yorkers*. (168 perf.). Friml, Romberg, McHugh and Fields all flopped.

1931   10 Feb.   *America's Sweetheart* (book by Herbert Fields and score by Rodgers and Hart) at the Broadhurst Theatre (135 perf.). 'I've Got Five Dollars', 'We'll Be The Same'. Lee Dixon, later in *Oklahoma!*, was in the chorus.

18 Feb. *The Gang's All Here* (book by Russel Crouse, with Hammerstein and Morris Ryskind, music by Lewis E. Gensler, lyrics by Owen Murphy and Robert A. Simon) at the Imperial Theatre (23 perf.).

15 Mar. *The Hot Heiress* (screenplay by Herbert Fields, score by Rodgers and Hart) released by First National. 'Like Ordinary People Do', 'You're The Cats'.

8 Sept. *Free For All* (book by Lawrence Schwab and Hammerstein, lyrics by Hammerstein and music by Richard Whiting) at the Manhattan (formerly Hammerstein) Theatre (15 perf.).

27 Oct. *East Wind* (music by Romberg, book by Frank Mandel and Hammerstein and lyrics by Hammerstein) at the Manhattan Theatre (23 perf.).

24 Nov. Max Dreyfus, Richard Rodgers and Lorenz Hart form Rodart Music Publishing Company, to publish the work of Rodgers and Hart.

13 Dec. Rodgers and Hart engaged by Paramount to write the score of a new movie for Maurice Chevalier: *Love Me Tonight*.

Theatregoers had to wait until December 26 to get the big show of the year 1931. It was *Of Thee I Sing* (book by Kaufman and Ryskind, music and lyrics by George and Ira Gershwin). Not a particularly great score (only 'Love Is Sweeping the Country' and 'Who Cares?' are known today) but it was a great show and deservedly won its Pulitzer Prize. *The Laugh Parade*, starring Ed Wynn, was another hit, drawing attention to a song-writer named Harry Warren ('You're My Everything'). Jerome Kern and Otto Harbach had a big success with *The Cat and The Fiddle*, which contained 'The Night Was Made For Love' and 'She Didn't Say "Yes"'. Lew Brown and Ray Henderson, now *sans* Buddy de Sylva, who had gone out to Hollywood to be a tycoon, provided a string of hits for the 11th *George White's Scandals*, including 'Life Is Just a Bowl of Cherries', 'The Thrill Is Gone', 'That's Why Darkies Were Born' and 'This is The Missus' (and gave a chance to a chorus girl named Alice Faye). Arthur Schwartz and Howard Dietz hit the jackpot with *The Band Wagon*, starring the Astaires, who sang 'I Love Louisa', and which also contained 'Dancing in the Dark'. Twelve shows flops, the most predictable of which has to have been a show which premièred on 10 September and closed four performances later called *The Singing Rabbi*.

1932   13 Aug. Paramount releases movie *Love Me Tonight*, starring Jeanette MacDonald and Maurice Chevalier. 'Mimi', 'Love Me Tonight', 'Lover', 'Isn't It Romantic?'

23 Sept. Paramount releases movie *The Phantom President* starring George M. Cohan. 'Somebody Ought to Wave a Flag', 'Give Her A Kiss'.

8 Nov. *Music in the Air* (music by Jerome Kern, book and lyrics by Hammerstein) at the Alvin Theatre (342 perf.). 'I've Told Ev'ry Little Star', 'The Song is You', 'There's a Hill Beyond a Hill'.

Kern and Hammerstein had the biggest hit of 1932 with *Music in the Air*, but it was a parlous year. Prior to September, a dozen shows opened and ten failed—including Vincent Youmans's *Through The Years*. Irving Berlin's *Face The Music* (book by Moss Hart) was a bright spot, with its invitation to enjoy 'Soft Lights and Sweet Music', as was the new Brown-Henderson offering, *Hot-Cha!* but until Max Gordon opened the new Schwartz-Dietz revue *Flying Colours* nothing but the deepest gloom was visible along the Great White Way. 'Louisiana Hayride', 'Alone Together' and 'A Shine On Your Shoes' brightened things up slightly, as did the Kern–Hammerstein show, but for these two successes there were five more flops. Fred Astaire and Cole Porter were the kind of team to sell tickets, and *Gay Divorce* ran for 248 performances (and produced Porter's best known song, 'Night and Day' as well as 'After You, Who?'). A Bea Lillie revue *Walk a Little Faster*, which introduced Vernon Duke's 'April in Paris' opened at the new St James's Theatre, formerly Erlanger's.

1933   27 Jan.   *Hallelujah, I'm a Bum*, starring Al Jolson and Madge Evans, released by United Artists. 'I'd Do It Again', 'You Are Too Beautiful'. Rodgers and Hart also made brief appearances in the film as a photographer and a bank clerk respectively.

19 May   *Music in the Air* by Kern and Hammerstein at Her Majesty's Theatre, London (275 perf.). The only bright spot in Oscar's year.

1 Nov.   Dick and Larry aren't doing much better. Their song 'That's The Rhythm of the Day', interpolated into MGM's film *Dancing Lady* starring Franchot Tone, Clark Gable and Joan Crawford, is sung (dreadfully) by Nelson Eddy.

16 Nov.   Two more of their songs 'Rhythm' and 'A Baby's Best Friend' originally in *She's My Baby*) sung by Bea Lillie in a British revue, *Please*, at the Savoy Theatre (108 perf.).

The only highlights of the musical theatre's year were again provided by the oldest of the old pros—Kern and Berlin. Kern's score for *Roberta* (book and lyrics by Otto Harbach) was one of his best and included 'You're Devastating', 'Yesterdays', 'The Touch of Your Hand' and the best-known of all Kern's songs, 'Smoke Gets in Your Eyes'. Irving Berlin's 'Easter Parade' and 'Heat Wave' enlivened *As Thousands Cheer*, a Moss Hart revue that starred Marilyn Miller and Clifton Webb, who was a 'mauve' dancer long before he became Waldo Lydecker or Mr Belvedere. Everything else in 1933 was disaster: the Gershwins' *Pardon My English* flopped, 'Lorelei' and 'Isn't It a Pity' notwithstanding, and so did Sigmund Romberg's *Melody*. Even Brown and Henderson seemed to have lost their touch; their new show *Strike Me Pink* managed only 105 performances; and when George and Ira Gershwin had a second try in October with a sequel to *Of Thee I Sing* called *Let 'Em Eat Cake* they did even less well than Henderson and Brown. There was only one other bright spot in the whole year. On 5 December, Utah became the 36th and deciding State to repeal Prohibition. YOU CAN DRINK! screamed the headlines in the New York *Daily News*: REPEAL

VOTED. Perhaps 1934 would be better, after all.

1934   1 Feb.   Anna Sten sings Rodgers and Hart's 'That's Love' in the Samuel Goldwyn movie *Nana*.

2 May   Shirley Ross sings 'The Bad in Every Man' (originally 'Prayer') in MGM's *Manhattan Melodrama*, which starred Clark Gable, William Powell, Myrna Loy. The song was published independently later in the year, with a new lyric, as 'Blue Moon'.

25 May   MGM's *Hollywood Party*, starring Jimmy Durante *et al* is released. Three Rodgers and Hart songs remain of the original fourteen: 'Reincarnation', 'Hello' and 'Hollywood Party'.

At this time MGM also releases *The Merry Widow*, starring Chevalier and Jeanette MacDonald. Although all the songs have their original titles, Larry Hart (collaborating with Gus Kahn) has rewritten all the lyrics for 'Vilia', 'Paris in the Spring' and the famous waltz.

7 June   *Ever Green* (now called *Evergreen*) released by Gaumont-British Pictures, starring Jessie Matthews and Sonnie Hale. Only three songs from the original production are retained. Three others by Harry M. Woods (including 'Over My Shoulder' and 'When You've Got a Little Springtime in Your Heart') and Joseph Tabrar's 'Daddy Wouldn't Buy Me a Bow-Wow' are added.

Rodgers and Hart's lowest ebb, but Cole Porter's finest hour, for this was the year he wrote *Anything Goes* (the book by Guy Bolton and P. G. Wodehouse had been revised by a new writing team, Howard Lindsay and Russel Crouse) and in which Ethel Merman belted out 'I Get a Kick Out of You', 'You're The Top', 'Blow, Gabriel, Blow' and the title song. Apart from this show and a *Ziegfeld Follies* staged by his widow and the Schuberts, there was nothing notable except the Schwartz-Dietz show *Revenge with Music* ('You And The Night And The Music', 'If There Is Someone Lovelier Than You') and a clutter of revues featuring such diverse talents as Imogene Coca, Henry Fonda, Charles Walters (*New Faces*), Bert Lahr, Ray Bolger, Brian Donlevy (*Life Begins at 8.40*), Jack Whiting, Mitzi Mayfair, Judy Canova, Martha Raye (*Calling All Stars*), and Hal LeRoy and Eunice Healey introducing 'Zing! Went the Strings of My Heart' (*Thumbs Up*). This last show also contained Vernon Duke's 'Autumn in New York' and in its chorus was a young man named John Fearnley.

1935   2 April   Paramount releases *Mississippi* starring Bing Crosby, Joan Bennett, W. C. Fields, with a Rodgers and Hart score that included 'Down By The River', 'Easy To Remember', 'Soon'.

29 April   Rodgers and Hart's song 'You're So Lovely and I'm So Lonely' sung by Walter Pidgeon in Adelaide Heilbron's play *Something Gay* at the Morosco Theatre (72 perf.).

16 Nov.   Billy Rose's *Jumbo* at the Hippodrome (233 perf.). The

Rodgers and Hart score included 'The Most Beautiful Girl in the World', 'Over and Over Again', 'My Romance' and 'Little Girl Blue' (also 'There's a Small Hotel', which had to be cut and was saved for later).

5 Dec.   *May Wine* (book by Frank Mandel, music by Sigmund Romberg and lyrics by Hammerstein) at the St James's Theatre (213 perf.).

No new show opened on Broadway in 1935 until 20 May, and only three prior to September, when Schwartz and Dietz gave the Schuberts another hit with *At Home Abroad* ('Love is a Dancing Thing', 'Got a Bran' New Suit'). The big theatrical event of the year was the Gershwins' *Porgy and Bess*. It was to run for only 124 performances, despite songs like 'I Got Plenty of Nuttin' ', 'It Ain't Necessarily So', 'My Man's Gone Now' and 'Summertime'. Cole Porter hit a high level again in *Jubilee*, providing 'Just One of Those Things', 'Begin the Beguine', 'Why Shouldn't I?' and 'A Picture of Me Without You' to go with Moss Hart's sprightly book.

1936   11 April   *On Your Toes* (book by George Abbott, Richard Rodgers and Lorenz Hart, score by Rodgers and Hart) at the Imperial Theatre (315 perf.). 'There's a Small Hotel', 'It's Got to be Love', 'The Heart is Quicker Than The Eye', 'Glad to be Unhappy', the title song, and the ballet 'Slaughter on Tenth Avenue'.

17 June   RKO releases *The Dancing Pirate*—in Technicolour—with a Rodgers and Hart score that included 'Are You My Love?' and 'When You're Dancing the Waltz'.

On Your Toes was far and away the biggest hit of the year. Others included yet another Schubert *Ziegfeld Follies* (memorable for a scene in which a young Bob Hope sang Vernon Duke and Ira Gershwin's 'I Can't Get Started' to Eve Arden), yet another *New Faces* (introducing an even younger Van Johnson) and another Vincente Minnelli revue with practically everyone providing the music called *The Show is On*: The Gershwins' 'By Strauss', Rodgers and Hart's 'Rhythm', Hoagy Carmichael's 'Little Old Lady' and songs by Harold Arlen, Vernon Duke, Arthur Schwartz and Herman Hupfeld. The Cole Porter show for 1935, *Red, Hot and Blue*, starred Jimmy Durante and Ethel Merman with Bob Hope in support, and included 'It's De-Lovely' and 'Riding High'. The longest-lived of all the year's shows, however, was to be *White Horse Inn*, which had been premièred at the London Coliseum on 8 April 1931 (223 perf. in New York; 651 in London). In the chorus of the American show was a young singer, Alfred Drake, one day to play the lead in *Oklahoma!* Despite this swing towards operetta, however, there was no work for Oscar. So he still languished in Hollywood, while Rodgers and Hart prepared to take Broadway by storm again.

1937   14 April   *Babes in Arms* (book, lyrics and music by Rodgers and Hart) at the Schubert Theatre (289 perf.). The score was phenomenal, and included 'My Funny Valentine', 'Where or When', 'I Wish I Were In Love Again', 'Johnny One Note',

'Imagine', 'The Lady is a Tramp' and 'Way Out West'.

May   Paramount releases *High, Wide, and Handsome* starring Irene Dunne and Randolph Scott, with music by Jerome Kern and lyrics by Hammerstein. 'Can I Forget You?', 'The Folks Who Live on the Hill'.

2 Nov.   Rodgers and Hart have their second big hit of the year with Moss Hart and George S. Kaufman's *I'd Rather Be Right* starring George M. Cohan, at the Alvin Theatre (290 perf.). 'Have You Met Miss Jones?'

In 1937, social significance was 'in' and the biggest hit was *Pins and Needles* (score by Harold Rome). Harold Arlen came in with a big one starring Ed Wynn and written by Lindsay and Crouse called *Hooray For What!* 'Down With Love'. Schwartz and Dietz tested failure with *Virginia* (Dietz had also written the book this time) despite 'Triplets', 'By Myself' and 'I See Your Face Before Me'. Even a show with Strauss music and lyrics by Clare Kummer, *Three Waltzes*, did better. What did the public want? Everyone was looking for the formula, but only Rodgers and Hart seemed to know it: the formula was not to have a formula.

1938   Warner Bros release *Fools for Scandal* starring Carole Lombard, with screen-play by Herbert and Joseph Fields, and Rodgers and Hart songs including 'How Can You Forget?' and 'There's a Boy in Harlem'.

11 May   *I Married an Angel* (book, music and lyrics by Rodgers and Hart) at the Shubert Theatre (338 perf.). 'Did You Ever Get Stung?', 'Spring is Here', 'At The Roxy Music Hall', 'A Twinkle in Your Eye' and the title song.

23 Nov.   *The Boys from Syracuse* (book by George Abbott, score by Rodgers and Hart) at the Alvin Theatre (235 perf.). 'Falling in Love With Love', 'This Can't Be Love', 'Sing for Your Supper', 'The Shortest Day of the Year'.

Dick and Larry had done it again: they had two of the six hits of 1938. The others were *Hellzapoppin*, that Goon Show of the Thirties; Harold Rome's *Sing Out The News* (with June Allyson in the chorus and 'Franklin D. Roosevelt Jones' in the score, yes sirree); Kurt Weill's *Knickerbocker Holiday*, with 'September Song', and Cole Porter's *Leave It To Me*, in which Mary Martin sang 'My Heart Belongs to Daddy', Sophie Tucker sang (?) 'Most Gentlemen Don't Like Love' and a youngster named Gene Kelly was in the ensemble.

1939   19 Sept. *Babes in Arms*, MGM's version of the Rodgers and Hart show, directed by Busby Berkeley and starring Judy Garland and Mickey Rooney, throws out everything except the title song and 'Where or When?' Six songs added, including 'I'm Just Wild About Harry', 'I Cried for You' and 'Good Morning'.

18 Oct.   *Too Many Girls* (book by George Marion, Jr, score by Rodgers and Hart) at the Imperial Theatre (249 perf.). 'Love Never Went to College', 'I Like to Recognise the Tune', 'Give it Back to the Indians', 'I Didn't Know What Time It Was'.

21 Oct.   Warner Bros releases *On Your Toes*, the movie version of the Rodgers and Hart show, starring Vera Zorina and Eddie Albert, but retaining only the ballet music 'Princess Zenobia' and 'Slaughter on Tenth Avenue'.

17 Nov.   *Very Warm For May* (book and lyrics by Oscar Hammerstein and music by Jerome Kern) at the Alvin Theatre (59 perf.). 'All The Things You Are', 'In Other Words, Seventeen', 'In The Heart of the Dark'.

The world was overshadowed now by the outbreak of war in Europe. Rodgers and Hart had yet another hit, outstripped only by an extravagant revue called *The Streets of Paris*, which featured Jean Sablon, Carmen Miranda, and Abbott and Costello, among others. The hit Jimmy McHugh–Al Dubin song was 'South American Way', sung by the irrepressible Miranda. In December, B. G. de Sylva, now a producer, unveiled Cole Porter's *Du Barry was a Lady*, book by himself and Herb Fields, starring Bert Lahr and Ethel Merman and providing her first Broadway vehicle for a cutie named Betty Grable, who sang a song later made more famous by Sinatra and Crosby in the movie *High Society*, 'Well, Did You Evah?' Porter's gifted score included 'But In The Morning, No!' and 'Do I Love You?'. 'Katie Went to Haiti' and the perfect blendship song 'Friendship'. The last show of the Thirties was one of its biggest (over 400 perf.).

1940   4 April   Rodgers and Hart's *Higher and Higher* (book by Gladys Hurlbut and Joshua Logan) opens at the Shubert Theatre (108 perf.). 'Nothing But You', 'From Another World', 'It Never Entered My Mind'. June Allyson and Vera-Ellen, who had been thrown out of work by the failure of *Very Warm for May* found a home in the specialty ensemble, and other Rodgers and Hart stalwarts included Shirley Ross, Lee Dixon and Robert Rounseville.

1 Aug.   Universal releases movie of *The Boys from Syracuse*, starring Allan Jones, Irene Hervey (later Mrs Jones and mother of Jack Jones) and Martha Raye. Rodgers and Hart wrote two new songs 'The Greeks Have No Word for It' and 'Who Are You?' for the movie.

22 Nov.   RKO releases movie version of Rodgers and Hart's *Too Many Girls*, starring Desi Arnaz, Lucille Ball. One new song added to the five retained from the original score: 'You're Nearer'.

25 Dec.   *Pal Joey* (book by John O'Hara, score by Rodgers and Hart) at the Ethel Barrymore Theatre (374 perf.). 'Bewitched, Bothered and Bewildered', 'I Could Write A Book', 'That Terrific Rainbow', 'Zip', 'Chicago' *et al.*

Oscar Hammerstein's best shot in 1940 was a song interpolated into the Abbott & Costello movie *One Night in the Tropics*, which also starred the ubiquitous Allan Jones. It was he who sang 'Your Dream is the Same as My Dream', written by Kern, Harbach and Hammerstein for a failed London show called *Gentleman Unafraid*. Irving Berlin had come back with a huge hit written by Morrie Ryskind called *Louisiana*

Purchase ('It's a Lovely Day Tomorrow' set just the right optimistic tone for the times.) Cole Porter, Herb Fields and Buddy de Sylva had another smash with *Panama Hattie*, starring the unquenchable Merman, introducing blonde bombshell Betty Hutton (Janis Carter, June Allyson, Betsy Blair, Lucille Bremer, Vera-Ellen and Doris Dowling were also in the cast). 'My Mother Would Love You' and 'Let's Be Buddies'. The all-black *Cabin in the Sky* produced a lesser hit for Vernon Duke, 'Taking a Chance on Love' (lyric by Ted Fetter). And when Paris fell, in June 1940, Oscar Hammerstein was moved to write a poem 'The Last Time I Saw Paris' which Jerome Kern would later put to music.

1941   8 May   RKO releases *They Met in Argentina*, starring Maureen O'Hara and Tim Ellison (also Joseph Buloff) with seven Rodgers and Hart songs including 'You've Got the Best of Me', 'Lolita', 'Simpatica' and 'Never Go To Argentina'.

May   Oscar's poem 'The Last Time I Saw Paris', set to music by Jerome Kern, is interpolated in MGM's movie version of the Gershwin show *Lady Be Good*. Later in the year the song was awarded an 'Oscar' as best song.

Sept.   Rodgers talks to Hammerstein about his problems with Hart.

1 Oct.   *Best Foot Forward* (score by Hugh Martin and Ralph Blane) is co-produced by Rodgers with George Abbott, but Rodgers takes no official billing.

4 Dec.   *Sunny River* (book and lyrics by Hammerstein and music by Sigmund Romberg) at the St James Theatre (36 perf.).

On 7 December 1941, Japanese bombers attacked the American naval base at Pearl Harbour, Hawaii, and the United States declared a state of war. This was the last year of America's innocence; from henceforward she would move towards being the dominant world power of the twentieth century. As in life, so in art: the American musical, too, would become pre-eminent within a few short years, as American culture invaded every corner of the world. The big shows of 1941 were extravagant fantasies like Kurt Weill's *Lady in the Dark*, written by Moss Hart with lyrics by Ira Gershwin. 'Jenny' and 'My Ship' provided Gertrude Lawrence with two solid hits, and a muscular actor named Victor Mature with a showcase that won him a Hollywood contract. Cole Porter hit the jackpot yet again with *Let's Face It*, written by Herb and Dorothy Fields and starring Danny Kaye and Eve Arden, the former making the song 'Let's Not Talk About Love' his own. And Larry Hart was skidding downhill at a prodigious rate; it was no longer a matter of whether he and Rodgers would have to split up, only when.

1942   May   Universal releases three-minute short *Keep 'em Rolling* in which Jan Peerce sings the Rodgers and Hart song of the same name.

2 June   *By Jupiter* (book, lyrics and music by Rodgers and Hart) at the Shubert Theatre (427 perf.). The last complete Rodgers and Hart score. 'Nobody's Heart', 'Life With Father', 'Ev'rything I've Got', 'Wait Till You See Her'.

9 July   MGM releases movie version of Rodgers and Hart's *I Married*

An Angel starring Jeanette MacDonald and Nelson Eddy with three songs from the original production, and 'Did You Ever Get Stung' changed to 'Little Workaday World' with lyric by Bob Wright and Chet Forrest.

23 July   The Theatre Guild announces a musical version of Lynn Riggs's play *Green Grow The Lilacs*, with book to be written by Hammerstein, score by Rodgers and Hart.

A smash-hit from Irving Berlin, *This Is The Army*, which had 'I Left My Heart at the Stage Door Canteen' and 'Oh, How I Hate To Get Up In the Morning'.

1943   31 Mar.   *Oklahoma!* at the St James Theatre (2,212 perf.) (book and lyrics by Oscar Hammerstein, music by Richard Rodgers). 'Oh, What a Beautiful Morning', 'Out of My Dreams', 'The Surrey with the Fringe on Top', 'I Cain't Say No', 'People Will Say We're In Love'.

17 Nov.   *A Connecticut Yankee*, revival of the Fields–Rodgers–Hart show of 1927, at the Martin Beck Theatre, with Rodgers as producer (135 perf.). New songs include 'Can't You Do A Friend A Favour?', 'You Always Love the Same Girl' and the last song written by Hart, 'To Keep My Love Alive'.

22 Nov.   Lorenz Hart dies at Doctors Hospital, New York City.

2 Dec.   *Carmen Jones* (book and lyrics by Hammerstein to the music of Georges Bizet) at the Broadway Theatre (502 perf.). 'Beat Out Dat Rhythm on the Drum', 'Stand Up and Fight'.

9 Dec.   RKO releases the movie version of Rodgers and Hart's *Higher and Higher*. The film, which has little resemblance to the original, stars Frank Sinatra, and retains only one song from the show ('Disgustingly Rich'). Eight new ones added by Jimmy McHugh and Harold Adamson, including 'A Lovely Way To Spend an Evening', 'I Couldn't Sleep A Wink Last Night' and 'The Music Stopped'.

What else did Broadway have to offer war-weary Americans in 1943? There was still the *Ziegfeld Follies*, even if the show bore little resemblance to the original. The Fieldses and Cole Porter had another hit with Ethel Merman, *Something For The Boys* ('Hey, Good Lookin' ' and 'By The Mississinewah!'). A new Mary Martin musical *One Touch of Venus* (music by Kurt Weill and lyrics by (of all people) Ogden Nash). Other musicals of the year included Lerner and Loewe's *What's Up*, revivals of *The Merry Widow* and *The Student Prince*. The year saw a decisive shift in the tide of the war, and there was a buoyant mood in the air.

1944   19 Jan.   *Broadway Rhythm*, MGM's version of the Kern–Hammerstein show *Very Warm For May* (and bearing no resemblance), starring George Murphy, Eddie 'Rochester' Anderson, and Nancy Walker, who introduced 'Milkman, Keep Those Bottles Quiet' by Martin and Blane, who had done extra songs for the movie.

19 Oct.   John van Druten's new play *I Remember Mama* (produced by

Rodgers and Hammerstein) starring Mady Christians as
Mama, Raymond Bishop, and a twenty-year-old actor named
Marlon Brando, at the Music Box Theatre (714 perf.).
Herb and Dorothy Fields and Cole Porter presented *Mexican Hayride*
(481 perf.), and Harold Arlen and E. Y. Harburg did even better with
Bloomer Girl (654 perf.). Just counting as a 1944 show (it opened on
28 December) Leonard Bernstein's musical *On The Town* (book and
lyrics by Betty Comden and Adolph Green, 463 perf.). Olsen and Johnson of *Hellzapoppin* fame had a new musical, *Laffing Room Only*; and
Song of Norway, with score and book based on the melodies and life
of Edvard Grieg, was also successful. There were some great movie
musicals: Rita Hayworth and Gene Kelly's *Cover Girl*, Deanna Durbin's
Can't Help Singing (both with music by Kern) Judy Garland in *Meet
Me in St Louis*, Ginger Rogers in *Lady in the Dark*, and Bing Crosby
in *Going My Way*, not strictly a musical but musical enough for all that.

1945   19 April   The Theatre Guild presents Rodgers and Hammerstein's
new musical, *Carousel* (890 perf.). Book and lyrics by Hammerstein based on Ferenc Molnar's play *Liliom*. Music by
Rodgers. 'If I Loved You', 'What's The Use of Wond'rin' ',
'You'll Never Walk Alone', 'A Real Nice Clambake', 'When
the Children Are Asleep'.

20 Aug.   20th Century Fox releases *State Fair*, starring Jeanne Crain,
Dana Andrews, Vivian Blaine and Dick Haymes, with a
Rodgers and Hammerstein score. 'It's A Grand Night For
Singing', 'That's For Me', 'Isn't It Kinda Fun?', and 'It
Might As Well Be Spring', which won the year's Oscar for
best song in a motion picture.

Movie musicals: *Anchors Aweigh* starring Gene Kelly and Frank Sinatra.
Wonder Man (Danny Kaye), and the first of the 'biopics', *Rhapsody in
Blue*, starring Robert Alda, and purporting to be the life story of George
Gershwin. On the Broadway stage, Herb and Dorothy Fields teamed
up with Sigmund Romberg for the highly successful *Up in Central Park*.
Lerner and Loewe had the unsuccessful *The Day Before Spring*, and other
musicals included *Billion Dollar Baby* (book by Comden and Green,
music by Morton Gould) and *Polonaise*, with Marta Eggerth and Jan
Kiepura.

1946   16 May   Rodgers and Hammerstein present Irving Berlin's new musi-
cal, *Annie Get Your Gun* (Book by Herbert and Dorothy Fields,
and starring Ray Middleton and Ethel Merman) at the Im-
perial Theatre (1,147 perf.). 'Doin' What Comes Naturally',
'I Got The Sun in the Morning', 'The Girl That I Marry',
'There's No Business Like Show Business', 'Anything You
Can Do', 'You Can't Get A Man With A Gun', 'Who
Do You Love, I Hope?', 'They Say It's Wonderful'.

31 Oct.   Rodgers and Hammerstein present Anita Loos's play *Happy
Birthday* starring Helen Hayes at the Broadhurst Theatre
(564 perf.). The play contained one song: 'I Haven't Got
a Worry in the World' by Rodgers and Hammerstein.

Harold Rome's *Call Me Mister* was no *Annie* but it chalked up a highly respectable 734-performance run (and had a huge hit in 'South America, Take It Away') which was a good deal better than most of the other musicals of the year: *Lute Song*, starring Mary Martin and the unknown Yul Brynner (only 142 perf.); Orson Welles produced and appeared in *Around The World in Eighty Days* but the Cole Porter score was listless, and it died after 75 performances, just three more than the Arthur Schwartz–Ira Gershwin show, *Park Avenue*; as did Harold Arlen and Johnny Mercer's *St Louis Woman*, directed by Mamoulian (113 perf.), despite the presence of Pearl Bailey and 'Come Rain or Come Shine', 'Legalize My Name', 'Anywhere I Hang My Hat Is Home' and 'Ridin' On The Moon'. A revival of *Show Boat* starring Jan Clayton, Charles Fredericks and Carol Bruce was successful, as was the Ray Bolger revue *Three to Make Ready*, but it wasn't a vintage year. Movie musicals included the life story of the (still-living) Cole Porter, played by Cary Grant, in *Night and Day*, inaccurate but a musical feast, produced by of all people, Arthur Schwartz. There was also the hugely-successful Larry Parks impersonation of the Singing Fool in *The Jolson Story*, Jeanne Crain and Cornel Wilde in Kern's *Centennial Summer*, Bing Crosby and Fred Astaire in *Blue Skies*, which had Irving Berlin songs, and Disney's *Song of the South*.

1947   4 Feb.   Rodgers and Hammerstein present Norman Krasna's play *John Loves Mary*, starring Nina Foch and Tom Ewell, at the Booth Theatre (421 perf.).

29 April   *Oklahoma!* opens at the Theatre Royal, Drury Lane, London (1,548 perf.), with Harold (Howard) Keel as Curly, Betty Jane Watson as Laurey, Dorothea MacFarland as Ado Annie. Also in the cast was Isabel Bigley.

10 Oct.   *Allegro*, at the Majestic Theatre (315 perf.). Book and lyrics by Hammerstein, music by Rodgers. 'You Are Never Away', 'The Gentleman Is a Dope', 'A Fellow Needs a Girl', 'So Far' and one Rodgers and Hart song, 'Mountain Greenery'.

Rodgers and Hammerstein were outclassed by three musicals this year: *Finian's Rainbow* (score by Burton Lane and Yip Harburg, 725 perf.). 'How Are Things in Glocca Morra?', 'If This Isn't Love', 'Old Devil Moon', 'When I'm Not Near The Girl I Love'. Lerner and Loewe hit the jackpot with *Brigadoon*. 'The Heather on the Hill', 'Waitin' For My Dearie', 'There But For You Go I', 'I'll Go Home With Bonnie Jean' and others. Jule Styne and his new collaborator Sammy Cahn gave director George Abbott yet another hit show: *High Button Shoes* (727 perf.). 'I Still Get Jealous' and 'Papa, Won't You Dance With Me?'.

1948   9 Dec.   *Words and Music*, the story of Rodgers and Hart, as filmed by MGM (screenplay by Fred Finklehoffe, adapted by Ben Feiner, Jr, from a story by Guy Bolton and Jean Holloway (no wonder it was bad!)). Twenty-three Rodgers and Hart songs are included and everyone who can either sing or dance at MGM is in the movie.

Cole Porter's most successful show ever, *Kiss Me Kate* (1,077 perf.). 'Wunderbar', 'So In Love', 'Why Can't You Behave', 'Brush Up Your Shakespeare', 'Too Darn Hot', 'Always True To You In My Fashion'. Frank Loesser, after years of obscurity as a lyricist, burst on to the scene with *Where's Charley?*, starring Ray Bolger (792 perf.). 'Once In Love With Amy'. Schwartz and Dietz's hit *Inside U.S.A.* (399 perf.), a revue starring Bea Lillie and Jack Haley. 'Rhode Island is Famous For You' and 'Come, O, Come to Pittsburgh'. Kurt Weill, too, had a hit with *Love Life* (lyrics by Alan Jan Lerner). The Shuberts tried a new Sigmund Romberg musical, *My Romance* (book and lyrics by Roland Leigh) but it failed.

The Hollywood musical was well represented by the Fred Astaire–Judy Garland *Easter Parade* (music by Irving Berlin); Gene Kelly and Garland again in a Cole Porter musical, *The Pirate* (vastly underrated at the time) and Deanna Durbin and Dick Haymes in Romberg's *Up in Central Park*.

1949 7 April Rodgers and Hammerstein, in association with Leland Hayward and Joshua Logan, present *South Pacific* (book by Hammerstein and Logan based on James Michener's *Tales of the South Pacific*, lyrics by Hammerstein, music by Richard Rodgers). 'Bali Ha'i', 'There Is Nothing Like a Dame', 'I'm In Love With a Wonderful Guy', 'I'm Gonna Wash That Man Right Out of My Hair', 'Some Enchanted Evening', 'This Nearly Was Mine', 'Bloody Mary', 'Younger Than Springtime', 'Carefully Taught', 'Honey Bun'. Majestic Theatre (1,925 perf.).

South Pacific obscured other hits like Kurt Weill's *Lost in the Stars* and Irving Berlin's *Miss Liberty*. Only the Styne–Comden–Green musical *Gentlemen Prefer Blondes* really made it (740 perf.) and skyrocketed Carol Channing to stardom (and some years later provided a useful vehicle for Marilyn Monroe and Jane Russell). The Hollywood musicals included June Haver and Ray Bolger in *Look for the Silver Lining*, which purported to be the life story of Marilyn Miller; and the reunion of Fred Astaire and Ginger Rogers in *The Barkleys of Broadway* with songs by Harry Warren and lyrics by Ira Gershwin. Sinatra, Kelly and Munshin danced and sang alongside Vera-Ellen, Betty Garrett and Ann Miller in the MGM version of *On The Town*, its score almost completely rewritten by Comden and Green. Paramount also filmed a new version of *A Connecticut Yankee*, but the score was by Jimmy van Heusen and Johnny Burke.

1950 24 Jan. Rodgers and Hammerstein present *The Happy Time*, a play by Samuel Taylor based on the novel by Robert Fontaine, at the Plymouth Theatre (614 perf.).

      4 Mar. *The Heart of the Matter*, a play by Grahame Green and Basil Dean, based on Green's novel and presented by Rodgers and Hammerstein, is closed during its tryouts at the Shubert Theatre, Boston, which had begun on 20 February.

      7 June Prince Littler, in association with the Theatre Guild, presents

Rodgers and Hammerstein's *Carousel* at the Theatre Royal, Drury Lane, London (566 perf.). Iva Withers plays Julie, Stephen Douglass, Billy Bigelow, and Margot Moser Carrie Pipperidge.

19 Oct.   Rodgers and Hammerstein present John Steinbeck's play *Burning Bright*, starring Kent Smith, Howard da Silva and Barbara Bel Geddes, at the Broadhurst Theatre (13 perf.). (Steinbeck's novelette of the same name published 21 Oct. with limited success.)

Frank Loesser enjoyed an enormous hit with *Guys and Dolls*; 'I'll Know', 'If I Were a Bell', 'A Bushel and a Peck', 'I've Never Been in Love Before', 'Luck Be a Lady' and 'Take Back Your Mink'. Irving Berlin's *Call Me Madam!* (644 perf.). 'The Hostess with the Mostest', 'It's a Lovely Day Today', 'Marrying for Love', 'You're Just in Love'. A new Cole Porter musical, *Out Of This World*, was not a success. At the movies Howard Keel and Betty Hutton starred in *Annie Get Your Gun*, Betty Grable warbled 'Baby Won't You Say You Love Me' in Fox's *Wabash Avenue*, Doris Day, Jimmy Cagney, Gordon MacRae and Virginia Mayo did what they could with Jule Styne's forgettable songs in Warners' *Fine and Dandy*, and that was the musical scene.

1951   29 Mar.   *The King and I* at the St James Theatre, New York (book and lyrics by Oscar Hammerstein based on the novel *Anna and the King of Siam* by Margaret Landon. Music by Rodgers). 'Getting to Know You', 'We Kiss in a Shadow', 'I Have Dreamed', 'Shall We Dance?', 'I Whistle A Happy Tune', 'Something Wonderful' and others (1,246 perf.)

1 Nov.   Williamson Music, Ltd. presents *South Pacific* at the Theatre Royal, Drury Lane, London (802 perf.).

Hollywood was trembling in fear and chaos as television cut audiences and box office receipts. The major studios forbade contract players to appear on TV at all, and the films that came out tended to be the certainties. Although MGM have to be credited with Gene Kelly's *An American in Paris* and the Howard Keel–Kathryn Grayson–Ava Gardner *Show Boat* there was little else of musical interest. Broadway's crop was also middling to fair: Lerner and Loewe's *Paint Your Wagon*, Arthur Schwartz and Dorothy Field's *A Tree Grows in Brooklyn*, the new Styne–Comden–Green revue *Two On The Aisle* and the Phil Silvers *Top Banana*.

1952   26 Oct.   NBC Television and the United States Navy present the TV première of *Victory at Sea*, a documentary written by Henry Salomon and Richard Hanser, music by Richard Rodgers orchestrated by Robert Russell Bennett. (Twenty-six weeks, each show half an hour in length.)

3 Jan.   Jule Styne and Leonard Key in association with Anthony Brady Farrell, present *Pal Joey* at the Broadhurst Theatre (524 perf.) starring Harold Lang, Patricia Northrop and Vivienne Segal. (Understudy for the role of Joey was Bob Fosse and Elaine Stritch played Melba Snyder.)

South Pacific and *The King and I* were still big hits. Vernon Duke's new show, *Two's Company*, brought Bette Davis on to the revue stage, if for only ninety performances. Josh Logan directed Harold Rome's new musical *Wish You Were Here* (598 perf.) and another success was the one-woman show *An Evening with Beatrice Lillie*. Hollywood hit back with one of its best-ever musicals, Gene Kelly's *Singin' in the Rain*.

1953　28 May　*Me and Juliet*, a musical comedy with book and lyrics by Oscar Hammerstein, music by Richard Rodgers, at the Majestic Theatre (358 perf.). 'Marriage Type Love', 'Keep It Gay', 'The Big Black Giant', 'No Other Love', 'We Deserve Each Other'.

　　　29 July　MGM releases the Lester Cowan movie *Main Street to Broadway* in which Rodgers and Hammerstein 'compose' a song called 'There's Music in You', sung by Mary Martin.

　　　31 Aug.　Rodgers and Hammerstein Week, New York City. Four musicals, *The King and I*, *South Pacific*, *Me and Juliet* and a revival of *Oklahoma!* running simultaneously.

　　　8 Oct.　*The King and I* at the Theatre Royal, Drury Lane, London (926 perf.) starring Herbert Lom and Valerie Hobson.

Kismet, with the music of Borodin, *Wonderful Town* (score by Leonard Bernstein, lyrics by Comden and Green) and Cole Porter's *Can Can* were the brightest-shining musicals on stage. On screen, it was Doris Day in *Calamity Jane* who provided the only really original musical score (by Sammy Fain and Paul Francis Webster). There were movie versions of *Kiss Me, Kate*, *The Band Wagon*, *Gentlemen Prefer Blondes* and *Call Me Madam*, none of which lived up to its original.

1954　28 Mar.　General Foods 25th Anniversary Show, on NBC-TV, CBS-TV, ABC-TV, honouring Rodgers and Hammerstein in a one-and-a-half-hour network television spectacular.

Movie musicals included *Carmen Jones*, Irving Berlin's *White Christmas*, *There's No Business Like Show Business* (also mostly Berlin), *Rose Marie*, *A Star Is Born*, and the only true original among them all, *Seven Brides for Seven Brothers*. Broadway's best was *The Pajama Game* with a score by Richard Adler and Jerry Ross, 'Hey, There!'. Joshua Logan and David Merrick co-produced *Fanny* (888 perf.), and Herb and Dorothy Fields, with composer Arthur Schwartz, got 270 performances out of *By The Beautiful Sea*, starring Shirley Booth. Newcomer Julie Andrews was a big hit in the imported musical, *The Boy Friend*, as was Mary Martin in *Peter Pan*.

1955　18 July　Rodgers and Hammerstein Festival, St Louis, Mo., in which the St Louis Municipal Opera devoted a week each to a Rodgers and Hammerstein symphony concert, productions of *Carousel*, *Allegro* and *The King and I*, and a two-week production of *South Pacific*.

　　　30 Nov.　*Pipe Dream* (musical play with book and lyrics by Hammerstein, based on the novel *Sweet Thursday* by John Steinbeck; music by Rodgers, Shubert Theatre, New York (246 perf.). 'Everybody's Got a Home But Me', 'All At Once You Love

Her', 'The Man I Used To Be', and 'The Next Time It Happens'.
Notable among musicals were *Damn Yankees* by Adler and Ross ('Whatever Lola Wants') and Cole Porter's final Broadway musical, *Silk Stockings*. From Hollywood, *Oklahoma!* (released 11 October 1955) did not repeat its stage success any more than MGM's *Guys and Dolls* with Brando, Sinatra, Jean Simmons and Vivian Blaine in her original stage rôle as Adelaide. Other musicals included a remake of *Hit The Deck*, and the 'life story' of Ruth Etting, *Love Me Or Leave Me*, which starred Doris Day and James Cagney.

1956   16 Feb.   20th Century Fox releases *Carousel* starring Shirley Jones and Gordon MacRae (who replaced Frank Sinatra).

28 June   20th Century Fox releases *The King and I*, starring Yul Brynner and Deborah Kerr.

Times were changing. Rodgers and Hammerstein musicals were getting competition from stars like Elvis Presley, who made his movie debut in *Love Me Tender*. Sinatra teamed with Bing Crosby and Grace Kelly in the movie *High Society* with music by Cole Porter ('True Love'), but it was about the only one worth mentioning. Broadway had much more to offer: A new Frank Loesser show of almost operatic dimensions called *The Most Happy Fella* (676 perf.) which introduced a big hit, 'Standing on the Corner'. Composer Jerry Bock and lyricists Larry Holofcener and George Weiss produced a couple of durable hits for a show called *Mr Wonderful* starring Sammy Davis Jr., the title song and 'Too Close For Comfort'. Styne, Comden and Green's *Bells Are Ringing* (924 perf.) had Judy Holliday and a fine score ('Long Before I Knew You' and 'The Party's Over'). Lerner and Loewe's *My Fair Lady*, with Rex Harrison and Julie Andrews, outdistanced them all (2,717 perf.), better than anything anyone had ever done before. It became the longest-running musical in theatrical history until it was outdistanced in 1964 by *Fiddler on the Roof*.

1957   31 Mar.   CBS Television Network premières *Cinderella* (television musical with book and lyrics by Oscar Hammerstein II, adapted from the fairy tale; music by Richard Rodgers). 'Do I Love You Because You're Beautiful?', 'A Lovely Night' and 'Ten Minutes Ago'.

9 Sept.   Columbia Pictures releases *Pal Joey*, movie version of the Rodgers and Hart show of 1940. The screenplay by Dorothy Kingsley owed little to the original, and 'I Didn't Know What Time It was', 'There's A Small Hotel', 'My Funny Valentine' and 'The Lady is a Tramp' were added. Only five original songs were kept.

Stanley Donen, a graduate of the original *Pal Joey*, directed Audrey Hepburn and Fred Astaire in a movie version of Gershwin's *Funny Face*, and Gene Kelly starred in Cole Porter's last movie musical, MGM's *Les Girls* (Porter wrote fourteen songs; only five were used). On Broadway, there was an immense hit, *The Music Man*, written by Meredith Willson, 'Till There Was You' and 'Seventy Six Trombones'. New composer-lyricist Bob Merrill (new, that is, to Broadway: his nontheatrical songs had been big, if brainless hits like 'How Much Is That Doggie in The Window?', 'Sparrow In The Treetop', 'Candy and Cake', 'Truly, Truly Fair' and 'Mambo Italiano') had a substantial success with *New Girl In Town*, starring Gwen Verdon. The most dramatic of the new musicals, however, was *West Side Story* (music by Leonard Bernstein, lyrics by Stephen Sondheim and breathtaking ballets staged by Jerome Robbins; 732 perf.

1958   19 Mar.   20th Century Fox release *South Pacific*, starring Mitzi Gaynor, Rossano Brazzi, John Kerr and France Nuyen. 'My Girl Back Home' (cut from the original show) reinstated. Brazzi's songs were sung by Giorgio Tozzi, Kerr's by Bill Lee and Juanita Hall's by Muriel Smith.

         1 Dec.   Rodgers and Hammerstein, in association with Joseph Fields, present *The Flower Drum Song* (musical play with book by Hammerstein and Fields based on C. Y. Lee's novel, lyrics by Hammerstein, and music by Rodgers; 600 perf. at the St James Theatre). 'Don't Marry Me', 'Sunday', 'I Enjoy Being a Girl', 'Grant Avenue', 'Love Look Away', 'A Hundred Million Miracles'.'

Publication of Jack Kerouac's *On The Road*, precursor of the 'Beat' generation to follow. *Gigi* was made into a movie with Leslie Caron in the original Audrey Hepburn part. Cole Porter's last score was heard: a television version of *Aladdin* produced by Richard Lewine for CBS, 'Come To The Supermarket In Old Peking' (Porter died in 1964). Styne, Comden and Green had another hit, *Say, Darling*. It was getting progressively harder to put on musicals, but the following year proved to be one of the best ever and, in many ways, the high water mark of the genre pioneered a quarter of a century earlier by Rodgers and Hammerstein.

1959   16 Nov.   Leland Hayward, Richard Halliday, Rodgers and Hammerstein present *The Sound of Music* (musical play with book by Howard Lindsay and Russel Crouse (suggested by 'The Trapp Family Singers' by Maria Augusta Trapp), music by Richard Rodgers, lyrics by Oscar Hammerstein, at the Lunt-Fontanne Theatre (1,443 perf.). 'Sixteen Going on Seventeen', 'The Lonely Goatherd', 'Edelweiss', 'Do-Re-Mi', 'My Favourite Things' and 'Climb Ev'ry Mountain'.

Huge though its success eventually became, Rodgers and Hammerstein's new show was not the only big musical of the year. Two newcomers, Jerry Bock and Sheldon Harnick, wrote a score for a George Abbott-Jerome Weidman book about New York's legendary Mayor La Guardia. *Fiorello!* (In 1964 they would write the most successful musical ever, *Fiddler on the Roof*.) Jule Styne, Arthur Laurents and Stephen Sondheim had a huge hit with *Gypsy* (702 perf.), the story of that same Gypsy Rose Lee whom Rodgers and Hart had so mercilessly lampooned in their song 'Zip' in *Pal Joey*. In the score, 'Everything's Coming Up Roses', 'Small World', 'All I Need Is The Girl', 'If Momma Was Married'. It starred Ethel Merman. TV personality

Jackie Gleason proved a big draw in a new Bob Merrill musical, *Take Me Along*; *Porgy and Bess* came to the screen; and Oscar Hammerstein personally arranged for the statue of George M. Cohan, sculpted by Georg Lober, to be erected in Times Square, eternally giving the Yankee Doodle Boy's regards to a Broadway he would no longer recognize.

1960   23 Aug.   Oscar Hammerstein died at Doylestown

The most influential theatrical team in the business was no more. Others were waiting in the wings, however: Charles Strouse and Lee Adams opened their *Bye Bye Birdie* on 14 April ('Got a Lot of Living To Do', 'Put On a Happy Face') and two weeks later, Tom Jones and Harvey Schmidt's fantastic *The Fantasticks* ('Try to Remember', 'Soon It's Gonna Rain') began its career. Cy Coleman's first show, *Wildcat*, starring Lucille Ball ('Hey, Look Me Over') heralded a career which would include *Little Me* and *Sweet Charity*. That same year, Jerry Herman had his second flop, *Parade*. Four more years and he would write the second-longest-running musical in Broadway history, *Hello, Dolly!*, and follow it two years later with *Mame*, which holds ninth position on the same list. Mitch Leigh and Joe Darion would collaborate on *Man of La Mancha*, and John Kander and Fred Ebb, whose first show *From A to Z* died after 21 performances in May, 1960 went on to create *Cabaret*. And there was Oscar's protégé and discovery, Stephen Sondheim, who has become the *wunderkind* of the contemporary musical, with a string of shows to his credit: *Company*, *A Funny Thing Happened On The Way To The Forum*, *Follies*, *A Little Night Music* and *Pacific Overtures* among them.

There were big changes in the musical air, and it is highly doubtful if Oscar would have liked any of them. Rock and roll, Presley's rhythm and blues, and early in the Sixties the advent of the Beatles, started a pop revolution. The new audience was not the affluent middle class theatregoer who bought an original cast album, but the new affluent youth who bought The Sound, who subscribed to the protest/drug/counterculture outlook that was apotheosized on the musical stage in 1967 in Galt MacDermott's *Hair*. If the end of the Rodgers and Hammerstein era has to be dated, then it must be the first night of *Hair*.

Bibliography

The following were the principal works consulted in preparing this book.

GEORGE ABBOTT, *Mr Abbott*, Random House, New York, 1963.

DESI ARNAZ, *A Book*, William Morrow & Co. Inc., New York, 1976.

BROOKS ATKINSON, *Broadway*, Macmillan, New York, 1970; Cassell, London, 1971.

DANIEL BLUM, *Pictorial History of the American Theatre 1900–56*, Greenberg, New York, 1950.

GUY BOLTON (See P. G. Wodehouse).

JAN CLAYTON (See Samuel Marx).

AGNES DE MILLE, *Dance to the Piper*, Little Brown, Boston, 1951.

HOWARD DIETZ, *Dancing in the Dark*, Quadrangle, *The New York Times*, New York, 1974.

DAVID EWEN, *Richard Rodgers*, Henry Holt & Co., New York, 1957.

LYNN FARNOL GROUP, *Richard Rodgers Fact Book*, Lynn Farnol Group, New York, 1968.

EDNA FERBER, *A Peculiar Treasure*, Copyright renewed 1966 by Edna Ferber.

HUGH FORDIN, *Jerome Kern, The Man and His Music*, T. B. Harms, Santa Monica Cal., 1974.

STANLEY GREEN, *The World of Musical Comedy*, A. S. Barnes & Co., New York, 1968.

——*Ring Bells! Sing Songs!* Arlington House, New Rochelle, New York, 1971.

MEL GUSSOW, *Don't Say 'Yes' Until I've Finished Talking*, Doubleday, New York, 1971.

REX HARRISON, *Rex*, Macmillan, London, 1974.

MOSS HART, *Act One*, Random House, New York, 1959.

MARGARET CASE HARRIMAN, *Take Them Up Tenderly*, Knopf, New York, 1944.

CHARLES HIGHAM, *Ziegfeld*, W. H. Allen, London, 1973.

JOHN KOBAL, *Gotta Sing, Gotta Dance*, Hamlyn, New York and London, 1971.

JOSHUA LOGAN, *Josh*, Delacorte Press, New York, 1976; W. H. Allen, London, 1977.

MARY MARTIN, *My Heart Belongs*, William Morrow & Co. Inc., New York, 1976.

SAMUEL MARX and JAN CLAYTON, *Rodgers and Hart*, G. P. Putnam's Sons Inc., New York, 1976; W. H. Allen, London, 1977.

JESSIE MATTHEWS, *Over My Shoulder*, W. H. Allen, London, 1974.

GEORGE OPPENHEIMER, *The Passionate Playgoer*, Viking, New York, 1958.

TONY PALMER, *All You Need Is Love*, Weidenfeld & Nicolson, London, 1977.

JOAN ROBERTS, *Never Alone*, McMullin, New York, 1954.

RICHARD RODGERS (ed.), *The Rodgers and Hart Song Book*, Simon & Schuster, New York, 1951.

—— *Musical Stages*, Random House Inc., New York, 1975; W. H. Allen, London, 1976.

CORNELIA OTIS SKINNER, *Life with Lindsay and Crouse*, Houghton Mifflin, Boston 1976.

JERRY STAGG, *The Brothers Shubert*, Random House, New York, 1968.

HOWARD TEICHMANN, *George S. Kaufman. An Intimate Portrait*, William Morrow, New York, 1974.

—— *Smart Aleck*, William Morrow, New York, 1976.

TONY THOMAS, *Harry Warren and the Hollywood Musical*, Citadel, New York, 1975.

ALEC WILDER, *American Popular Song*, Oxford University Press, 1972.

MAX WILK, *They're Playing Our Song*, Atheneum, New York, 1974.

P. G. WODEHOUSE and GUY BOLTON, *Bring on the Girls*, Simon & Schuster, New York, 1953.

CRAIG ZADAN, *Sondheim & Co*, Macmillan, New York, 1974.

Index

of names, shows and songs

Note: For reasons of space the Chronology is not covered by this index

Aarons, Alex A., 42, 88, 101
Abbott, George, 6, 14, 87, 102, 108, 110, 180, 187, 188, 189, 265
Adams, Edith, 198
Adams, Franklin P., 36
Adler, Larry, 6, 240
Adler, Richard, 234
'Ah, sweet mystery of life', 47
Aleichem, Sholom, 166
'Alice blue gown', 75
All About Eve, 36, 234
'All at once you love her', 196
'All the things you are', 63
'All through the day', 136
All You Need Is Love, 233, 235, 265
Allegro, 6, 141–3, 157, 189
Allen, Elizabeth, 229, 230
Allyson, June, 13, 109
Alton, Robert, 185, 189
'Always room for one more', 72, 237
Always You, 40, 43
ASCAP (American Society of Composers, Authors and Publishers), 4, 46, 47, 136, 239
America's Sweetheart, 91
'An ordinary couple', 216
Anderson, John Murray, 64, 77, 80
Andrews, Dana, 126, 127
Andrews, Julie, 194, 197, 198, 215, 219, 222, 224
Androcles and The Lion, 232
Anna and The King of Siam (see also *The King and I*), 167
Annie Get Your Gun, 6, 121, 137–9, 141, 144, 147
Ann-Margret, 226
'Any old place with you', 68
'Anything you can do', 139
Applause, 234
Arlen, Harold, 227
Arlen, Michael, 79
Arnaz, Desi, 108, 239, 265
Arsenic and Old Lace, 207
Astaire, Adele, 77
Astaire, Fred, 63, 77, 101, 145
Atkinson, Brooks, Jr, 28, 107, 113, 139, 180, 265
'Auto show girl', 69
Away We Go! (see also *Oklahoma!*), 24–7
Awe, Jim, 148
Axelrod, George, 36, 140, 145
Axelrod, Herman, 36, 37
Ayres, Lew, 126
Babes in Arms, 22, 66, 104–5

Bacall, Lauren, 234
Backer, George, 16
'bad in every man, The', 98
Balanchine, George, 102, 104, 106
'Bali Ha'i', 152, 201
Ball, Lucille, 108
Ball at the Savoy, 64
Ballard, Kaye, 198
Ballard, Lucinda, 6, 109, 177, 209, 217, 218, 239
Bancroft, Anne, 229
Barnett, Lincoln, 236
'Barney google', 70
Barrie, Sir James M., 197
Battles, John, 143
Bayliss, Jean, 222
Bear Flag Cafe, The (see also *Sweet Thursday* and *Pipe Dream*), 192
'Beat out dat rhythm on the drum', 119
Beauty of Bath, The, 50
Behrman, Samuel N., 24, 32, 95, 191
Bel Geddes, Norman, 16
Benchley, Robert, 81
Bender, 'Doc' Milton, 11, 87, 108, 113, 118, 238
Ben-Hur, 224
Bennett, Joan, 101
Bennett, Robert Russell, 182, 184
Bergman, Ingrid, 125
Berkeley, Busby, 53, 61
Berle, Milton, 36
Berlin, Irving, 6, 57, 77, 82, 99, 101, 137, 138, 141, 191, 207
Bernstein, Leonard, 6
Best Foot Forward, 13, 14
Betsy, 57, 82
'Bewitched, bothered and bewildered', 112, 114, 239
'Beyond the blue horizon', 136
'big black giant, The', 189, 240
Bigley, Isabel, 32, 186, 187, 188
Bikel, Theodore, 209, 210, 213, 218, 220
'Bill', 50, 59
Birch, Peter, 134
Blaine, Vivian, 126
Bledsoe, Jules, 54
Blond Beast, The, 71, 237
Blondell, Joan, 159
Blossom Time, 28
Blow, Richard M., 172
'Blue moon', 98
'blue room, The', 96
Blyden, Larry, 200, 203
Bock, Jerry, 166
Bolger, Ray, 15, 192

Bolton, Guy, 42, 48, 49, 50, 52, 57, 69, 84, 85, 265
'Bombay bombashay, The', 74
Bonci, A., 33
Bonwit, Elise, 74
Boone, Pat, 226
Booth, Shirley, 229
Boy Friend, The, 192, 194
'Boys and girls like you and me', 26
Boys From Syracuse, The, 22, 107, 164
Bracken, Eddie, 108
Brady, 'Diamond Jim', 237
Brando, Marlon, 203
Brazzi, Rossano, 162, 201
Brent, Romney, 78
Brice, Fanny, 75
Brigadoon, 141
Broadway Melody, The, 89
Broadway Rhythm, 238
Brooks, Geraldine, 241
Brown, Nacio Herb, 97
Brynner, Yul, 164, 168, 170, 171, 172, 173, 175, 176, 184, 201, 235
Buloff, Joseph, 23, 29
Burning Bright, 164, 166
Burton, Richard, 224
Buttons, Red, 203
By Jupiter, 11, 12, 14, 15, 22, 114, 115
Cabaret, 240
Cagney, James, 93
Cahn, Sammy, 6
Caldwell, Anne, 53
Call Me Madam, 207
'Camelot samba, The', 116
'Campfire days', 69
Can-Can, 192
'Can I forget you?', 63
'Can't help lovin' dat man', 58, 59
Can't Help Singing, 127
'Can't you do a friend a favour?', 117
Capote, Truman, 227
Carmen Jones, 119
Carousel, 6, 128–34, 135, 151, 187, 223
Carpenter, Constance, 175
Carr, Charmian, 215
Carroll, Diahann, 227
Cartwright, Angela, 215
Cassidy, Jack, 241
Casto, Jean, 129, 133
CBS Television, 184, 197, 198
Centennial Summer, 128, 136
Cerf, Bennett, 36
Cesar, 191
Champagne and Orchids, 63
Champion, Gower, 240
Chaplin, Saul, 241

Chappell & Co., 15, 120, 238
Charley's Aunt, 192
Charnin, Martin, 232
Chase, Duane, 215
Chase, Ilka, 198
Chee Chee, 86
Chevalier, Maurice, 93, 94, 98, 151
'Chicago', 112
Children of Dreams, 237
Chocolate Soldier, The, 48, 69
'Chop suey', 205
Christine, Audrey, 107
Christy, Ed, 85
Churchill, Winston, 221
Cinderella, 6, 197–8
Citizen Kane, 36
City Chap, The, 53
Claire, Ina, 139
Clark, Edward, 37
Clayton, Jan, 6, 128, 129, 133, 177, 180, 265
Cleopatra, 224
'Climb ev'ry mountain', 216, 223
Clurman, Harold, 193
Cochran, C. B., 82, 85, 89, 91
Cochrane, June, 97
'cockeyed optimist, A', 148
Cocktail Party, The, 167
Cohan, George, M., 95, 105, 106, 238
Cohn, Harry, 24, 114, 140, 239
Columbia Pictures, 24, 39, 140, 239
Columbia University Shows, 37, 39, 73, 75, 121, 140
Colvan, Zeke, 59
Comden, Betty, 241
Comstock, F. Ray, 48
A Connecticut Yankee, 83, 84, 85, 115–17
Connery, Sean, 153
Conried, Richard, 40
Cook, Edward, F., 172
Copeland, Joan, 235
Copland, Aaron, 22
Cornell, Katharine, 44
'Cotton blossom', 59, 237
Courtneidge, Cicely, 81
Coward, Noel, 81, 86, 89, 232
Crain, Jeanne, 126, 127, 226
Crawford, Joan, 96
Crosby, Bing, 100, 101, 164, 175
Crouse, Russel, 119, 151, 207, 208, 209, 211, 216, 218
'Cuddle up a little closer, lovey mine', 40
Cukor, George, 93

Cullman, Howard, 172
Cypher, Jon, 198
da Silva, Howard, 32
Daffy Dill, 42
Dailey, Dan, 105
Daisy, The, 125
Damn Yankees, 6
'Dance', 188
Dancing in the Streets, 27, 236
Dancing Lady, 96
'Dancing on the ceiling', 89, 91
Danish Yankee in King Tut's Court, A, 75, 83
Dann, Roger, 222
Darin, Bobby, 226
Dauphin, Claude, 164
Davidson, Jim, 164
Davies, Brian, 216
Davis, Bette, 93
Davis, Meyer, 172
Davis, Owen, 88
Dawson, Mark, 187
Day, Doris, 158, 201
Day, Edith, 42
De Cuir, John, 171
de Mille, Agnes, 6, 22, 24, 128, 134, 141, 142, 265
de Mille, Cecil, 22, 239
de Sylva, B. G. 'Buddy', 50
de Vries, Peter, 201
Dean, Basil, 164
'Dear, oh dear!', 86
Dear Sir, 43
Dearest Enemy, 40, 77, 79, 80, 81
Deep in My Heart, 193
dell'Isola, Salvatore, 163, 185
D'Erlanger family, 83
Desert Song, The, 41, 52, 53, 62, 238
Dexter, John, 229
'Diamonds are a girl's best friend', 136
'Did you ever get stung?', 107
Dietz, Howard, 6, 36, 43, 72, 73, 96, 97, 238, 265
Dillingham, Charles, 52, 53, 85
Dixon, Lee, 29, 30
Do I Hear A Waltz?, 229–30
'Do I love you because you're beautiful?', 198
Dr Zhivago, 224
'Doin' what comes naturally', 137
Donahue, Jack, 53
Donaldson, Walter, 97
Donehue, Vincent J., 206
Donen, Stanley, 112, 193
Donnelly, Dorothy, 57
'Don't blame me', 240
'Don't love me like Othello', 72, 74
'Don't marry me', 205
'Do-re-mi', 216, 218
Doughgirls, The, 201
Dovey, Alice, 49
'Down at the lake', 72
'Down by the river', 101
Drake, Alfred, 22, 23, 29, 32, 164, 170

Drake, Tom, 97, 99
Dreyfus, Louis, 14
Dreyfus, Max, 15, 75, 76, 80, 120, 191, 238
Du Barry Was A Lady, 115
Duke, Vernon, 27
Duncan, William Cary, 44
Dunn, Kathy, 209
Dunne, Irene, 58, 59, 85, 167
Durante, James, 102
Durbin, Deanna, 127
Durgin, Cyrus, 26
Dvonch, Fred, 209
Dyrenforth, James, 69
East Wind, 64
Easter Parade, 99
'Easy to remember', 101
Ebb, Fred, 240
'Edelweiss', 219, 220
Eddy, Nelson, 63, 96
Edwards, Cliff (Ukelele Ike), 53
Eisenhower, Dwight D., 164
Eliot, T. S., 167
Ellis, Mary, 6, 44, 45, 46
Elmo, Ann, 201
Erickson, Leif, 109
Ernst, Deila, 111
Ever Green, 89, 91
'Every little movement has a meaning of its own', 40
'Everybody loves you', 105
Ewell, Tom, 140, 226
Ewen, David, 6, 236, 265
Ewing, Sherman, 172
The Exorcist, 241
Fabray, Nanette, 241
Fairbanks, Douglas, 98
Fairchild, Edgar, 104
'Falling in love with love', 107
Fanny, 191
Farrell, Anthony, B., 172, 176
Faye, Alice, 226
Fearnley, John, 151, 170, 233
Feiner, Benjamin, 82
Feiner, Benjamin, Jr, 82
Feiner, Dorothy (see Rodgers, Dorothy)
'fellow needs a girl, A', 142
Ferber, Edna, 53, 54, 86, 265
Fetter, Theodore C., 6
Feuer, Cy, 191, 192, 193
Fiddler On the Roof, 166, 197, 234
Fielding, Harold, 198
Fields, Dorothy, 6, 36, 68, 72, 135, 136, 137, 182, 198, 240
Fields, Frances, 68
Fields, Herbert, 36, 68, 72, 75, 77, 80, 81, 82, 83, 84, 85, 88–90, 92, 97, 115, 135, 198
Fields, Joseph, 36, 68, 135, 198, 199, 200, 201, 202, 203
Fields, Lew, 36, 50, 68, 72–4, 81, 84, 85, 101
Fields, W. C., 75, 99, 101
Fifth Avenue Follies, The, 81

'fine romance, A', 240
Finian's Rainbow, 6, 141
Finn, Myra (see Hammerstein, Myra Finn)
Firefly, The, 40
First National Picture Corp., 90
Fitelson, William, 207
Five Columbians, The, 237
Flower Drum Song, The, 40, 199–205, 207, 208, 211, 221, 223
'flower garden of my heart, The', 112
Flowering Peach, The, 232
Fly With Me, 40, 72
Flynn, Errol, 68
Fogarty, Frank, 35
'folks who live on the hill, The', 63
Fonda, Henry, 144, 145, 172, 194, 241
Fonda, Susan, B., 172
Fontaine, Robert, 164
Fontanne, Lynn, 79
Foran, Dick, 116
Ford, George, 6, 77, 80
Ford, Harry, 80
Ford, Helen, 6, 40, 77, 79, 80, 82, 86, 117, 182, 241
Foster, Stephen C., 85, 101, 136
Fox, Paul, S., 171, 203
Franchi, Sergio, 229, 230
Freaky Friday, 232
Free For All, 61, 64
Freed, Arthur, 24, 97, 115
Freedley, Vinton, 88, 101
Friml, Rudolf, 5, 17, 37, 39, 40, 44, 45, 53, 77
'From afar', 234
Froman, Jane, 184
Fuller, Penny, 234
Gable, Clark, 96, 97
Gabor, Eva, 164
Gallico, Paul, 115
Gang's All Here, The, 64, 119
Garde, Betty, 29, 30
Garden, Mary, 33
Garland, Judy, 13, 127, 145
Garrick Gaieties, The, 79, 81, 164, 193, 239
Gaxton, William, 184
Gaynor, Janet, 126
Gaynor, Mitzi, 158, 161, 162, 201
'gentleman is a dope, The', 142
Gentleman Unafraid, 64
George White's Scandals of 1920, 75
Gerber, Alex, 75
Gershwin, George, 14, 36, 42, 43, 51, 53, 61, 62, 65, 75, 76, 77, 95, 108, 136, 161, 237
Gershwin, Ira, 14, 36, 42, 43, 61, 62, 75, 76, 77, 95, 161
'Getting to know you', 157, 175, 203
Ghostley, Alice, 198
Gibbs, Wolcott, 28, 113

Gingham Girl, The, 77
'girl friend, The', 96
'*Girl Friend, The*, 59, 81
'girl that I marry, The', 137
'Give it back to the indians', 108
Give Us This Night, 237
'Glad to be unhappy', 102, 114
Glaenzer, Jules, 28
Glazer, Benjamin, 125, 239
'Gliding through my memoree', 40, 205
Godfather, The, 241
Golden Dawn, 61
Goldwyn, Frances, 120
Goldwyn, Samuel, 96, 120, 232
Gone With The Wind, 224
Good Boy, 61
Good Morning, Dearie, 52
Gordon, Anita, 226
Gordon, Max, 24
'gown is mightier than the sword, The', 238
Grafton, Gloria, 102
Grahame, Sheilah, 83
Grand Street Follies, The, 44
'Grant Avenue', 205
Great Waltz, The, 237
Greatest Show On Earth, The, 239
Green, Abel, 81
Green, Adolph, 241
Green Grow The Lilacs (see also *Oklahoma!*), 11, 15, 18, 20, 236
Green Hat, The, 79
Green, John, 6, 182, 241
Green, Mitzi, 104
Greene, Graham, 164
Greenstone, Hal, 172
'Guadalcanal March', 184
Guardsman, The, 79, 239
Guinness, Alec, 169
Guinness family, 83
Guys and Dolls, 6, 187, 192
Gypsy, 6, 229
Hale, Alan, 68
Hale, Sonny, 83
Hall, Juanita, 151, 154, 161, 163, 203, 205
Hallelujah, I'm a Bum, 95, 96
Hallelujah, I'm a Tramp (see above)
Halliday, Hildegarde, 6
Halliday, Richard, 139, 172, 206, 207, 208, 209
Halliday, Robert, 53
Happy Birthday, 139
'Happy Christmas, little friend', 191
'Happy talk', 152, 154, 155, 203
Happy Time, The, 164, 227, 240
Hammerstein, Arthur, 33, 37, 39, 40, 41, 44, 45, 53
Hammerstein, Dorothy Blanchard, 8, 60, 121, 123, 124, 167, 172, 179, 188, 208, 221, 238
Hammerstein, Myra Finn, 37

Hammerstein, Oscar I., 33,
34, 35, 47, 56, 57
Hammerstein, Reginald,
35, 172, 193
Hammerstein, William
('Billy'), 141, 177, 221,
223, 237
Hammerstein, William
('Willie'), 33, 35
Harbach, Otto, 5, 37, 40–1,
42, 44, 53, 61, 63, 75
Harburg, E. Y., 136, 239
Harlow, Jean, 96, 97, 98
Harms, T. B., Inc., 42, 75,
80, 238
Harnick, Sheldon, 166, 234
Harrigan, William, 144
Harris, Sam, 238
Harrison, Rex, 6, 167, 169,
265
Hart, Dorothy, 5, 6, 12, 70,
87, 88, 95, 115, 117, 118,
239
Hart, Frieda, 69, 70, 95,
115
Hart, Max, 69–70, 71
Hart, Moss, 96, 105, 160,
239, 265
Hart, Teddy, 69, 118, 239
Have A Heart, 50
'Have you met Miss
Jones?', 105, 114
Havoc, June, 112
Hawks, Nancy (Mrs
Leland Hayward), 172,
240
Hayden, Rita, 83
Hayden, Sterling, 79
Hayes, Bill, 186, 187, 188
Hayes, Helen, 139, 145
Haymes, Dick, 126
Hayward, Leland, 39, 145,
146, 151–2, 160, 172,
174, 207, 208, 209, 240
Hayworth, Rita, 128
Heads Up!, 88
Heart of the Matter, The,
164, 166
Hecht, Ben, 95, 102
Heggen, Thomas, 144
Helburn, Theresa, 11, 22,
24, 25, 26, 124, 125, 128,
131, 139, 172
Held, Anna, 57
Hello, Dolly!, 191, 240
'Hello, young lovers', 173,
176, 240
Hellzapoppin, 233
Henderson, Florence, 32
Henky (see *The Melody
Man*)
Hepburn, Audrey, 206
Hepburn, Katharine, 229
Herbert, Victor, 42, 45, 46,
47, 51
'Here in my arms', 80, 82,
96
Herman, William, 209
Heyward, du Bose, 61
High Chaparral, The, 109
High, Wide and Handsome,
63, 237
Higham, Charles, 237, 265
Higher and Higher, 108–9
Hit The Deck, 43, 85
Hobson, Valerie, 176

Hogan, Luanne, 126, 127
Hollywood Party, 96–7
Holm, Celeste, 23, 29, 30,
32, 164, 168, 175, 198
Holman, Libby, 79
Holtzmann, Fanny, 167
Home James, 37
'Honey bun', 158, 175
Hornblow, Arthur, Jr, 45,
46
Hot Heiress, The, 90, 91, 93
House of Flowers, 227
Hovick, Rose, 112
'How can I ever be
alone?', 73
'How can love survive?',
216
Howard, Sydney, 79, 192
Hughes, Elinor, 26
Hulbert, Jack, 81, 82
'hundred million miracles,
A', 205
Hutchinson, Leslie
('Hutch'), 83
'I cain't say no', 21
'I can't give you anything
but love, baby', 240
'I could write a book', 113,
114
'I didn't know what time it
was', 108, 114
'I enjoy being a girl', 204,
205
'I feel at home with you',
85
'I guess I'll have to change
my plan', 72
'I have confidence in me',
222, 225
'I haven't got a worry in
the world', 139
'I know my girl by her
perfume', 73, 238
'I like to recognise the
tune', 108
I Love Lucy, 108
I Married An Angel, 96, 105,
106–7, 109
'I might fall back on you',
59
'I must love you', 86
I Picked A Daisy, 228
I Remember Mama, 120, 124
'I Surrender', 238
'I whistle a happy tune',
173, 240
'I wish I didn't love you
so', 192
'I wish I were in love
again', 105
'I'd love to poison Ivy', 76
I'd Rather Be Right, 105, 108
'If I loved you', 131, 133
'If I weren't King', 198
'If they could see me
now', 240
I'll Take Romance, 237
'I'm an Apache', 94
'I'm falling in love with
someone', 46
'I'm gonna wash that man
right out of my hair',
155, 159, 201
'I'm in love with a
wonderful guy', 154,
159

'I'm in the mood for love',
240
'I'm talking to my pal', 128
'In love in vain', 136
Irene, 75
'Isn't it kinda fun?', 126
'Isn't it romantic?', 93
'It might as well be spring',
126–7
'It never entered my mind',
109, 114
'It's a grand night for
singing', 126
It's Always Fair Weather,
105
'It's got to be love', 102,
114
'It's the little things in
Texas', 226
'I've told ev'ry little star',
61
Jackson, Fred, 42
Jackson, Robert, 79
Jackson, Roberts, 4
Jacobs, Morris, 120, 172
Jaws, 241
Jazz A La Carte, 75
Jazz King, The (see *The
Melody Man*)
Jazz Singer, The, 95
Jimmie, 42
John Loves Mary, 140
'Johnny one note', 105
Johnson, Bill, 194
Johnson, Van, 108, 112,
193
Jolson, Al, 61, 95
Jonay, Roberta, 143
Jones, Shirley, 21, 196, 241
Jongleur de Notre Dame, Le,
33
Jumbo, 102, 103
'June is bustin' out all
over', 134
Kahn, Gus, 97, 98
Kalman, Emmerich, 61,
115
Kalmar, Bert, 61, 85
Kander, John, 240
Kapp, Jack, 32
Karath, Kym, 215
Kaufman, George S., 96,
105, 160, 161, 238, 239,
265
Kaye, Benjamin, 40, 78
Kaye, Danny, 223–3
Kaznar, Kurt, 164, 216
Keel, Howard, 32, 151
Keith, Robert, 144
Kelly, Gene, 6, 110, 111,
112, 114, 145, 200, 202–
3, 205, 241
Kenney, Ed, 203
Kent, Duke of, 89
Kent, William, 45
Kern, Eva, 136
Kern, Jerome, 5, 17, 43,
47–52, 53, 54, 55, 56, 57,
58, 59, 61, 63, 65, 69, 75,
84, 101, 115, 124, 128,
136, 137, 139, 208, 223,
237, 238, 239, 240, 241,
265
Kerr, Deborah, 172, 201
Kerr, Donald, 74
Kerr, John, 161, 219

Key, Leonard, 176
Kiley, Richard, 228
King, Dennis, 45, 107
King, Henry, 133
King and I, The, 6, 23, 157,
161, 164, 168–76, 180,
183, 193, 197, 201, 223,
235
Kirk, Lisa, 142, 184, 241
'kiss in the dark, A', 46
'Kiss me again', 46
Kiss Me, Kate, 6, 170, 180
Krasna, Norman, 140
Kron, William, 118, 239
Kroop, Milton, 40
Krupa, Gene, 108
Krupska, Dania, 234
Kwan, Nancy, 205
'La bambalina', 42
La, La, Lucille, 42, 43
'Ladies of the box office',
79
Lady Be Good, 77
Lady In The Dark, 167
'lady is a tramp, The', 105
Lady Objects, The, 237
'Lady Raffles—Behave',
238
Lake, Harriette (see
Sothern, Ann)
Landon, Margaret, 167,
172
Lane, Burton, 6, 115
Lang, Charles, 99
Lang, Harold, 180
Lang, Walter, 127, 171,
201
Langner, Lawrence, 11, 22,
27, 125, 131, 139, 172
Lannin, Paul, 42
Lark, Charles Tressler, 83,
84
Laurents, Arthur, 229, 230
Lawrence, Gertrude, 157,
167, 168, 170, 173, 175,
176, 223
Laye, Evelyn, 62, 83
Layton, Joe, 218, 227
Lazar, Irving ('Swifty'),
224
Leave It To Jane, 50
Leave It To Me, 139
Leavitt, Philip, 66, 68, 69,
238
Lee, Bill, 219
Lee, Chin Y., 201
Lemmon, Jack, 114
Lerner, Alan Jay, 6, 115,
192, 194, 227, 228–9
Lester, Ed, 148
'Let me drink in your eyes',
238
Let's Face It, 115
Levy, Jacob, 68
Levy, Rachel, 68
Lewine, Richard, 233
Lido Lady, 81
Lien, Evanna, 209
'Life upon the wicked
stage', 54, 59
Life With Father, 119, 198,
207
Light, The, 39
Liliom (see also *Carousel*),
124, 126, 128, 129, 239
Lillie, Beatrice, 85

Lindsay, Howard, 119, 151, 198, 207, 208, 209, 211, 216, 218, 223
'Little girl blue', 102
Little Show of 1929, The, 72
'Loads of love', 228
Locke, Mary Susan, 209
Loesser, Frank, 6, 192
Loewe, Frederick, 6, 192, 194, 227
Logan, Joshua, 6, 15, 88, 106, 109, 113, 134, 137, 138, 139, 140, 141, 142, 144, 145, 146, 147, 148, 149, 151, 152, 154, 155, 156, 158, 159, 160, 161, 162, 163, 167, 172, 173, 174, 176, 177, 182, 191, 192, 199, 201, 203, 207, 265
Logan, Nedda Harrigan, 138, 145, 148, 149, 172
'Loneliness of evening', 159, 198
'lonely goatherd, The', 210
Lonely Romeo, A, 54
'Lonely room', 21
Long Dark Hall, The, 167
'Look no further', 228
Loos, Anita, 139
'Lord only knows, The', 238
Louise, 33
'Love look away', 205
'Love makes the world go', 228
Love Me Tonight, 93-4, 95, 96, 108
Love o' Mike, 50, 69
'lovely night, A', 198
'Lover', 93
Loving Ann, 88
Loy, Myrna, 97
Lubitsch, Ernst, 98
Luke, Keye, 203, 205
Luna, Barbara, 157
Lund, Art, 228
Lunt, Alfred, 79
Lynn, Bambi, 151
Lynn, Eve, 68
Lyon, Ben, 90
Lyons, Leonard, 160
MacArthur, Charles, 102
McConnell, Lulu, 82
McCormick, Myron, 153, 161, 163
McCracken, Joan, 186, 187
McDaniels, Hattie, 58
MacDonald, Jeanette, 63, 93, 94, 96, 98
McGuffie, Bill, 239
McKenna, Kenneth, 144
McRae, Gordon, 19, 21, 196, 241
Mad Show, The, 232
Mademoiselle Modiste, 69
Magnificent Seven, The, 164
Main Street to Broadway, 190
'Make believe', 54, 59
Mamoulian, Rouben, 6, 22, 24, 25, 26, 28, 92, 93, 95, 120, 128, 129, 131, 134
'man I used to be, The', 194
Man of La Mancha, 228, 240

Mandel, Frank, 42, 75, 76, 91, 101
'Manhattan', 75, 76, 78, 79, 80, 96, 108, 175
Manhattan Melodrama, 97-8
Mankiewicz, Herman, 36, 37
Mankiewicz, Joseph, 36
Mantle, Burns, 28
'Many a new day', 21
Marbury, Elizabeth, 48
March, Frederic, 77
Marion, George, Jr, 108
Marius, 191
Marlowe, Marion, 216
Marsh, Howard, 55
Marshall, Armina (Mrs Lawrence Langner), 172
Martin, Ernie, 191-3
Martin, Hugh, 137
Martin, Mary, 6, 22, 27, 118, 139, 146, 147, 148, 150, 151, 154-5, 157, 158, 159, 161, 163, 164, 172, 175, 180, 182, 190, 197, 205, 206, 207, 208, 209, 210, 213, 214, 215, 216, 217, 218, 221, 229, 265
Marx, Groucho, 22, 163
Marx, Samuel, 6, 14, 62, 63, 69, 91, 97, 238, 265
Mary Jane McKane, 43
'Mary, Queen of Scots', 72
'Mary's a grand old name', 95
Mason, James, 167
Masters of Melody, 76, 96
Matthews, Jessie, 6, 83, 89, 91, 265
May Wine, 62
Mayer, Edwin Justus, 237
Mayer, Louis B., 96
Me and Juliet, 6, 185-9, 198, 232
'Me and my shadow', 70
'Meat and potatoes', 189
Meet Me In St Louis, 127
Meiser, Edith, 6, 78-9, 82
Melody Man, The, 76
Menzies, Heather, 215
Mercer, Johnny, 136, 239
Mercer, Mabel, 6
Meredith, Burgess, 125
Merman, Ethel, 91, 135, 138, 139, 194
Merrick, David, 191, 240
Merry Widow, The, 48, 98
Metro-Goldwyn-Mayer, 24, 36, 60, 62, 63, 96, 97, 99, 106, 107, 108, 109, 115, 127, 128, 151, 190, 193
Michaelis, Arnold, 236, 240
Michell, Keith, 234
Michener, James, A., 143, 144, 145, 147, 152, 160, 163, 192, 240
Midnight Cowboy, 216
'midnight supper, the', 238
Mielziner, Jo, 102, 107, 109, 133, 144, 146, 152, 154, 163, 170, 172, 173, 176, 184-5
Milestone, Lewis, 96
Millais, Geoffrey, 241

Miller, Marilyn, 51, 53, 237
Miller, Norman, 121
'Mimi', 93
Miss 1917, 50, 237
Mississippi, 99, 100, 101
Mister Roberts, 144, 145, 159
'Mister Snow', 131, 134
Molnar, Ferenc, 124, 126, 128, 130, 131, 134, 239
Monroe, Marilyn, 224
Montgomery, James, 53
Montgomery, Robert, 167
'Moonlight mama', 76
'Moon of my delight', 86
Moore, Constance, 15
'More than just a friend', 226
Morgan, Helen, 58, 59, 61
Morrow, Doretta, 175, 176
Moskewitch, Joseph H., 170
'most beautiful girl in the world, The', 102, 114
Most Happy Fella, The, 192
Mother Wore Tights, 105
'Mountain greenery', 81
Munson, Una, 90
Murrow, Ed, 190
Music Box Revue, 77, 101
Music In The Air, 61, 62, 65
Music Man, The, 192
'My best love', 205
'My boy Bill', 128, 134
My Fair Lady, 6, 96, 192, 194, 197, 209, 210, 227, 240
'My favourite things', 215, 217
'My friend, my friend', 156
'My funny Valentine', 105
My Gal Sal, 128
'My girl back home', 159, 201
'My heart belongs to Daddy', 139
'My heart stood still', 83, 84, 85
My Lady Liza (see *My Fair Lady*)
'My little girl', 134
'My lord and master', 174
'My romance', 102, 114
My Sister Eileen, 201
Myers, Carmel, 172
Myers, Henry, 61, 71, 237
Nammond, Nicholas, 215
Nana, 96
Naughty Marietta, 47
NCB Television, 164, 176, 179, 232
'Never say "No" to a man', 226
New Moon, The, 52, 61, 237
Nichols, Lewis, 28
Night Boat, 75
Night Is Young, The, 63, 237
Nimmo, James, 35
9.15 Revue, The, 89
Nixon, Marni, 172
No, No, Nanette!, 41, 43, 44, 61, 77
'No other love', 185, 188, 198
No Strings, 228
Nobody Home, 49

'Nobody loves a riveter', 90, 91
'No way to stop it', 216
Northrop, Patricia, 166
Norton, Elliott, 26, 129, 175
'Nothing but you', 109
'Now is the time', 156
'Now you leave', 174
O'Connor, Donald, 241
Odets, Clifford, 232
Of Thee I Sing, 36
O'Hara, John, 109-10, 166, 180
Oh, Boy!, 50
Oh, Lady, Lady, 50
'Oh, what a beautiful morning', 19, 20
Oklahoma! (see also *Away We Go* and *Green Grow The Lilacs*), 6, 17, 18, 20, 21, 23, 26-32, 64, 95, 115, 116, 119, 120, 124, 126, 127, 129, 131, 139, 144, 151, 159, 160, 161, 166, 170, 175, 182, 187, 189, 193, 194, 196, 197, 198, 220, 223, 232, 236, 240
'old folks at home, The', 85, 101
'Ol' man river', 54, 59, 237, 241
'On a desert island with thee', 85, 174
'On a slow boat to China', 192
'On the sunny side of the street', 240
'On your toes', 104, 114
On Your Toes, 65, 101, 102, 103, 104, 107, 109
Once In A Lifetime, 105
Once Upon A Mattress, 232
'One alone', 53
One Dam' Thing After Another, 83
One For The Money, 22
'One kiss', 61
One Minute, Please, 66, 69
One Night In The Tropics, 237
One Touch of Venus, 118, 139
Oppenheimer, George, 182, 265
Osterman, Lester, Jr, 233
'Our State Fair', 126
'Out of my dreams', 21
'Over and over again', 102
'Over there', 95
Pagnol, Marcel, 191
Pal Joey, 66, 110, 114, 176, 179, 180, 193, 235, 239
Palmer, Tony, 233, 235, 265
Panama Hattie, 115
Paramount Pictures, 63, 93, 95, 96, 99, 100, 101, 108, 206, 223, 239
'Paris in the spring', 98
Parson's Bride, The, 55
Peace Pirates, 37
Peculiar Treasure, A, 54
Peggy-Ann, 82
'People will say we're in love', 21